CW01430845

BRITISH BIRDS

A Pocket Guide

Rob Hume, Robert Still, Andy Swash,
Hugh Harrop & David Tipling

WILDGuides

PRINCETON
press.princeton.edu

Published by Princeton University Press,
41 William Street, Princeton, New Jersey 08540
In the United Kingdom: Princeton University Press, 6 Oxford Street,
Woodstock, Oxfordshire OX20 1TR
press.princeton.edu

Requests for permission to reproduce material from this work should be
sent to Permissions, Princeton University Press

First published 2019

British Library Cataloging-in-Publication Data is available

Library of Congress Control Number 2019940867
ISBN 978-0-691-18167-7

Production and design by **WILD**Guides Ltd., Old Basing, Hampshire UK.
Printed in Italy

10 9 8 7 6 5 4 3 2 1

Contents

Foreword

The face of British birding has changed beyond recognition since the days of the Victorian forefathers who practiced shotgun ornithology. Thumbing through the pages of a well-used field guide did not conclude tricky bird identification conundrums in those dark days. Instead, the identification was usually conducted in the hand or on the desk top, with the unfortunate bird lying dead from its wounds and a massive set of volumes to hand. Fortunately, over time we managed to put down the guns and pick up binoculars and telescopes. Our thirst for knowledge about the birds we were observing gave rise to the early field guides, distilling identification details into one small book, and by the 1950s the modern birder, replete with an identification armoury, was truly born.

Field guides – books to be used outside or 'in the field' as much as indoors – started out as fairly complex tomes, featuring every bird that might be seen in the regions that they covered. Being confronted with such an array of species is a daunting prospect for many beginners. Some worry about confusion species that, frankly, are not very likely to be seen, whilst others lose the will to live and give up! As a kid I was forever on the lookout for Azure Tits, the eastern counterpart of the far more familiar Blue Tit, because they were featured and compared on the same page. Most misleading!

Fast-forward to the present day and at last there is a field guide that goes the extra mile to help beginners (and more experienced birders) get to grips with identification. *British Birds – A Pocket Guide* will be a game changer. The opening spreads feature shapes and colour pictures of the various 'types' of birds, be they gulls or finches, linked by what they are doing and where they are. These guide you directly to the right section of the book, where you can read up more about each group and then move on to the individual species. It really could not be easier. And the photographs – stunning!

I know what book I will be recommending to all the budding new birders that I meet!

David Lindo
The Urban Birder
22 April 2019

Introduction

This book aims to help you set out on an enjoyable, lifelong interest in birds. It illustrates 300 species but focuses on the identification of the 248 that are most likely to be seen in Britain and Ireland. Some of these birds are scarce and localized, but all may be found in the right area, at the right time. The others include a handful of 'escapes' that may be encountered flying free, and 45 rarer birds that turn up each year in small numbers, just to give a flavour of what else might be found.

Being able to recognize a penguin, a flamingo, an owl – perhaps more specifically a Puffin and a Kingfisher – while still too young to read about them, instils a basic, simplistic knowledge of some kinds of birds. Later, learning pigeons, Blackbirds, Blue Tits and a few others begins to build familiarity with a steadily increasing stock of common birds. There is simply no substitute for time and practice; expert birdwatchers who have been observing birds for years are still learning. An experienced expert might identify a bird at a glance, like someone being able to recognize a familiar person in a crowd (it might be by their face, posture, actions or a bit of each, but rarely by fine details such as the colour of their eyes). For a beginner, identifying a bird may be difficult, but much easier next time. This book gives you the 'identikit' elements, but also tries to convey the overall 'feel' of each bird that will become increasingly obvious with experience.

Although it is an introductory guide, which will lead on to the more advanced *Britain's Birds – An Identification Guide to the Birds of Great Britain and Ireland* that covers in detail all 640+ species recorded in these islands, this book will also be invaluable for experienced birdwatchers to have in their pocket, since it covers well over 99% of the individual birds that are likely to be seen.

Avocets with Black-headed Gulls – not photographed in southern Europe, but in North Norfolk.

How to use this book

The book has been designed specifically with identification in mind, by grouping together similar-looking birds for ease of comparison and highlighting the key features. It is structured to help you put a name to a bird by taking the minimum number of steps.

Identifying birds (*page 10*) covers the key factors that influence identification, such as size and shape, voice and behaviour. It shows the parts of a bird that are useful to know when reading descriptions and understanding what you see on the living bird.

The identification process

1 When you first see an unfamiliar bird, go to **Getting to the right group of birds** (*pages 13–25*), which shows a range of birds both in silhouette and colour. Silhouettes replicate the view you may get of a distant bird; in many cases shape is often the most straightforward way to identify a type of bird. There are five sections, grouping similar birds together by behaviour/location and size:

▶ **Birds on water** (*pages 14–15*)
▶ **Standing birds – larger** (*pages 16–17*)
▶ **Perched birds – larger** (*pages 18–19*)
▶ **Small landbirds** (*pages 20–21*)
▶ **Birds in flight** (*pages 22–25*)

Simply glance through the relevant images and look for the one that most closely matches your bird.

2 The cross-reference from your chosen image will take you to the relevant **group introduction** or **species account** (see *page 8*). For larger groupings this introduction may refer you to a sub-group and, if needed, further subdivisions with identification information, before referring you to a **species account**.

3 By now you should be in the part of the book that matches your bird. Details in the accounts should enable you to put a name to the species you are looking at.

If something is not right then:

a) refer back to the introductory section for that species group, where information on commonly confused groups/species can be found.

b) it may be an exotic escape (such as a parrot) or it may be a rare bird. In the case of rare birds that look similar to more common species a cross-reference is given; if it does not look like any of our regular species you might still find it in the *Rare migrants and regular vagrants* section (*pages 256–261*).

Example identification

A small bird bathing doesn't seem to be a 'waterbird' and would suggest checking the **Small landbird** section first.

Identifying the bird as a **Finch/Sparrow/Bunting** you go to that section, which helps establish that it is a **'yellow-winged' finch**.

Finches compared. **'Fringilla finches'** – peaked head, broad wingbar; **'yellow-winged'** – broad yellow wingpanels, streaks but otherwise differ; **'brown'** – streaks brown with pale wing bar or white streaks; **'specialist'** – individual

By looking at the three species in that sub-group you can conclude that it is a **Goldfinch** (juvenile).

Hoopoe – a good example of a rare migrant that looks nothing like any of the the regular species covered in this book.

The species accounts

These follow a consistent format, with text and information boxes as follows:

ACCOUNT TEXTS

ENGLISH NAME and *SCIENTIFIC NAME* – English names are those in popular usage in the context of Britain and Ireland; scientific names and taxonomy are those used by BirdLife International.

SIZE – measured bill tip to tail tip (L), and wingtip to wingtip across spread wings (WS).

IDENTIFICATION [ID] – summarizes general characteristics, colours, patterns or shapes typical of all ages and both sexes of the species at any time of year. The description refers to a perched bird, with the plumages covered in the following order: ADULT (*i.e.* able to breed), subdivided as BREEDING and NON-BREEDING if there are seasonal plumage changes; MALE and FEMALE (where sexes differ, separate descriptions are given); JUVENILE (in its first covering of feathers after leaving the nest) and/or IMMATURE (when bird has shed and replaced some feathers but is not yet of breeding age; in some cases (*e.g.* gulls) this can cover a number of years). **Bold lettering** highlights key identification features. In instances where no distinction is made, the text refers to adult plumage.

IN FLIGHT – summarizes features that are usually or best seen in flight or on a spread wing.

VOICE – includes representations of typical calls and songs, some of which may be crucial to correct identifications.

COMPARISON SPREADS and TABLES

Throughout the book are plates or boxes that show various groups or species to scale and in comparable poses, often in flight (*e.g.* wildfowl, waders, birds of prey and gulls). In addition, tables giving key identification features for similar species are provided where useful. Look at these in conjunction with the individual species accounts, as these often add important information that cannot be covered entirely on the species pages. Comparisons are cross-referenced from the main species accounts.

IMAGE ANNOTATIONS and LABELS

Annotations – highlight key identification features (blue text for birds in flight).

Labels – where relevant, images are labelled with age and sex information as follows:

M male **F** female
B breeding plumage
N non-breeding plumage
A adult (sex undetermined)
I immature **J** juvenile **C** chick
1Y, **2Y**, **3Y** age up to 1, 2 or 3 years old

Months following a label indicate the period during which a particular plumage can be seen – for plumages that can be seen year round no dates are given.

Month [in square brackets] is the month in which the bird was photographed.

BOXED INFORMATION and MAPS

STATUS – a summary of current status in Britain and Ireland (colour-coded as maps); for migrants, the MONTHS when usually present and their typical origin are also given.

OBSERVATION TIPS – information, such as behaviour and location, that may help in gaining a better viewing experience.

WHERE — indicates the typical habitat(s) (for individual or groups of species)

EATS — summarizes the type(s) of food taken (by individual or groups of species)

Map colour-coded as:
■ all-year ■ summer ■ winter
■ passage migrant (spring/autumn)
NB arrows show origin/direction of migration routes

! Reference to rare migrant or regular vagrant

Knowing the parts of a bird

When trying to describe a bird or relate a description in a book to reality, it is useful to know a bird's structure and the way its feathers lie and how patterns appear as the wings are folded or spread. As far as possible, specialist terms have been avoided in this book, although they can make written descriptions of such patterns more precise. For example, "stripe over eye" is used instead of 'supercilium' and "moustache" rather than 'malar stripe'.

These annotated images show the basic, essential terms used throughout this book (other terms specific to a particular group are covered in the relevant introductory section).

Wingbars: The term "wingbar" is used to describe any obvious 'bar' along the spread wing. This is typically formed of contrasting tips to the wing coverts and/or pale bases to the flight feathers. On some species such as **Blue Tit** (*right*) this bar is obvious on the closed wing, in others, such as **Sanderling** (*below*), it is barely discernible or not visible – particularly any pale bases to the flight feathers.

stripe over eye
eyestripe
cap
wingbar

BLUE TIT

SANDERLING

covert tips barely discernible

covert tips

pale bases to flight feathers

covert tips (visible on closed wing)

UPPERWING

rump

back

midwing
greater coverts

innerwing
wing coverts and secondaries

forewing
lesser and median coverts

primary coverts

outerwing
primary coverts and primaries

SECONDARIES
PRIMARIES

hindwing
secondaries and inner primaries

wingtip
outer primaries

UNDERWING

flight feathers
PRIMARIES
SECONDARIES

'wingpit'

trailing edge

FIELDFARE

wingtip (closed)

back

wing coverts
greater   median   lesser

'shoulder'   neck

nape

crown

eyering

forehead

upper mandible

bill

rump

throat   chin

'moustache'   cheek

tail

flank

thigh

belly   breast

Identifying birds

Size, shape and actions, colour and pattern, voice, habitat, location and time of year all play a part in identifying birds. Shape, which is key to identifying many birds, is reflected in *Getting to the right group of birds* on *pages 13–25*, where silhouettes help pinpoint various species groups. A bird's actions, even in silhouette, may be invaluable, but colour adds more clues, shown by examples of the *types of bird*. When you see a bird you cannot identify immediately, the best approach is to get an overall impression and then look for the important detail. Using this book will gradually show what features are useful (and which can be ignored) for each group of birds. But always remember to check where and when you might expect to see the species you are considering.

Size and shape

Judging size is important: try to estimate size against a familiar bird (Mute Swan, Pheasant, Mallard, Feral Pigeon, Blackbird and Robin give a handy scale). Shape includes details of bill shape (long or short, triangular or slender, straight or curved), leg length and tail shape, as well as the general impression. Remember that shape is affected by many factors: a bird may be rounder when relaxed, or fluffed out in cold weather, but slim and taut when alert or alarmed, or in hot weather.

Colour and pattern

Colour (in general) and pattern (specific details) may be vital, yet many birds can be told even at a distance or in silhouette when such details are not clear (increasingly so with experience). Don't forget the influence that different lighting conditions, reflections from foliage, *etc.* can have on the way a bird looks, as well as the real changes caused by wear and fading of feathers.

SIZE AND SHAPE: even though they show a wide variation of plumages as they age, the shape of a **Gannet** is always distinctive.

SIZE AND SHAPE: seen in isolation the size of an egret may be difficult to determine – but if seen together the size difference between **Little Egret** (*left*) and **Great White Egret** (*right*) is very obvious.

COLOUR AND PATTERN: the surroundings and lighting conditions have a profound effect on how a bird appears: *e.g.* **Curlew** look bright and buff in sunshine or against a dark background, but dull and grey in poor light or against bright water, when they are more likely to be confused with Whimbrel.

Voice

Birds' calls and songs are usually distinctive and in some cases vital to identification: try to describe what you hear as clearly as possible in a way that you will understand later.

VOICE: some species, for example **Willow Warbler**, are most simply identified from similar species by their song.

Behaviour

Behaviour includes broad tendencies (*e.g.* solitary or in flocks, walking or hopping on the ground, or climbing trees) and finer detail (*e.g.* wing and tail flicks, head bobbing). It is in part linked with habitat, especially where and how a bird feeds (*e.g.* swimming and diving, wading and probing with the bill, or hopping on a lawn).

Habitat

Habitats can be broadly divided into **water**, **waterside** and **land**, with various subdivisions (*e.g.* salt and fresh water, saltmarsh, reedbed, moorland, farmland, woodland, *etc.*). A bird on water is clearly a water or swimming bird; if wading in the shallows or walking along the water's edge it is a waterside bird. Birds on heaths or in fields, or in trees or bushes, are equally clearly land birds. Remember, however, that exceptions are frequent: almost any 'land bird' will drink or bathe at the waterside and many 'water birds', will rest on the shore. The broad habitat types are illustrated on *pages 26–33*, each of which has a list of the types or species of birds typically associated with it.

BEHAVIOUR: a small sandpiper wading belly deep is worth a second glance – though not diagnostic **Curlew Sandpipers** are far more likely to do this than Dunlin.

HABITAT: **Buzzards** can be encountered concealed in woodland, on open ground, or perched high in the open (*e.g.* on a post).

Location and time of year

Location and time of year are useful: relatively few birds are seen in the wrong place or at the wrong time of year, although unusual occurrences do happen! Our resident species are present all year round within Britain and Ireland but may move between breeding and wintering areas (*e.g.* upland species moving to the coast in winter). 'Summer migrants' come to our region in spring (from *e.g.* Africa) and leave in the autumn. 'Winter visitors' breed elsewhere, migrate to Britain and Ireland in autumn and leave in spring. 'Passage migrants' can be seen in spring as they head north (to *e.g.* the Arctic) and in autumn as they return south. Hard weather may also cause movements of large numbers of some species both within Britain and Ireland and from continental Europe and Scandinavia.

LOCATION + TIME OF YEAR: a 'Meadow/Tree' Pipit during Nov–Mar will almost certainly be a **Meadow Pipit** but it is worth checking any pipit for Tree Pipit during migration (Apr/May and Aug–Oct) and on open heath with trees in the breeding season (Apr–Aug).

Birds in flight: identification at a distance

Identifying a large bird soaring overhead may be easy. Identification is more difficult, but often possible from even a distant view or the briefest glimpse of a bird flying away. Some species have a distinctive flight action: the flapping rise and curved, downward glide of a Collared Dove, the rounded, 'rowing' wings of a Jay, or the rising into a hover of a Kestrel. Some flight actions are more subtle but characteristic once you are familiar with the bird. For example, a Blackbird tends to fly moderately fast and low with a turning dip into cover, but the similar-looking Ring Ouzel appears more purposeful, dashing and direct as it goes off into the distance.

Many birds gather in flocks, and at a distance the shape of a flock can be a good identification clue. Golden Plovers form a distinctive rounded bunch, trailing off at the rear, before sometimes settling into long lines and 'V' shapes, often separating out from slower Lapwings as they go. Woodpigeon flocks over fields and woods have little clear shape but the individual birds have a steady, direct action. Jackdaws often fly together from a cliff, building or tree, sweep round in a glide and return. Starling flocks are tight and bunched and fly fast, with changes in height and direction that sweep through the flock like a 'Mexican wave'.

Learning these distinctive clues takes time, but gradually many species become more easily identified even at a glance.

The shape and flock style of distant **Starlings** are distinctive with experience.

Getting to the right group of birds

This section compares 'types' or categories of birds, based on a broad assessment of behaviour, habitat, size and shape:

▶ **Birds on water** (*pages 14–15*) – all types of bird likely to be seen on water, whether in freshwater habitats or at sea.

▶ **Standing birds** (*pages 16–17*) – types of (larger) bird that habitually stand on the ground or on mud, on a rock or on some other relatively flat surface.

▶ **Perched birds** (*pages 18–19*) – types of bird that are generally seen on a branch, top of a bush, post or wire, or clinging to a tree trunk or side of a rock.

▶ **Small landbirds** (*pages 20–21*) – various smaller birds up to the size of a Blackbird that are likely to be seen in gardens, woodland, scrub, urban areas, farmland or areas of open ground.

▶ **Birds in flight** (*pages 22–25*) – subdivided into
1) **those that are strongly associated with water**, and
2) **those found in a wide range of habitats**.

When faced with an unfamiliar bird, rather than looking for fine details, first assess its overall size and shape. You may be surprised to find that the silhouettes shown on the left page of each comparative spread are often easier to recognize than the same 'full colour' image shown on the right, as the vagaries of different plumages do not then confuse the issue. The full colour images can, however, be used to confirm the general 'look' of the bird.

The birds on each page-spread are shown approximately to scale, providing additional clues to the type of bird you are looking at. Check the various page-spreads, focusing on the 'look for' points, and once you think you have found the right type, go to the section to which it is cross-referenced and read the introduction. This should help to confirm that you are in the right area and ultimately enable you to put a name to the bird.

In some cases a 'type' of bird, such as a gull, may be found in more than one category and adopt significantly different shapes depending on their activity.

Birds on water

LOOK FOR:
- ► bill shape
- ► neck length
- ► tail profile
  – flat to surface or uptilted

SKUA *p. 101*

GULLS, SKUAS, TERNS *p. 82*

FULMAR *p. 77*

GULL (larger) *p. 88*

GULL (smaller) *p. 86*

SEABIRDS *p. 70*

SHEARWATER *p. 78*

GANNET *p. 80*

PHALAROPE *pp. 111, 138*

DIVER *p. 66*

CORMORANT *p. 64*

AUK *pp. 70, 72*

WATERBIRDS *p. 63*

GREBE (larger) *p. 68*

GREBE (smaller) *p. 69*

COOT/MOORHEN *p. 144*

DUCK (sawbill) *p. 56*

DUCK (diving) *p. 54*

DUCK (surface-feeding) *p. 50*

WILDFOWL *p. 36*

NB Shelduck and Egyptian Goose are intermediate between ducks and geese

SWAN *p. 38*

GOOSE *p. 40*

14

Some species are only confusing in certain plumages

juvenile gulls resemble skuas but are typically paler and larger-headed

SKUA

FULMAR

GULL (larger)

GULL (smaller)

J (adult black-and-white)

SHEARWATER

GANNET

PHALAROPE

DIVER

CORMORANT

AUK

GREBE (larger)

GREBE (smaller)

COOT/MOORHEN

DUCK (sawbill)

DUCK (diving)

DUCK (surface-feeding)

SWAN

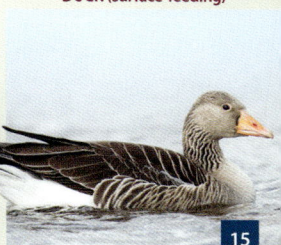

GOOSE

Standing birds (larger)

LOOK FOR:
► body shape and posture
► tail shape
► bill length
► leg length

SANDPIPER *p. 122*

PLOVER (smaller) *p. 117*

WADERS
p. 109

'SHANK' *p. 132*

PLOVER (larger) *p. 118*

PIGEON/DOVE
p. 154

RAIL *p. 146*

MOORHEN/COOT *p. 144*

'GAMEBIRD' *p. 147*

GULLS, SKUAS,
TERNS *p. 82*

GULL *p. 88*

TERN *p. 104*

BIRD OF PREY (larger) *p. 158*

WILDFOWL
p. 36

GOOSE *p. 40*

DUCK *p. 46*

CROW *p. 232*

BITTERN *p. 140*

LARGE
WATERSIDE
p. 139

EGRET *p. 141* HERON *p. 142* SPOONBILL *p. 143*

CRANE *p. 143*

16

LOOK FOR:
▶ bare part (leg and bill) colours
▶ overall colour/pattern
▶ streaks, spots or bars

SANDPIPER

PLOVER (small)

DOVE

'SHANK'

PLOVER (larger)

'GAMEBIRD'

RAIL

MOORHEN/COOT

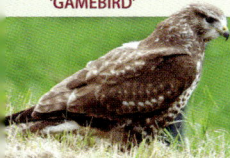
BIRD OF PREY (larger)

GULL

TERN

CROW

GOOSE

DUCK

BITTERN

EGRET

HERON   SPOONBILL

CRANE

17

Perched birds (larger)

LOOK FOR:
- ▶ body shape and posture
- ▶ tail shape
- ▶ bill length
- ▶ leg length

PARAKEET
p. 185

WOODPECKER
p. 186

AUK *pp. 70, 72*

PIGEON *p. 154*

OWL *p. 176*

CORMORANT *pp. 63, 64*

CROW *p. 232*

CUCKOO *p. 184*

BIRDS OF PREY
p. 139

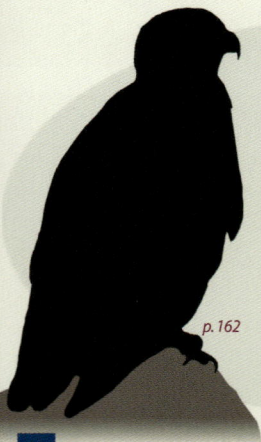

p. 162

EAGLE

p. 164/166/168

BUZZARD/KITE/
OSPREY/HARRIER

p. 172

FALCON

p. 170

HAWK

LOOK FOR:
- ▶ overall colour/pattern
- ▶ streaks, spots or bars
- ▶ bare part (leg and bill) colours

PARAKEET

WOODPECKER

AUK

PIGEON

OWL

CORMORANT

CROW

CUCKOO

EAGLE

BUZZARD

FALCON

HAWK

19

Small landbirds

PASSERINES
p. 190

LOOK FOR:
▶ overall shape
▶ size comparison (if possible)
▶ bill shape
▶ leg length and gait

NUTHATCH
p. 226

TREECREEPER
p. 226

WAXWING
p. 200

SWALLOW/MARTIN p. 188

'TRUE' TIT
p. 228

TITS
p. 227

pp. 227, 228
LONG-TAILED/BEARDED

p. 219

CREST

p. 222

PHYLLOSCOPUS

WARBLERS
p. 215

p. 216

SYLVIA

p. 220

'WETLAND'

FLYCATCHER p. 224

CHAT p. 203

FINCHES, BUNTINGS, SPARROWS
p. 240

DUNNOCK p. 202

WREN p. 202

p. 241

FINCH

p. 255

SPARROW

p. 250

BUNTING

LARK p. 194

PIPIT
p. 196

WAGTAIL
p. 198

STARLING p. 200

DIPPER p. 201

THRUSH p. 203

LOOK FOR:
- overall colour/pattern
- streaks, spots or bars

WAXWING

NUTHATCH

TREECREEPER

SWALLOW/MARTIN

'TRUE' TIT

LONG-TAILED TIT

CREST

PHYLLOSCOPUS WARBLER

SYLVIA WARBLER

WETLAND WARBLER

FLYCATCHER

CHAT

DUNNOCK

WREN

FINCH

SPARROW

BUNTING

LARK

PIPIT

WAGTAIL

STARLING

DIPPER

THRUSH

21

Birds in flight 1/2

Species strongly associated with water

LARGE WATERSIDE
p. 139

HERON, EGRET, BITTERN
p. 140

SWAN
p. 44

WILDFOWL
p. 36

SPOONBILL
p. 143

WATERBIRDS
p. 63

CORMORANT
p. 64

GOOSE
p. 44

DIVER
p. 66

GREBE
p. 68

DUCK
p. 48

AUK
p. 72

GANNET
p. 80

SKUA
(larger)
p. 102

KINGFISHER
p. 183

SEABIRDS
p. 70

GULL
(larger)
p. 90

SHEARWATER
p. 78

SKUA
(smaller)
p. 102

GULLS,
SKUAS,
TERNS
p. 82

FULMAR
p. 77

STORM PETREL
p. 76

GULL
(smaller)
p. 87

SANDPIPERS
p. 112

TERN
p. 108

PLOVERS
p. 112

WADERS *p. 109*

22

LOOK FOR:
▶ head and neck shape   ▶ tail length
▶ wing shape and posture   ▶ flight action

HERON, EGRET,
BITTERN

SWAN

SPOONBILL

CORMORANT

GOOSE

DIVER

GREBE

DUCK

AUK

GANNET

KINGFISHER

SKUA
(larger)

SHEARWATER

GULL
(larger)

SKUA
(smaller)

FULMAR

STORM PETREL

GULL
(smaller)

TERN

PLOVERS

SANDPIPERS

23

Birds in flight 2/2

Species seen in a wide range of habitats

LARGER SPECIES

BIRDS OF PREY
p. 158

KITE
p. 167

BUZZARD
p. 164

EAGLE
p. 162

CROW
p. 232

HARRIER
p. 168

HAWK
p. 170

FALCON
p. 172

NIGHTJAR
p. 182

PIGEON
p. 154

PARAKEET
p. 185

CUCKOO
p. 184

OWL
p. 176

WOODPECKER
p. 186

'GAMEBIRD'
p. 147

SWIFT
(to scale)

SMALLER SPECIES

NB Swift is shown to scale in both sections

SWALLOW/
MARTIN
p. 188

SWIFT
p. 188

FINCH,
BUNTING,
SPARROW
p. 240

PIPIT
p. 196

LARK
p. 194

THRUSH
p. 205

WAGTAIL
p. 198

STARLING *p. 200*

NB Waxwing (*p. 201*)
has a similar profile

LARGER SPECIES

LOOK FOR:
- overall shape
  tail length, body bulk,
  wing length and shape
  head shape and size
- size comparison (if possible)
- flight action

KITE

BUZZARD

EAGLE

CROW

HARRIER

HAWK

NIGHTJAR

FALCON

PIGEON

PARAKEET

CUCKOO

OWL

WOODPECKER

'GAMEBIRD'

SWIFT
(to scale)

SMALLER SPECIES

LOOK FOR:
- overall shape
  tail length and shape,
  wing length and shape
- flight action (*e.g.* direct, undulating)

SWALLOW/
MARTIN

SWIFT

PIPIT

STARLING

LARK

FINCH,
BUNTING,
SPARROW

WAGTAIL

THRUSH

25

Bird habitats

Understanding their habitat needs is fundamental to finding many birds. Most are limited to particular habitats by their preferred food, or the way they find it. Check the summaries for each species to see whether they may be found more widely or only in restricted habitats. The following broad habitat types have characteristic suites of birds; the lists included are not intended to be exhaustive but give an idea of the range of species that might be found in each.

Urban and suburban areas and gardens will have birds at any time, many of which can be seen from the comfort of an armchair or even during a daily commute. Variety is restricted, but town parks may have **Jay** and **Nuthatch**, town centres even have **gulls** and **Jackdaw**, perhaps even **Peregrine**, and gardens anywhere may be made attractive to various **tits**, **thrushes**, **finches** and more. Many urban areas include water, such as park lakes, ponds, canals and reservoirs – the birds found in these habitats are covered in their relevant watery category.

TYPICAL SPECIES

Gulls (*p. 82*)
Grey Heron (*p. 141*)
Pigeons: (*p. 154*)
Collared Dove (*p. 157*)
Birds of Prey: Peregrine (*p. 175*),
   Kestrel (*p. 173*)
Ring-necked Parakeet (*p. 185*)
Aerial feeders: Swift (*p. 188*),
   Swallow (*p. 189*),
   House Martin (*p. 189*)
Wagtails: Pied Wagtail (*p. 198*),
   Grey Wagtail (*p. 199*)
Starling (*p. 200*)

Dunnock, Wren (*p. 202*)
Thrushes (*p. 204*)
Robin (*p. 208*)
Tits: Blue Tit, Great Tit (*p. 229*),
   Coal Tit (*p. 231*), Marsh Tit
   (*p. 230*), Long-tailed Tit (*p. 228*)
Crows (*p. 232*)
Finches: Chaffinch (*p. 242*),
   Brambling (*p. 243*), Greenfinch
   (*p. 245*), Siskin (*p. 245*)
House Sparrow (*p. 255*)

Peregrine

Some common garden birds

Dunnock

Great and Blue Tits

Robin

Chaffinch

Wren

Blackbird

Starling

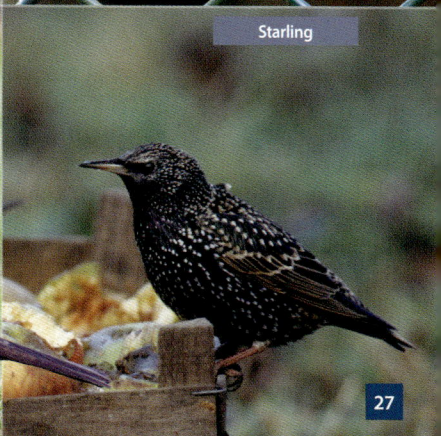

Woodland habitats are mostly rich in birds but woods can seem 'empty' in late summer (when migrants are leaving and many residents are moulting and keeping quiet) and in winter (when many birds join nomadic flocks). Some species use all or most woods, others have preferences. Even in a mostly deciduous wood, **Coal Tit** prefer to be around an isolated conifer; **Goldcrest** favour coniferous woods, and **Crossbill** must have conifers for their specialist diet and feeding techniques. **Spotted Flycatcher** prefer woodland edges or clearings; **Firecrest** sing from the depths of a dense old Holly or tangle of Ivy; **Redstart** are elusive singing from the tops of woodland oaks; while **Robin** hop down from the lower canopy to feed on the ground, and **Wren** scuttle about on the ground. 'Woodland' has many subtle sub-habitats, all of which are worth exploring.

Deciduous woodlands:
TYPICAL SPECIES

Woodcock (*p. 121*)
Birds of Prey: Buzzard (*p. 164*),
   Hawks (*p. 170*), Red Kite (*p. 167*)
Owls (*p. 176*)
Woodpeckers (*p. 186*)
Tree Pipit (*p. 196*)
Dunnock, Wren (*p. 202*)
Thrushes (*p. 204*)
Chats Robin (*p. 208*), Redstart (*p. 210*)
***Phylloscopus* Warblers** (*p. 222*)
***Sylvia* Warblers:** Blackcap (*p. 218*),
   Garden Warbler (*p. 218*)
Crests (*p. 219*)
Flycatchers (*p. 224*)
Nuthatch, Treecreeper (*p. 226*)
Tits (*p. 228*)
Crows (*p. 232*)
Finches: Chaffinch (*p. 242*), Bullfinch
   (*p. 243*), Greenfinch (*p. 245*),
   Redpoll (*p. 247*), Hawfinch (*p. 249*)

Wood Warbler

Lesser Spotted Woodpecker

Nuthatch

Woodcock

Coniferous woodlands:

TYPICAL SPECIES

Capercaillie (*p. 153*)
Great Spotted Woodpecker (*p. 187*)
Tree Pipit (*p. 196*)
Coal Tit, Crested Tit (*p. 231*)
Goldcrest (*p. 219*)
Siskin (*p. 245*)
Crossbills (*p. 248*)

Crested Tit

Crossbill

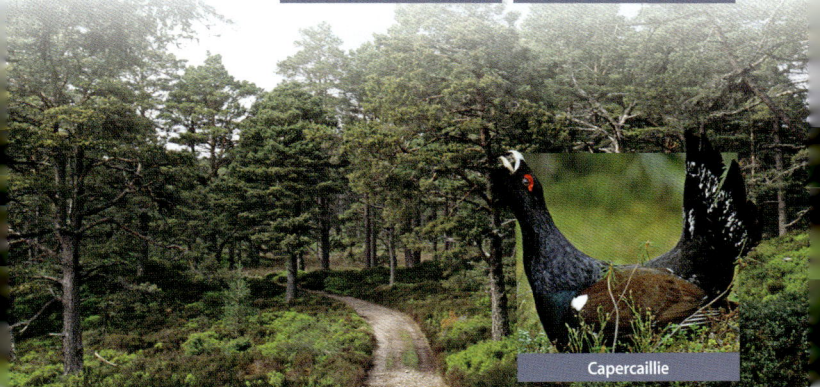
Capercaillie

Scrub is a valuable habitat, with bushes kept low by browsing animals or poor soils. It provides an abundance of food (*e.g.* insects and autumn berries that are exploited by migrants). Breeding birds include those that prefer patches of bushes on open ground and those that need dense vegetation down to ground level.

TYPICAL SPECIES
Dunnock, Wren (*p. 202*)
Chats: Robin (*p. 208*), Stonechat (*p. 212*), Whinchat (*p. 213*), Nightingale (*p. 209*)
Sylvia **Warblers** (*p. 216*)

Long-tailed Tit (*p. 228*)
Finches: Greenfinch (*p. 245*), Bullfinch (*p. 243*), Linnet (*p. 246*)
Buntings: Yellowhammer (*p. 252*), Cirl Bunting (*p. 253*)

Stonechat

Farmland can be rich in birds if there are pastures and hedgerows, orchards and farm ponds, or almost empty where modern intensive farming has created vast areas of weed-free crops with almost nothing for birds to eat.

TYPICAL SPECIES

Hedgerows:
Pigeons and Doves (*p. 154*)
Sparrowhawk (*p. 170*)
Little Owl (*p. 177*)
Cuckoo (*p. 184*)
Dunnock,Wren (*p. 202*)
Thrushes (*p. 204*)
Whitethroat (*p. 216*)
Crows (*p. 232*)
Buntings: Yellowhammer (*p. 252*),
   Cirl Bunting (*p. 253*),
   Reed Bunting (*p. 254*)
Sparrows (*p. 255*)

Arable:
Swans (*p. 38*)
Geese (*p. 40*)
Waders: Lapwing (*p. 116*),
   Golden Plover (*p. 119*),
   Dotterel (*p. 118*)
Gulls (*p. 82*)
'Gamebirds': Pheasant (*p. 148*),
   partridges (*p. 149*),
   Quail (*p. 147*)
Birds of Prey: Marsh (*p. 168*) &
   Montagu's (*p. 169*) Harriers
Pigeons and Doves (*p. 154*)
Larks (*p. 194*)
Meadow Pipit (*p. 196*)
Pied Wagtail (*p. 198*)
Thrushes (*p. 204*)

Crows (*p. 232*)
Wheatear (*p. 214*)
Finches: Chaffinch (*p. 242*),
   Brambling (*p. 243*), Goldfinch
   (*p. 244*), Greenfinch (*p. 245*),
   Linnet (*p. 246*), Twite (*p. 247*)
Buntings (*p. 250*)
Sparrows (*p. 255*)

Pasture:
Swans (*p. 38*)
Grey geese (*p. 40*)
Gulls (*p. 82*)
Waders: Lapwing (*p. 116*),
   Golden Plover (*p. 119*),
   Black-tailed Godwit (*p. 134*),
   Redshank (*p. 133*)
'Gamebirds': Pheasant (*p. 148*),
   partridges (*p. 149*)
Birds of Prey: Harriers (*p. 168*),
   Kestrel (*p. 173*), Hobby (*p. 174*)
Owls Barn Owl (*p. 178*),
   Short-eared Owl (*p. 180*)
Skylark (*p. 194*)
Meadow Pipit (*p. 196*)
Wagtails: Pied Wagtail (*p. 198*),
   Yellow Wagtail (*p. 199*)
Starling (*p. 200*)
Thrushes (*p. 204*)
Crows (*p. 232*)

Skylark

Little Owl

Lapwing

Open ground may include anything from extensive pastures or floodplains, heaths and moors to high peaks and plateaux. Grassland is exploited by swans and geese, some waders, pipits and wagtails. Heaths have their own birds such as **Stonechat**, **Linnet** and **Meadow Pipit**, and many more on the edges; moors may have these as well as **Raven**, foraging **Starling** flocks in summer, **Wheatear**, or **Red Grouse**, even **Hen Harrier**. Higher ground has fewer birds but there are specialists such as **Golden Eagle** and **Ptarmigan**.

TYPICAL SPECIES

Mountain:
Dotterel (*p. 118*)
Ptarmigan (*p. 151*)
Golden Eagle (*p. 162*)
Crows (*p. 232*)

Heathland:
Hobby (*p. 174*)
Nightjar (*p. 182*)
Cuckoo (*p. 184*)
Larks (*p. 194*)
Pipits: Meadow Pipit, Tree Pipit (*p. 196*)
Wren, Dunnock (*p. 202*)
Chats: Stonechat (*p. 212*), Whinchat (*p. 213*), Wheatear (*p. 214*)
Dartford Warbler (*p. 217*)
Linnet (*p. 246*)
Yellowhammer (*p. 252*)

Moorland:
Gulls (*p. 82*)
Skuas (*p. 101*)
Waders: Golden Plover (*p. 119*), Greenshank (*p. 133*), Dunlin (*p. 124*)
Grouse: Red Grouse (*p. 150*), Black Grouse (*p. 152*)
Birds of Prey: Kestrel (*p. 173*), Merlin (*p. 172*), Peregrine (*p. 175*), Hen Harrier (*p. 169*)
Skylark (*p. 194*)
Pipits: Meadow Pipit, Tree Pipit (*p. 196*)
Chats: Stonechat (*p. 212*), Whinchat (*p. 213*), Wheatear (*p. 214*)
Crows (*p. 232*)
Finches: Linnet (*p. 246*), Twite (*p. 247*)

Open downland:
Partridges (*p. 149*)
Kestrel (*p. 173*)
Swallow (*p. 189*)
Skylark (*p. 194*)
Meadow Pipit (*p. 196*)
Wheatear (*p. 214*)
Crows (*p. 232*)
Corn Bunting (*p. 250*)

Golden Eagle

Nightjar

Wheatear

Freshwater wetlands (open water) include some of the best and most popular birdwatching habitats, where other habitats may come together alongside water: rivers, lakes, flooded gravel pits and their associated hinterland offer opportunities for a great variety of birds. A lake, especially, will attract **wildfowl**, **gulls** and a range of small birds, with different ones appearing or moving on almost daily – these are the places to see migrant **waders**, **terns**, **ducks** and **grebes**, **pipits** and **wagtails**, **Swift** and **Swallow** flocks, **birds of prey** and so much more.

TYPICAL SPECIES

Lakes and reservoirs:
Swans (p. 38)
Geese: Canada Goose (p. 42),
  Greylag Goose (p. 40)
Ducks:
  surface-feeding (p. 50),
  diving (p. 54)
Cormorant (p. 64)
Divers (p. 66)
Grebes (p. 68)
Coot (p. 145)
Terns: Common Tern (p. 106),
  Black Tern (p. 105)
Aerial feeders (p. 188)

Rivers:
Ducks:
  surface-feeding (p. 50),
  diving (p. 54)
Little Grebe (p. 69)
Moorhen (p. 144)
Dipper (p. 201)

Water's edge:
Waders (p. 109)
Herons and Egrets (p. 141)
Birds of Prey: Osprey (p. 166),
  Peregrine (p. 175)
Kingfisher (p. 183)
Pipits: Water Pipit (p. 197),
  Meadow Pipit (p. 196)
Wagtails: Pied Wagtail (p. 198),
  Grey Wagtail (p. 199)

Osprey

Little Grebe

Little Egret

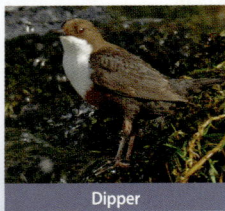

Dipper

Freshwater wetlands (marshes, reedbeds and fen) Reedbeds and wet fen vegetation may attract **Reed** and **Sedge Warblers**, **Water Rail**, **herons** and **egrets**, hunting **Barn Owl** and **harriers**.

TYPICAL SPECIES

Herons and Egrets (*p. 141*)
Bittern (*p. 140*)
Rail and Crakes: Coot (*p. 145*),
Moorhen (*p. 144*),
Water Rail (*p. 146*)

Birds of Prey: Marsh Harrier
(*p. 168*), Hobby (*p. 174*)
Barn Owl (*p. 178*)
Cuckoo (*p. 184*)
Wetland Warblers (*p. 220*)
Bearded Tit (*p. 227*)

Hobby

Cuckoo

Barn Owl

Bittern

Bearded Tit

Water Rail

Coastal wetlands include tidal rivers leading to wider estuaries, which may be deep or shallow, muddy or sandy, or have sand and shingle bars at the outer edge; inside these exposed areas, sheltered saltmarshes and creeks often form and artificial seawalls may protect wet pastures or shallow, brackish lagoons. Different species occupy different habitats here, but the coast and its associated wetland, rough grazing, etc. is always a productive place to look for birds.

TYPICAL SPECIES

Geese: grey geese (p. 40), Barnacle Goose, Brent Goose (p. 43)
Shelduck (p. 45)
Ducks: surface-feeding (p. 50)
Gulls (p. 82)
Terns (p. 104)
Waders (p. 109)
Osprey (p. 166)
Pipits: Meadow Pipit (p. 196), Rock Pipit, Water Pipit (p. 197)
Wagtails: Pied Wagtail (p. 198), Yellow Wagtail (p. 199)
Wetland Warblers (p. 220)
Finches: Linnet (p. 246), Twite (p. 247)
Buntings: Reed Bunting (p. 254), Snow Bunting (p. 251)

Common Tern

Black-headed Gull

Redshank

Wigeon

Snow Bunting

Pink-footed Geese

Open coasts and sea include sheer rock cliffs, islands and lower rock, shingle, sand and mud shores; sand dunes form on the inland edge of lower coasts. Many migrants that normally use other habitats rest on the coast, often in low thickets or small woods, and this is where most rarities also appear. Urban areas, including seaside resorts, harbours, piers and industrial/dockland sites, often have seabirds, especially in rough weather.

TYPICAL SPECIES

Sea ducks (p. 60)
Cormorants (p. 64)
Divers (p. 66)
Grebes (p. 68)
Auks (p. 72)
Petrels (p. 76)
Shearwaters (p. 78)
Gannet (p. 80)
Gulls (p. 82)
Terns (p. 104)
Waders (Turnstone (p. 115),
    Oystercatcher (p. 114),
    Purple Sandpiper (p. 128),
    Ringed Plover (p. 117)
Rock Dove (p. 155)
Peregrine (p. 175)
Rock Pipit (p. 197)
Crows (p. 232)

Fulmar

Gannet

Puffin

Peregrine

Turnstone

Eider

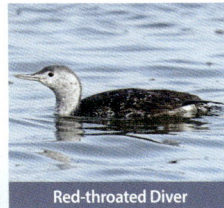
Red-throated Diver

Wildfowl
are typically associated with open water, though many can be seen in fields or marshy grassland. They can be found alone, in pairs or in flocks – often comprising mixed species.

Swans (p. 38)
Obviously very large and long-necked; pure white when adult but brown feathering when young.

Geese (pp. 40–44)
Large, long-necked, short-legged – two broad groups. Flocks tend to be of a single species, though individuals of one species may become 'caught up' in flocks of others.

'Grey' geese (p. 40)
Mostly grey-brown; legs and all or part of bill orange or pink.

'Black' geese (p. 42)
Black on the head and neck; black legs and bill.

WHOOPER SWAN

PINK-FOOTED GOOSE

BRENT GOOSE

SHELDUCK

EGYPTIAN GOOSE

Shelduck (p. 45)
Distinctive: large, piebald; red bill, pink legs.

Egyptian Goose (p. 45)
Distinctive: pale with white wing patches; long, pink legs

Ducks (pp. 46–62) ▶ MALE DUCKS COMPARED p. 46
Medium–large, short-legged; all swim, some dive, some feed on land; sexes differ markedly, juveniles like adult female; seasonal differences marked in males – three broad groups.

Surface-feeding ('dabbling') ducks (pp. 50–53)
Bill tapered but rather broad-tipped. In flight, wings show distinct pattern ('speculum') on inner hindwing. Feed by dabbling or upending. Can take off from and land on dry ground. Walk well on land; tail held clear of surface when swimming.

WIGEON | M

Diving ducks (pp. 54–57)
Bill broad-tipped or narrow (cutting edges serrated in 'sawbills'). In flight, wings show patches or central stripe of white or grey. Take off from water with short run. Feed by diving from surface. Do not walk well on land; tail low on surface when swimming.

SCAUP | F

Sea ducks (pp. 60–62)
Bill short, thick or wedge-shaped. In flight, wings all-dark and/ or with patches of white. Feed by diving from surface. Mostly aquatic; stand but do not walk on land.

EIDER | M

▶POSSIBLE CONFUSION WITH | **Grebes, Divers, Coot/Moorhen, Cormorant** | see *pp. 14, 16, 22*

In flight

Swans in pairs, small shapeless groups or 'V'- formation; **geese** typically in flocks, often large numbers; in straight lines, 'V's or shapeless masses; **ducks** are seen singly, in pairs, small groups or flocks (particularly sea ducks and Wigeon).

▶IN FLIGHT
SWANS AND GEESE *p. 44*
DUCKS *p. 48*

PINK-FOOTED GOOSE

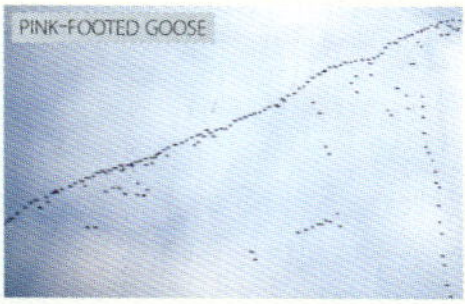
PINK-FOOTED GOOSE

BEWICK'S SWAN

SHOVELER

Plumages

Swans and geese do not show seasonal changes, but differ according to age: young **swans** are brown, becoming whiter with age; young **geese** are very similar to adults with only minor differences in feather edging. **Duck** breeding plumages differ between male and female; while females appear the same year-round, males can look very similar to females once they have moulted into 'eclipse' plumage (June to September); younger birds of either sex look very like females until their first moult from July to April, when males become apparent.

MALLARD M

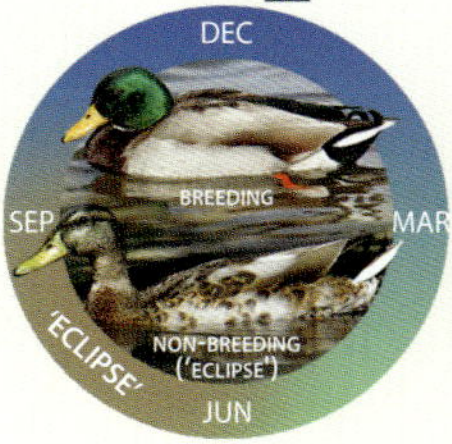
DEC
BREEDING
SEP
MAR
NON-BREEDING ('ECLIPSE')
'ECLIPSE'
JUN

MALLARD F

DEC
SEP
MAR
JUN

Identification

The features that are particularly important in the identification of wildfowl are shown in the annotated image here.

midwing
forewing
head
wing patch (speculum)
M
underwing
belly

GADWALL

Behaviour

Can help in identifying the type of duck if plumage details are hard to discern. **Surface-feeding ducks**, such as this Teal, sift through the water surface, or may 'upend', with their head submerged, like these Mallards; they may also feed on land.

Diving ducks such as this Goldeneye will either dive with a leap. or simply submerge.

M

TEAL **dabbling**

F
M

MALLARD **upending**

F

GOLDENEYE **diving**

Swans are unmistakable when adult: white with long neck but short legs and tail. Juveniles, the same shape but drab, usually remain with their parents, but may be told by a hint of the adult bill pattern, in duller colours. In most areas, swans will be **Mute Swan**, but locally, from October to March, two migrant species appear.

IDENTIFY BY:
▶ bill colours and pattern
▶ calls and wing noise in flight

WHERE rivers, lakes, farmland, coasts

EAT **All**: grass, aquatic plants, grain
Winter swans: also waste potatoes, root crops

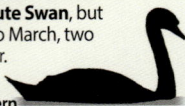

| MUTE SWAN | WHOOPER SWAN | BEWICK'S SWAN |

Mute Swan is the familiar swan often seen on park lakes, riversides and ponds. Well known for forming strong pair-bonds, they remain faithful for life – a key strategy for large birds that must care for their growing young for months. Sociable most of the time but in spring both sexes swim powerfully with aggressive, arch-winged postures to drive off other swans. They make enormous nests of thick plant stems, near water.

In breeding pairs, the bird with the largest black 'knob' on the bill will be the male, but most of the time sexes are hard to tell apart.

Young birds have a grey bill with a black triangle at the base.

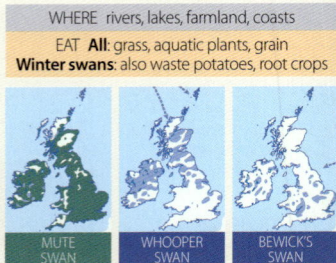

WHOOPER

longer neck
yellow bill
shorter neck
BEWICK'S
MUTE
orange bill

M

Common, locally numerous

Widespread, on rivers, lakes, sheltered coasts, marshes, pastureland.

Mute Swan *Cygnus olor*

L 140–160 cm | WS 200–240 cm

ID **Black-and-orange bill** with a black 'knob', pointed tail; frequently arches wings. JUVENILE: patched brown and for a year or two has a duller bill without a 'knob'.

VOICE Quiet, strangled, trumpeting notes and hisses. More obvious is a loud, rhythmic, throbbing hum from wings in flight.

At distance **Mute Swan** has a rounded body and a curled neck; **Whooper** and **Bewick's Swans** are slimmer and usually, but not always, have a straight neck. **Mute Swan's** downtilted bill is a more consistent clue.

J

I

long, pointed tail

A

orange bill

BEWICK'S SWANS

Very locally numerous OCT–MAR	Very locally numerous OCT–MAR
From Siberia. On floods, lakes, arable land; mostly on nature reserves in southern England, where easy to see. Rare away from regular sites.	From Iceland and Scandinavia. On floods, lakes, pastures, saltmarsh; mostly in north and west and on the Ouse Washes in East Anglia. Easy to see at regular sites, rare elsewhere.

Bewick's Swan
Cygnus columbianus

L 115–130 cm | WS 170–195 cm

ID Relatively small with shortish neck, short, square tail, rounded head; bill **black with a yellow rounded patch** each side JUVENILE: plumage greyish; bill similar pattern to adult but grey/pink/whitish and black.

VOICE Loud, bugling, ringing or bubbling calls; no loud wing noise.

Whooper Swan
Cygnus cygnus

L 140–160 cm | WS 205–235 cm

ID Large, long-necked, short-tailed; bill **black with a long, pointed yellow 'wedge'**. JUVENILE: plumage greyish; bill as adult but 'wedge' grey.

VOICE Loud, bugling or trumpeting calls; wings whistle but do not have the wing noise of a Mute Swan.

WHOOPER

BEWICK'S

A

WHOOPER

BEWICK'S

J

yellow 'wedges' on bill meet across top

long neck

WHOOPER SWAN

A

Yellow on bill varies from isolated 'blobs' (here) to large patches joined across top (head: above right).

short tail

BEWICK'S SWAN

A

39

'Grey' Geese

are actually grey-brown; they lack black on the head and have a greyer forewing and white tail with a dark central patch, most obvious in flight. They are usually found in flocks at regular sites, but odd ones or small groups turn up in unexpected places from time to time (sometimes amongst other species); they are fun to pick out but need to be studied closely for correct identification.

IDENTIFY BY:
▶ bill/leg colour combination
▶ plumage contrasts/markings

Adult **White-fronted Geese** also have distinctive head and belly markings.

The **Greylag Goose** is Britain's only native breeding goose but it is now difficult to tell wild birds (in W Scotland) from widespread introductions. Often tame, these lack the romance of true 'wild' winter visitors, but are still dramatic birds in the landscape. In winter thousands of **Greylag** and **Pink-footed Geese** arrive from Iceland as well as smaller numbers of **White-fronted Geese** from Russia and Greenland; and **Bean Geese** (rare) from Arctic NE Russia.

WHERE farmland, marshes, lakes, damp river meadows

EAT grass, sedges, roots and waste crops (*e.g.* sugar beet)

GREYLAG GOOSE | BEAN GOOSE | PINK-FOOTED GOOSE | WHITE-FRONTED GOOSE

Common, locally numerous winter migrant OCT–MAR from N Europe, and introduced resident

Introduced birds easy to see but wild migrants are found mainly in Scotland/Ireland.

Greylag Goose
Anser anser

L 74–84 cm | WS 149–168 cm

ID **Largest and palest brown of the 'grey' geese**, with a large, bright **orange bill** and pink (sometimes orange) legs.

VOICE Distinctive loud, harsh, staccato "*kya-gaa-gaa*" or "*ang-ang-ank*" with a clanging/clattering quality.

Many domesticated geese originate from the Greylag Goose but are usually stockier in the belly and have some obvious plumage differences, most often at least some white feathers.

upperwing pale at front, dark at rear

strongly contrasted dark and very pale grey underwing

orange bill

pink legs

WINTER GEESE Tens of thousands of grey geese, mostly **Pink-footed** (shown) and **Greylag**, arrive here each autumn, mostly in Scotland, north-west England and Norfolk. Wild and unapproachable, they look and sound spectacular as they fly to roost against a winter sunset. Family groups remain together all winter – young birds are duller, less neatly barred above.

PINK-FOOTED GEESE

Rare and local OCT–APR	Locally abundant SEP–APR	Uncommon OCT–MAR
Best seen in Norfolk at the RSPB reserve near Buckenham. Occasional individuals appear with other geese elsewhere.	In their wintering areas, flocks are usually easy to see flying over each evening to roost but can be elusive when feeding.	Small numbers at Slimbridge (Glos.) and in Norfolk. Greenland birds in Ireland, W Wales and SW Scotland.

Taiga/Tundra Bean Goose
Anser fabalis/serrirostris

L 69–88 cm | WS 140 cm–174 cm
ID Slightly larger, **longer-necked and browner** than the more numerous Pink-footed Goose, with neat pale bars above and **orange legs**. 'TAIGA BEAN GOOSE' bill mostly **orange with a dark tip**, 'TUNDRA BEAN GOOSE' bill **black with narrow orange band**.
VOICE *"Ung-ung," "yak-ak-ak;"* lower than other grey geese.

Pink-footed Goose
Anser brachyrhynchus

L 64–76 cm | WS 137–161 cm
ID Small, round, all-dark head, barred blue-grey back; **black-and-pink bill**; **pink legs**.
VOICE Distinctive loud babbling chorus in flight; intermixed with double *"ang-ung"* notes and much higher *"wink-wink"* calls.

White-fronted Goose
Anser albifrons

L 64–78 cm | WS 130–160 cm
ID **White forehead** and **black patches on belly**; **orange legs**. JUVENILE: no white on forehead until midwinter, and no black below.
VOICE Slightly yodelling, high notes *"lyo-lyok."* Flock chorus a high, yapping/yodelling.

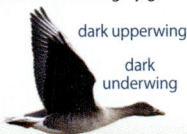

dark upperwing

dark underwing

The two species are sometimes treated as forms of one species.

mid-grey upperwing

pale grey underwing

narrow grey upperwing band

pale grey underwing

dark belly patches

Birds from Russia have a pink bill, those from Greenland an orange bill.

white forehead, pink/orange bill

'TAIGA'

'TUNDRA'

orange-and-black bill

rear flank same tone as back

orange legs

dark bill with pink band

rear flank darker than back

pink legs

young birds; no white forehead; pinkish-orange bill and orange legs

orange legs

41

'Black' Geese are dark geese with black on the head and neck (extending onto a broad 'breastplate' in some); they all have a black bill, black legs and a diagnostic pattern of white on the head and neck. **Canada Goose** is widespread, but introduced; **Brent** and most **Barnacle Geese** are wild birds with a more limited distribution, from autumn to spring.

IDENTIFY BY:
▶ face pattern
▶ extent of black on neck and breast

WHERE pastures, marshes, rivers, lakes, coasts
EAT grass, aquatic and saltmarsh plants, algae

CANADA GOOSE
BARNACLE GOOSE
BRENT GOOSE

Canada Geese, especially flying flocks with their loud, honking calls, add drama to many suburban landscapes. They are equally at home on water or on land. There are a few resident feral **Barnacle Geese** in the south; truly wild Barnacle Geese arrive in autumn from the Arctic and are far less approachable. **Brent Geese**, also from the Arctic, can be shy, though some are less so, even feeding on grassy areas in suburban areas. All geese spend the winter in identifiable family groups: young birds learn migration routes from their parents.

CANADA
BARNACLE
BRENT

Common, locally numerous (introduced)

Introduced from North America, commonplace even in parks and along town centre riversides, most on lakes/flooded pits.

Canada Goose *Branta canadensis*

L 80–105 cm | WS 155–180 cm

ID Big, brown, with characteristic **black neck and white 'chinstrap'**, and a large white rear end ('stern'). **IN FLIGHT**, long-necked and dark, with white above the tail.

VOICE Loud, honking notes; clamour from flocks.

dark underwing
black forehead
white breast

white 'chinstrap'
white breast
black legs

Locally numerous SEP–APR	Locally numerous winter visitor OCT–APR; introduced population resident
Dark-bellied birds are from the Russian Arctic and pale-bellied from the Canadian Arctic and Svalbard: look for lines of close, dark shapes on coastal fields, saltmarshes and mudflats; the birds keep up a low 'conversation' as they feed.	Birds from Greenland winter mostly in Ireland and W Scotland, from Svalbard on the Solway Firth, Loch of Strathbeg and Lindisfarne. Watch for flocks in flight or settling on coastal grassland.

Brent Goose *Branta bernicla*

L 55–62 cm | WS 105–117 cm

ID Small; ADULT: **black head and breast**, **white neck-patch**. JUVENILE: as adults but no neck-patch; pale bars across wings. Two forms. 'DARK-BELLIED' (NE, SE, S England) **steel-grey above**, **grey-brown belly**, white 'stern'; 'PALE-BELLIED' (NE England and Ireland) **browner above**, **whitish belly**. IN FLIGHT, very dark with large white patch surrounding tail.

VOICE Quiet grunting notes, become loud, croaking chorus as flock takes flight.

Barnacle Goose *Branta leucopsis*

L 58–70 cm | WS 120–142 cm

ID Grey, black and white (no brown); **white face**, **black neck and breast**; white underparts. IN FLIGHT, contrasted black front and white belly, grey upperwing, two-tone underwing. JUVENILE: duller, upperpart barring less regular.

VOICE Short, sharp notes, barking chorus from flocks.

black forehead

white forehead

prominent white 'stern'

black breast

white belly

white forehead

black breast

'PALE-BELLIED' form (above) is browner on back, more contrasted beneath than the widespread 'DARK-BELLIED' form.

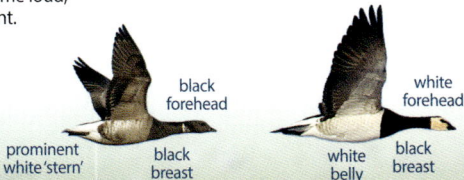

white neck-patch

black head and breast

white face

black 'breastplate'

black legs

black legs

43

Swans and Geese in flight

MUTE SWAN (p. 38)
very large, 'bump' on bill; loud wing noise

BEWICK'S SWAN (p. 39)
large, pointe bill, ringing hooting call

WHOOPER SWAN (p. 39)
very large, pointed bill bugling/ honking call

contrasting white

wholly dark

dark

dark grey

HEAD wholly dark

BRENT GOOSE (p. 43)

pale

BELLY (ADULT) barred

WHITE-FRONTED GOOSE (p. 41)
HEAD + BODY grey-brown

mid-grey outer

PINK-FOOTED GOOSE (p. 41)

black + white

pale

FOREHEAD white

pale grey

HEAD dark brown
BODY grey-brown

plain grey

BARNACLE GOOSE (p. 43)

white

HEAD + BODY dark brown

dark

'TAIGA' BEAN GOOSE (p. 41)

dark grey-brown

brown

FOREHEAD dark

contrasted dark grey and white

CANADA GOOSE (p. 42)

contrasting white

brown

HEAD + BODY grey-brown

pale blue-grey

GREYLAG GOOSE (p. 40)

Egyptian Goose and **Shelduck** are two larger wildfowl that show large white wing-patches in flight.

SHELDUCK

| WHERE ornamental parks with pools; grassy shores of flooded pits and reservoirs, nearby fields | EATS grass, leaves | WHERE coasts, inland lakes and marshes, estuaries | EATS small invertebrates: insects, molluscs, crustaceans |

| Locally common (introduced) | Common resident/winter visitor from N Europe |

Native to Africa; introduced to a few lakes in Norfolk but has spread and is increasing in southern Britain; usually in pairs or small flocks. Sometimes perches high up on dead branches.

Eyecatching on shallow pools and mud; between late July and September most migrate to the Baltic Sea to moult, leaving a few with crèches of juveniles.

Egyptian Goose *Alopochen aegyptiaca*

L 63–73 cm | WS 110–120 cm

ID Pale; olive-brown above, rufous towards rear; **pale head with dark brown 'eye-patch'**; **short, pink bill**; sandy-brown underparts; **long, pink legs. IN FLIGHT,** big white patch above and below on otherwise dark wing.

VOICE Various harsh calls; rough, unmusical quality.

EGYPTIAN GOOSE

Shelduck *Tadorna tadorna*

L 55–65 cm | WS 100–120 cm

ID Large, **strikingly white**; black head, **orange breast-band**. Vivid red bill (large 'knob' on MALE'S); legs pink. JUVENILE: dark crown and hindneck, white face; bill and legs grey at first, soon turn pink. **IN FLIGHT,** mostly white with black head and flight feathers.

VOICE In spring, short whistling notes and quick, grunting quacks, otherwise quiet.

SHELDUCK

J

large bill 'knob'; face all-black

no bill 'knob'; face smudged white

M

F

Male ducks compared

MALLARD
(p. 50)

TEAL
(p. 52)

GARGANEY
(p. 52)

PINTAIL *(p. 53*

SHOVELER
(p. 51)

**RED-BREASTED
MERGANSER**
(p. 56)

POCHARD
(p. 55)

WIGEON *(p. 53*

TUFTED DUCK
(p. 54)

GOOSANDER
(p. 56)

RED-CRESTED POCHARD
(p. 59)

SMEW *(p. 57*

SCAUP
(p. 55)

SHELDUCK
(p. 45)

GADWALL
(p. 51)

**LONG-TAILED
DUCK**
(p. 60

GOLDENEYE
(p. 57)

COMMON SCOTER
(p. 62)

VELVET SCOTER
(p. 62)

EIDER *(p. 61*

Female dabbling ducks compared

Female surface-feeding ducks can look very similar. On birds flying overhead, take note of underwing patterns and underwing/body contrast (see *page 48*). On standing birds check overall shape, bill size and colour, head shape, belly colour and leg length.

WHITE-BELLIED

WIGEON (*p. 53*)

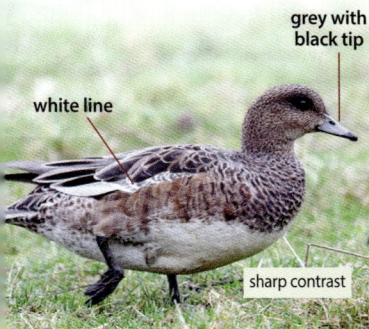

white line

grey with black tip

sharp contrast

TEAL (*p. 52*)

30% smaller than other dabbling ducks shown

well-marked 'stripy' face

GARGANEY (*p. 52*)

all dark

green (if visible)

PINTAIL (*p. 53*)

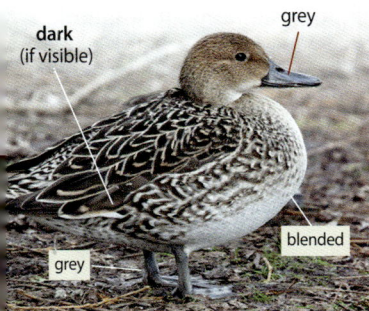

dark (if visible)

grey

grey

blended

GADWALL (*p. 51*)

sharp orange sides

white (if visible)

pale orange

sharp contrast

BROWN-BELLIED

SHOVELER (*p. 51*)

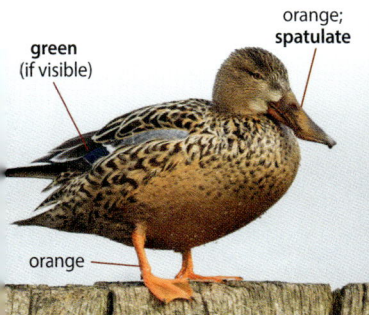

green (if visible)

orange; spatulate

orange

MALLARD (*p. 50*)

diffuse orange and brown

blue (if visible)

orange

47

Ducks in flight

M

MALLARD
(p.50)

M

SHOVELER
(p.51)

M

PINTAIL
(p.53)

F

F

F

M

M

POCHARD
(p.55)

F

GADWALL
(p.51)

F

M

M

TEAL
(p.52)

M

GARGANEY
(p.52)

F

F

WIGEON
(p.53)

SHOVELER
(p.51)

MALLARD
(p.50)

GADWALL
(p.51)

PINTAIL
(p.53)

UNDERWING dark
BELLY white

UNDERWING white
BELLY brown

UNDERWING white
BELLY white

UNDERWING white
BELLY brown

GARGANEY
(p.52)

TEAL
(p.52)

WIGEON
(p.53)

**FEMALE DABBLING
DUCKS FROM BELOW**

UNDERWING white with
black leading edge

UNDERWING white with
speckled leading
edge

UNDERWING grey

GOLDENEYE
(p. 57)

SMEW
(p. 57)

F

M

F

M

RED-BREASTED MERGANSER
(p. 56)

F

SHELDUCK
(p. 45)

GOOSANDER
(p. 56)

F

M

M

M

MI

F

EIDER
(p. 61)

M

LONG-TAILED DUCK
(p. 60)

F

M

F

SCAUP
(p. 55)

M

COMMON SCOTER
(p. 62)

M

VELVET SCOTER
(p. 62)

M

F

TUFTED DUCK
(p. 54)

F

F

Surface-feeding (or 'Dabbling') Ducks

typically feed while swimming, or on the shore or nearby grassy areas, arable fields and marshes; rarely dive underwater. Males are distinctive, females more difficult. Males are brightly plumaged from September/October to April/May but moult into 'eclipse' plumage and look like females between June and September. Juveniles are like females, but young males develop adult colouring through the winter.

IDENTIFY BY:
- ▶ plumage patterns and head shapes
- ▶ bill and leg colours
- ▶ wing patterns

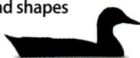

Mallard is common, but not always the most numerous duck. It is the one on park lakes and riversides that comes to be fed, and the dabbling duck to learn as a comparison. **Wigeon** and **Teal** are locally numerous; **Gadwall** is becoming more common; **Shoveler** and **Pintail** are more localized; and **Garganey** is rare. During the winter, resident birds are joined by **Mallard** from N and W Europe and **Gadwall**, **Shoveler**, **Wigeon** and **Teal** from Iceland and N/W Europe (with some Teal from Siberia). **Pintail** is a winter visitor from Iceland, Scandinavia and Arctic Russia. **Garganey** is a summer visitor that winters in sub-Saharan Africa.

WHERE lakes, rivers, park ponds, marshes, coastal sites and adjacent farmland

EAT grass, roots, seeds, cereals, aquatic vegetation, small invertebrates

MALLARD   GADWALL   SHOVELER

Common, locally numerous

Visit town lakes/riversides for close-up views; also look around edges of any freshwater lake.

Mallard *Anas platyrhynchos*

L 50–60 cm | WS 81–95 cm

ID Large; **orange legs.** MALE **glossy green head**, white collar, burgundy breast, yellow bill, dark eye. FEMALE/JUVENILE streaky brown with brown belly; mainly orange bill. **IN FLIGHT, purple-blue wing patch edged white.** FEMALE/JUVENILE white underwing contrasts with belly.

VOICE MALE whistles and quacks quietly. FEMALE makes typical loud, coarse *"quaark-quark-quack quack quack ack."*

All ducks are flightless for a brief period when moulting from JUN–SEP; during this time MALE Mallards look like females but have a yellow bill.

blue-and-white wing patch

brown belly

glossy green

yellow

OCT–MAY

burgundy

blue wing patch not always visible

grey

Locally common resident/winter visitor from N Europe

Check groups of ducks milling around diving Coot; listen for courtship calls in early spring.

Gadwall *Mareca strepera*

L 46–56 cm | WS 78–90 cm

ID Large; **pale orange legs**, **white wing patch** (not always visible). MALE buff-brown and **grey**; **black bill**; **black rear** (no white). FEMALE streaky brown with **white belly**; orange sides to bill. **IN FLIGHT**, **white** square or diamond **near base of wing**. FEMALE/JUVENILE no underwing/belly contrast.

VOICE Low quack; MALE has nasal, double "*nhek-nhek*" in flight and in display.

white diamond on wing

M

white belly

F

F

white wing patch (not always visible)

MALES as females JUN–SEP, but retain some finely barred grey feathers.

M SEP–MAY

Locally common resident/winter visitor from N Europe

Look for white-breasted males in groups strung out on the shore or in shallow bays; sometimes feeds in tight, rotating flocks.

Shoveler *Spatula clypeata*

L 44–52 cm | WS 73–82 cm

ID Large; **long, 'shovel' bill**; short, **orange legs**. MALE green-black head, black bill, **yellow eye**, **white breast**, **rufous flank**. FEMALE streaked brown, orange bill. **IN FLIGHT**, **blue/grey upper forewing**; **white midwing**; **green wing patch**.

VOICE Rather quiet, short quacks; wings make loud 'woof' on take-off.

M

blue/grey forewing

F

MALES as females JUN–SEP, but with a greyer head.

F

Long, flat head and bill profile

green-black

black

green wing patch (not always visible)

white

rufous

M NOV–JUN

51

TEAL

Common resident/winter visitor from N Europe

Look around the water's edge and in flooded vegetation; often feeds in shallows at night.

WHERE marshes, creeks, lagoons, lakes, floods; breeds rushy pools on upland moors

EATS aquatic invertebrates, but mainly seeds in winter

TEAL

Teal *Anas crecca*

L 35–40 cm | WS 50–60 cm

ID Small, dark; bill and legs grey. MALE grey; **thin white line** along body; brown head with **band of dark green**; triangle of **mustard-yellow** near tail. FEMALE grey-brown; **white streak** near tail.
IN FLIGHT, wing patch grass-green with broad, whitish band in front.

VOICE MALE has short, high, ringing double note. FEMALE gives a short quack.

speckled leading edge

green-and-white wing patch

rather plain 'face'

M SEP–MAY

MALES as females JUN–SEP, but retain some grey feathers.

white streak

Scarce MAR–OCT; winters in Africa

Check for autumn migrants swimming in flocks of Teal or Shoveler (*p. 51*): the distinctive head pattern is usually the first clue.

WHERE lakes, reservoirs, grassy floods, reedbeds, marshes

EATS leaves, shoots, insects

GARGANEY

Garganey *Spatula querquedula*

L 37–41 cm | WS 59–67 cm

ID Small; bill and legs **grey**. MALE **white stripe** on red-brown head; grey flank. FEMALE/JUVENILE/'ECLIPSE' MALE brown; blackish spots edged buff; head **striped** with pale band over eye, dark band across cheek.
IN FLIGHT, wing patch dark between two parallel white lines (like Mallard *p. 50*).

VOICE Quiet; male has dry rattling call in spring.

black leading edge

white-dark-white wing patch

well-marked 'face'

white stripe on red-brown head

Common, locally numerous winter visitor
SEP–MAR from N Europe; rare breeder, most in N

Look for flocks feeding on the shore or nearby areas of short grass, rarely feeds on open water.

WHERE coastal marshes, grassy pastures, floods, lakes

EATS aquatic plants, grasses and roots

WIGEON

Wigeon *Mareca penelope*

L 43–50 cm | WS 72–85 cm

ID Medium–large; **short grey bill and legs**. MALE **blue-grey**; white band on wing edge; red-brown head, **yellow forehead**. FEMALE dark or pale, greyish- or tawny-brown, more mottled than streaked; **white belly, plain** flank. IN FLIGHT, MALE **forewing white**, wing patch black-and-green; FEMALE forewing grey-buff, hindwing dark brown, belly white.

VOICE MALE makes wild, clear, emphatic double whistle, "*whee-oo.*" FEMALE has a deep, gruff, growling note.

M white forewing

grey underwing

F

white belly

F

yellow front to red-brown head

M NOV–APR

! American Wigeon (p. 256)

Locally common SEP–APR, from N Europe

Generally seen in small numbers on open water, saltmarsh or flooded grassland, usually dabbling or upending to feed in shallow water.

WHERE mostly estuaries; also floods, marshes, lakes, reservoirs

EATS small invertebrates, roots, seeds

PINTAIL

Pintail *Anas acuta*

L 51–62 cm | WS 79–87 cm

ID Large, heavy-bodied; slender neck, pointed tail (long on MALE). **Bill dark grey/ black, legs grey**. MALE **white breast**, white line on **brown head**. FEMALE streaked brown; head/neck pale ochre-buff. IN FLIGHT, long neck; dark wing patch with white rear edge.

VOICE Quiet quacks and quick gabbling notes.

long tail

M

dark/ white wing patch

long-necked

white trailing edge

F

white line on brown head

F

M NOV–JUN

Diving Ducks

swim on open water and dive under to feed. Males resemble females from May–September. In flight, diving ducks have long wingbars or white patches. 'Sawbills' have a hooked, finely serrated bill (for grasping fish). Diving ducks are usually loosely scattered across the water when feeding but cluster together if alarmed or sleeping, head-to-wind. On a dull day with silver-grey water, ducks can look very dark: shapes and patterns are more important than colour.

IDENTIFY BY:
▶ plumage patterns and head shapes
▶ pattern on spread wing
▶ bill colour

WHERE freshwater: rivers, reservoirs, gravel pits, sheltered coasts	EAT aquatic plants, molluscs, crustaceans, other invertebrates

TUFTED DUCK | POCHARD | SCAUP

Common, locally numerous resident/winter visitor from N Europe

Look for large flocks usually on freshwater, but also scan for pairs on grassy banks in spring.

Tufted Duck *Aythya fuligula*

L 40–47 cm | WS 65–72 cm

ID Medium–large; head round with tuft on nape. Bill grey with wide black tip; eye yellow. MALE **black with white flank**; **black 'tuft'** droops from nape. FEMALE/JUVENILE/'ECLIPSE' MALE unstreaked dark brown, often a little white by bill and under tail. Small **tuft on nape** nearly always obvious. **IN FLIGHT**, barrel-bodied, short-winged; long, white wingbar.

VOICE Low growling calls.

Diving ducks mix together on open water. During the winter **Scaup** from Iceland and N Europe (two centre birds) may join flocks, such as this mixed group of **Tufted Duck** and **Pochard** (with a single **Coot**). During the winter our resident **Tufted Duck** are joined by birds from Iceland and N & W Europe, and our **Pochard** by birds from E & W Europe.

MALES as females MAY–SEP, but usually blacker on the back and paler on the flanks.

black back

M

little/no white on face

F

pale eye

little or no white on 'face'

forehead rather rounded

tuft

F

black back

M SEP–MAY

Locally common resident/winter visitor from Europe

Look on lakes for pairs to hundreds, often sleeping amongst active Tufted Ducks before feeding at night.

Pochard *Aythya ferina*

L 42–49 cm | WS 67–75 cm

ID Medium–large; forehead slopes into long, dark bill with **grey band**. MALE 'black both ends', **grey body** with no white; head **red-brown**, eye red. FEMALE dull, greyish with liver-brown head and breast; **white around eye**, bill and throat. **IN FLIGHT**, broad, grey wingbar.

VOICE Insignificant growling notes; "*ah-ooh*" in display.

M

F

dark eye

F

M SEP–MAY

MALES duller
MAR–OCT

Scarce SEP–APR from Iceland and N Europe

Scan from vantage points over estuaries or open bays for Pochard-like flocks; look carefully through commoner diving ducks inland.

Scaup *Aythya marila*

L 42–51 cm | WS 71–80 cm

ID Marine equivalent of Tufted Duck. Bill broad, grey with **small** black tip (wider, blurred, on JUVENILE); eye yellow. MALE 'black both ends', **grey back** with **white flank**; head green-**black**. FEMALE/JUVENILE broad-bodied, pale brown; **extensive white 'face' patch** and often a pale 'ear' spot (lacking in Tufted Duck). **IN FLIGHT**, long, white wingbar.

VOICE Low growling notes.

grey back

M

white face

F

F/J

extensive white 'face' patch

no tuft

grey back

M SEP–JUN

55

'SAWBILL' DUCKS
Goosander, **Red-breasted Merganser** and **Smew** have a serrated ('saw') bill to help grasp fish underwater.

IDENTIFY BY:
▶ male: pattern + crest
▶ female: head and neck
▶ shape of crest

WHERE rivers, lakes, estuaries, open sea

EATS fish, sometimes other small aquatic creatures

RED-BREASTED MERGANSER

GOOSANDER

Locally common resident/winter visitor from N Europe

Look for long, dark shapes, diving frequently, males with a broad white streak along the body, on sheltered coastal waters.

Red-breasted Merganser *Mergus serrator*

L 52–58 cm | WS 67–82 cm

ID Large, long-bodied; **slim**, **orange-red bill**; **orange-red legs**. MALE black, white and grey, **dark brown breast**; **spiky crest**; **red** eye. FEMALE/MALE (JUN–NOV)/JUVENILE **brownish-grey**; reddish head **blends** into whitish foreneck and breast.
IN FLIGHT, swift, elongated; straight wings with white patches.
VOICE Usually silent.

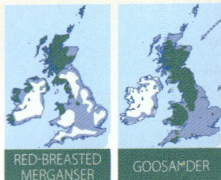

no head/breast contrast

dark breast

brown blends into breast

spiky crest

red eye

brown breast

dark side with broad white streak

M NOV–MAY

Locally common resident/winter visitor from NE Europe

Watch for elongated diving ducks on freshwater, males very white-bodied; also scan low banks. Flocks may gather in bays to roost.

Goosander *Mergus merganser*

L 58–68 cm | WS 78–94 cm

ID Large, long-bodied; **thick, red bill**; **red legs**. MALE **white**, tinged **salmon-pink** or yellowish, black back; **green-black** head; **dark** eye. FEMALE/MALE (JUN–NOV)/JUVENILE **blue-grey**; red-brown head and foreneck **sharply defined** against white breast; **white chin**; drooping crest. **IN FLIGHT**, swift, powerful, elongated; narrow, straight wings with white squarish patches.
VOICE Usually silent.

dark head and white breast contrast

brown contrasts sharply with white breast

dark eye

white/pink breast

white side

M NOV.

Fairly common winter visitor from Scandinavia & NE Europe SEP–APR; rare breeder in north

Scan lakes for dispersed, dark shapes diving frequently or groups that have gathered to display and/or roost.

WHERE coastal areas, lakes, including open, bleak reservoirs

EATS insects, molluscs, crustaceans

GOLDENEYE

Goldeneye *Bucephala clangula*

L 40–48 cm ¦ WS 62–77 cm

ID Medium-sized; **bulky**, **round-backed**, with **large head**, low tail. MALE underparts **pure white**, back and tail black; **head black** with **large white spot** between yellow eye and black bill. FEMALE/JUVENILE dark **grey**, small **white patches** along body; head **dark brown**, eye yellow or white. IN FLIGHT, big white patch on innerwing.

VOICE Low growls and rhythmic, mechanical "*airr-ik*" in display. Wings of male make loud whistle in flight.

MALES as females JUN–OCT, but usually with at least a faint white spot on the face.

F

M

Males look their best NOV–APR; courtship display includes extravagant, ritualized postures and jerky movements.

grey body looks dark at distance F

all-dark head, pale eye

black-and-white body M OCT–JUN

white face spot

Rare NOV–MAR (from Scandinavia)

Most frequent in south-east England, often around reeds and flooded willow thickets.

WHERE lakes, ponds, reservoirs with overhanging vegetation

EATS fish, some invertebrates

SMEW

Smew *Mergellus albellus*

L 38–44 | WS 56–69 cm

ID Small. MALE **white** with **grey flank**, **black face patch**, black back, fine black lines across side of breast, and **drooping crest**. FEMALE/JUVENILE **lead-grey**; red-brown head with **pure white patch** on lower face and throat. IN FLIGHT, quite elongated; white patches on narrow wing.

VOICE Usually silent.

F

M

dark eye

body lead-grey

white patch F

body white with black marks

M OCT–MAY

Introductions and escapes

Wildfowl are kept in 'ornamental' collections, wings 'clipped' to prevent them flying off, but some escape and can appear almost anywhere: the excitement of seeing a rare duck is often reduced by the chance of its being an escapee.

Some have been released (now illegal) and established themselves as regular breeding birds in the wild (*opposite page*); others are regularly encountered but have not (yet) become established (*this page*).

Rare (introduced)

Escaped Australian swan, sometimes breeds: lakes, estuaries, rivers, meadows.

Black Swan *Cygnus atratus*

L 110–140 cm | WS 160–200 cm

ID Black with white in wings (obvious in flight); red bill.

Uncommon (introduced)

Rare vagrant from N America, or, more regularly, escape: lakes, reservoirs, pastures.

Snow Goose *Anser caerulescens*

L 65–79 cm | WS 135–165 cm

ID Either white with black wingtips, or dark grey-brown with white head. Bill and legs pink.

Uncommon (introduced)

Escaped Asian goose: lakes, reservoirs and adjacent grassland.

Bar-headed Goose *Anser indicus*

L 71–76 cm | WS 140–160 cm

ID Pale grey with white head crossed by two black bars on nape. Bill and legs orange.

Uncommon (introduced)

From America: lakes, reservoirs.

Muscovy Duck (domesticated)
Cairina moschata

L 66–84 cm | WS 120–14 cm

ID Large; generally **glossy black** and white (but many varieties including white, brown and black) with red bill, **knobbly or warty** at base.

Common (introduced)

Lakes, reservoirs, rivers.

Mallard (domesticated)
Anas platyrhynchos

L 50–60 cm | WS 81–95 cm

ID Many varieties: may be white with yellow bill (so-called 'Aylesbury' Duck), dark brown, beige with dark brown head (vague pattern of male Mallard (*p. 50*)) or black-brown with a white breast.

Possible vagrant from Europe, but introduced populations established: lakes/reservoirs, often with Tufted Duck and Pochard.

Red-crested Pochard *Netta rufina*

L 53–57 cm | WS 85–90 cm

ID MALE pale brown and white with black breast and belly, fuzzy **orange crown** and **red bill**. FEMALE **pale plain brown** with **whitish face** and long, grey, pale-tipped bill. **IN FLIGHT**, long, **broad, white wingbar**.

MALES as females JUN–OCT, but bill and eye red.

RED-CRESTED POCHARD

recalls a high-crowned female Common Scoter (p.62) with a pale-tipped bill

'fuzzy' crown

red eye and bill

white flank obvious at long range

M OCT–MAR

Established introduction from Asia: wooded lakes and rivers, with large trees providing nest holes (readily uses nest boxes).

Mandarin Duck L 41–49 cm | WS 65–75 cm

ID MALE unmistakable: multicoloured, with unique **orange 'sails'**. FEMALE **mottled dark and light grey** with fine white 'spectacles'.

VOICE High, squeaky quacks from birds flying around wooded watersides in spring.

MALES as females JUN–OCT, but bill red.

MANDARIN DUCK

Often perches up on branches.

fine white 'spectacles'

distinctive orange 'sails'

M OCT–JUN

spotted flanks

F

59

Sea Ducks are diving ducks that are most likely to be seen offshore from September to March, particularly in sheltered bays (**Eider** and **Common Scoter** year-round). These species and **Long-tailed Duck** often form large flocks, sometimes numbering hundreds/thousands, occasionally mixed, and are best looked for by scanning from a raised viewpoint in likely areas. They are rarely seen inland, although Common Scoter breeds on freshwater lakes. (See also **Scaup** (p. 55), **Goldeneye** (p. 57) and **Red-breasted Merganser** (p. 56).)

Identify by:
▶overall colour
▶pattern on spread wing

WHERE coasts, islands, open sea, especially in large bays

EAT shellfish, crabs, other marine invertebrates

LONG-TAILED DUCK | EIDER

Long-tailed Duck in winter looks brown-and-white with complex patterns; the short, thick bill is distinctive. **Eider** is much larger, has a wedge-shaped bill and shows a variety of age/sex-related plumages. Scoters are all-dark and slightly smaller than Eider. **Common Scoter** is slightly less bulky, more round-headed than the white-winged **Velvet Scoter**.

Scarce; locally numerous AUG–MAY (from N Europe)

Look a few hundred metres offshore for lively flocks, frequently flying low over the sea, sometimes with scoters (p. 62) and/or Eiders.

Long-tailed Duck *Clangula hyemalis*

MALE L 49–62 cm (incl. 10–15 cm tail); FEMALE L 39–47 cm | WS 65–82 cm

ID Small, squat; square head and **short, triangular bill**; dives frequently. MALE **largely white**, patched with black and brown, including **dark cheek patch**; long, slender tail. FEMALE dark with white flank and **white face and dark cheek mark** (the size of which differs between individuals) JUVENILE like female but darker head/face/neck. IN FLIGHT, **all-dark wings**.

VOICE MALE gives frequent, nasal, yodelling "*ar-ar-ardl-ow*;" quiet "*gag*" notes. FEMALE has nasal quack.

white sides to dark rump

all-dark wings

F
MJ
F
M

triangular bill

F OCT–APR [light]

circular dark patch on cheek

F OCT–APR [dark]

pink band on bill (males only)

MN OCT–APR

Eider look distinctive, the white-backed males unlike any other common duck.

Females are grey-brown to rufous, with black and pale bars – not streaked.

Locally common resident/migrant

Look for family parties inshore in summer and scan well offshore for larger flocks at other times. Also look in harbours, where you may be able to get closer views.

Eider *Somateria mollissima*

L 60–70 cm | WS 95–105 cm

ID Large, bulky, with 'wedge'-shaped head; long, triangular, pale-tipped bill, with a 'wedge' of feathers extending either side. Short tail often raised. MALE **black below**, **white above**, with **pink breast**. FEMALE/JUVENILE brown, **barred crosswise** with black and buff. IMMATURE/'ECLIPSE' MALE patched black-brown and white (mature after three years).

VOICE MALE has sensuous, evocative courtship call, *"ooo, wu-vooooo."* FEMALE gives short, rapid quacks.

❗ King Eider (p.256)

long, 'wedge'-shaped head/bill profile

MI ALL YEAR

ADULT MALE black-brown with white breast JUL–OCT.

M OCT–JUN

Velvet Scoter, Common Scoter and Long-tailed Duck are easy to separate in flight, but can present a confusing black-and-white flicker as they fly together.

COMMON SCOTER　　LONG-TAILED DUCK　　VELVET SCOTER　　LONG-TAILED DUCK

WHERE coasts, islands, open sea, especially in large bays

EAT shellfish, crabs, other marine invertebrates

Locally common winter/passage migrant from Iceland/N Europe/ W Siberia; small numbers all year; rare breeder Ireland/N Scotland

Scan offshore for feeding flocks, or for lines of 'dark' ducks flying past; also check inland waters for small numbers in late summer.

Common Scoter *Melanitta nigra*

L 44–54 cm | WS 70–84 cm

ID Heavy body; rounded forehead; **pointed tail** often raised. Grey-black legs. MALE **black with slightly paler wingtips; yellow on top of bill.** FEMALE **dark brown with pale face;** black bill. IN FLIGHT, **all-dark wings.**

VOICE MALE gives whistled, piping notes. FEMALE has a growling note.

COMMON SCOTER

A **Common Scoter** flaps its wings to reveal paler wingtips but no white.

pale cheek

yellow on top of bill

F

M

Scarce winter/passage migrant from Scandinavia JUL–APR

Check flocks of Common Scoters for a telltale white wing flash.

Velvet Scoter *Melanitta fusca*

L 51–58 cm | WS 79–97 cm

ID Large, bulky; angular forehead; tapered bill faintly upcurved; short tail. **White patch on wing.** Dark red legs. MALE **black; white 'tick' under eye; yellow on sides of bill.** FEMALE dark brown with **two whitish spots** on side of head; black bill. IN FLIGHT, dark wings with **prominent white patch.**

VOICE Rarely heard: whistle from MALE; cackling note from FEMALE.

VELVET SCOTER

A suspected **Velvet Scoter** may eventually flap its wings, revealing big white patches.

two white patches on head

white 'tick' under eye

yellow on sides of bill

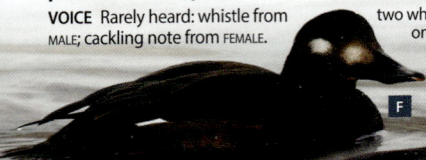

F

M

white wing patch (not always visible)

Waterbirds are a collection of small to large, swimming birds that dive from the surface to feed.

Cormorants
(*pp. 64–65*)

Large; long-bodied with long, broad tail; bill slightly hooked. All four toes joined by webs. Swim low in water, head uptilted; dive frequently; stand upright on cliff ledges, shorelines, rafts, buoys (Cormorant also in trees).

CORMORANT

Divers
(*pp. 66–67*)

Large; long-bodied with very short tail; bill dagger-like, straight or very slightly upturned. Three front toes webbed. Swim low in the water with slim neck upright, head held horizontal or uptilted; unable to stand.

GREAT NORTHERN DIVER

Grebes
(*pp. 68–69*)

Small–medium-sized; round-bodied with almost no tail; bill dagger-like or blunt. Toes unwebbed but broadly lobed along sides. Swim buoyantly with neck erect or withdrawn onto breast; rarely stand, cannot walk.

RED-NECKED GREBE

In flight

Cormorants in groups, lines, 'V' shapes; direct, strong, quick beats; Cormorant also glides with slight droop/kink in neck. **Divers** solitary; direct, long, slender wings, long head/neck slightly drooped, feet trailed. **Grebes** low over water, neck outstretched, feet trailed.

CORMORANT

Plumages

Cormorants black (juveniles dark brown, or white below); mature over 5 years; sexes alike. **Divers** and **grebes** distinctive in breeding plumages; non-breeding plumages more alike; juveniles like non-breeding adults; sexes alike.

GREAT CRESTED GREBE
J
N AUG–MAR
B MAR–JUL

Behaviour

Cormorants feed alone or in flocks, sometimes in 'feeding frenzy' around shoals of fish. **Divers** make distinctive loud wailing calls both day and night during the breeding season. **Grebes** have remarkable courtship displays; chicks may ride on parent's back.

GREAT CRESTED GREBE

LITTLE GREBES do not fly readily, but flap their wings and skitter across the water surface

Cormorants

Cormorants are heavy, long-bodied waterbirds with a slim neck, hook-tipped bill, rather long tail and short, thick legs. Perch (often with wings spread) on flat ground, rocks or (Cormorant only) trees, and swim and dive expertly.

IDENTIFY BY:
▶ head and bill shape ▶ facial pattern

Cormorant feed in salt or fresh water; inland, they perch (and nest) in trees (often obvious by copious white droppings). **Shag** swim and dive expertly in the roughest seas off rocky shores, and breed colonially on sea cliffs.

Locally common resident/winter migrant from N & W Europe; regular inland but more widespread and numerous SEP–APR

Look for birds swimming, perched or flying close inshore along all types of coast, from cliffs to saltmarsh; frequent inland on large rivers and lakes, where may be seen roosting in trees, or gathered in small flocks on lake shores before flying off to roost elsewhere.

WHERE Both: water and adjacent shore, rocky coasts, estuaries, harbours **Cormorant**: also large rivers, lakes, reservoirs

EAT fish, small marine invertebrates, caught during long dives from surface

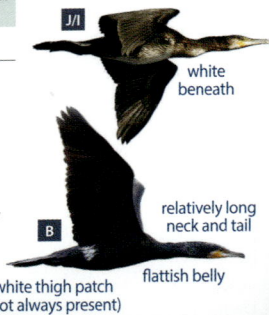

CORMORANT   SHAG

Cormorant *Phalacrocorax carbo*

L 77–94 cm | WS 121–149 cm

ID Very large. Blue-black with **white chin**. BREEDING angular yellow and white face patterns and bold **white thigh** patch. NON-BREEDING blackish, with yellow around bill, whitish throat. IMMATURE brown, **white beneath**, becoming darker with age. **IN FLIGHT**, graceful; flocks fly in lines, frequently synchronizing movements. Soar and glide surprisingly well, turning into the wind to settle deftly on water or a perch.

VOICE Low, unmusical grunts and growling notes.

J/I
white beneath

B
relatively long neck and tail

flattish belly

white thigh patch (not always present)

crest on nape

white throat

B JAN–JUN

B FEB–JUN

sloping forehead   long, thick bill

yellow throat patch

N JUN–FEB

J/I

white head plumes

white throat

B JAN–JUN

Locally common resident, disperses along coasts AUG–FEB; rare inland, chiefly after storms

Look on rocky coasts and cliffs, particularly near breeding colonies; often seen in flight low over the sea. Frequent in outer parts of estuaries, especially in winter, where regularly perches on buoys. Non-breeders occur widely around coasts of Britain and Ireland.

Cormorant (*top*) and **Shag** (*bottom*) both dive under with a forward roll, but Shag **leaps clear** of the surface.

Shag *Phalacrocorax aristotelis*

L 68–78 cm | WS 95–110 cm

ID Large but **smaller** than Cormorant, with rounded head, steep forehead, slim bill. **Black** (glossed green) with bright **yellow facial skin**. BREEDING neat, **upstanding crest**. IMMATURE birds brown with **white chin and/or throat**, paler brown but **no white beneath**. IN FLIGHT, more often in twos and threes than larger groups, with quicker wingbeats than Cormorant, low over the waves, and only rarely taking short cuts over land.

VOICE Grunting and hissing calls from male.

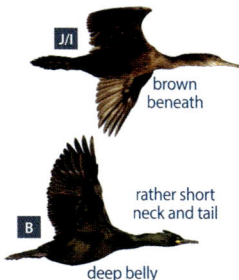

J/I

brown beneath

rather short neck and tail

B

deep belly

upright crest

dark throat

N JUN–FEB

B MAR–JUN

rounded head

slim bill

white chin spot

J/I

dark throat

B MAR–JUN

Divers are long-bodied, slim-necked and have a dagger-shaped bill with a tip that is not hooked. They dive frequently and travel long distances underwater, and never stand on dry land, buoys, *etc*. Flight is direct and fast, on slender wings, with neck outstretched and large feet trailing.

IDENTIFY BY:
▶ bill shape
▶ pattern on back in summer
▶ head/neck pattern in winter

WHERE northern lakes (summer); coasts, reservoirs (winter)	EAT fish, crabs and molluscs, caught in prolonged dives

RED-THROATED DIVER

BLACK-THROATED DIVER

GREAT NORTHERN DIVER

Scarce, local breeder and winter visitor/passage migrant from Iceland/Scandinavia; rare inland

Look on small pools and watch/listen for birds flying between breeding sites and the sea where they fish; scan far out at sea in winter.

Red-throated Diver *Gavia stellata*

L 55–67 cm | WS 91–110 cm

ID Smallest, commonest diver. Head and **tapered bill** held slightly **uptilted**. **Plain brown** above with grey head; narrow **dark red patch on foreneck**. NON-BREEDING/JUVENILE grey-brown and white; white on face extends **above eye**; narrow dark crown (dark crown reaches eye on other divers); back **finely speckled white**. **IN FLIGHT**, **quick** wingbeats; head and feet **drooped**; **waggles head up and down**.

VOICE Wailing calls and loud, staccato quacking notes, including guttural "*kuk-uk-uk-uk*" IN FLIGHT in summer.

The moult between breeding and winter plumages takes a few weeks, during which time a range of 'in-between' stages can be seen, such as this Red-throated Diver in October. These intermediate plumages can be seen during SEP–DEC and again during FEB–APR.

N

N

droop-necked

sloping forehead

white almost to back of head

N/J AUG–MAR

bill slightly uptilted

B MAR–SEP

Check large lakes with islands in Scotland in summer; at other times, scan bays and estuaries for birds drifting by on the tide.

Black-throated Diver *Gavia arctica*

L 63–75 cm | WS 100–122 cm

ID Middle-sized diver (slimmer than Great Northern Diver) with **slender, straight bill**. BREEDING back barred black-and-white; **head grey**; **black patch bordered with white stripes on foreneck**. NON-BREEDING/JUVENILE dark brown and white; grey-brown nape **paler than back**; **white patch** on rear flank. IN FLIGHT, head/neck **thick, straight out**; feet trailed.

VOICE Loud wailing calls in summer.

N

hindneck/cap paler than back

'tube'-necked

rounded forehead

bill slender, straight

N JUN–APR

pale front/dark rear of neck well defined

B FEB–OCT

white patch

Look close inshore or in estuaries – but keep scanning as birds can spend more time underwater than on the surface.

Great Northern Diver *Gavia immer*

L 73–88 cm | WS 122–148 cm

ID Largest diver; heavy, **dagger-like bill**, steep forehead. BREEDING **back chequered black-and-white; black head with white stripes on neck**. NON-BREEDING/JUVENILE brown above with pale bars; **black half-collar**; hindneck **darker than back**. IN FLIGHT, **whippy** wingbeats, **large head** barely drooped, feet trailed, wings long and slim.

VOICE Laughing or wailing notes in summer.

N

large-headed

pronounced 'bump' on forehead

hindneck/cap darker than back

N AUG–APR

black half-collar

bill thick, straight

B APR–OCT

Grebes spend almost all their time on water, diving frequently to feed, and only rarely stand on the shore and never walk or stand on buoys *etc*. They can travel some distance underwater and can be difficult to track in rough conditions or when far offshore.

IDENTIFY BY:
▶ size   ▶ bill size and shape   ▶head patterns

WHERE lakes, rivers, reservoirs and coasts -- especially wide, sandy bays and estuaries

EAT fish, small aquatic invertebrates

GREAT CRESTED GREBE

RED-NECKED GREBE

Common resident and winter visitor from N and W Europe

Widespread on lakes (watch for displaying pairs early in spring) and groups in sheltered coastal bays from autumn to spring; in winter, look for loose flocks of up to 100 (sometimes more) on larger lakes.

Great Crested Grebe *Podiceps cristatus*

L 46–51 cm | WS 59–73 cm

ID Largest grebe; slim **white neck held upright** or curled into 'shoulders'; bill slim, pink. **Black cap**; **white stripe** over eye. Black crest, **chestnut ruff**, spread in display. NON-BREEDING lacks chestnut ruff. JUVENILE brown; head striped black-and-white. IN FLIGHT, long, drooped neck, trailing legs; wings have large **patches of white**.

VOICE Loud barks in spring. Young birds call a loud, musical whistle.

white above eye

pink bill

white foreneck

N AUG–MAR

B MAR–JUL

Red-necked Grebe *Podiceps grisegena*

L 40–46 cm | WS 55–60 cm

ID Large grebe, **stockier** than Great Crested Grebe; bill thick, **yellow** at base. **Black cap extends to eye**. **Grey-white face**, **red neck**. NON-BREEDING black-and-white; **no white over eye**; cheek white, foreneck grey. IN FLIGHT, extended neck and trailing legs; large white patches on innerwing.

Rare winter visitor from W Europe AUG–MAY (declining)

Mostly in estuaries/bays on NE coast of England and Scotland, occasionally on coast and inland lakes farther south.

dark cap to below eye

yellow base to bill

N SEP–FEB

foreneck rusty or greyish

B MAR–SEP

Little Grebe *Tachybaptus ruficollis*

L 23–29 cm | WS 40–45 cm

ID Smallest grebe. **Very dark**; face **rusty red** with **pale spot** by bill. NON-BREEDING **brown**, with **dark cap**, **buff cheeks**; pale bill spot less contrasted. **IN FLIGHT**, skitters over water, trailing legs (*p. 63*); **wings all-dark**.

VOICE In summer, a **long, whinnying trill**, fading away; various short whistles and peeps.

LITTLE GREBE

N SEP–MAR

pale spot by bill

B APR–SEP

obvious white 'stern'

Black-necked Grebe *Podiceps nigricollis*

L 28–34 cm | WS 45–50 cm

ID Small. **Bill slightly upturned**; **head peaked**; eye bright red. BREEDING **black head and neck**, **drooping** yellow ear-tufts; **coppery-red flank**. NON-BREEDING **black cap extends below eye**. Front of neck **grey**; white patch hooks upwards behind cheek. **IN FLIGHT**, **white trailing edge** to wing.

VOICE Mostly silent but weak trills and rising whistles when nesting.

BLACK-NECKED GREBE

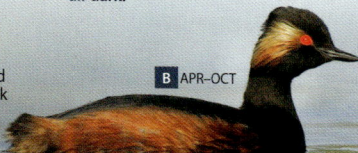

N SEP–APR

ill-defined pale cheek

B APR–OCT

Slavonian Grebe *Podiceps auritus*

L 31–38 cm | WS 46–55 cm

ID Small. **Straight** bill; crown rounded; eye bright red. BREEDING black head, **'wedge'-shaped** yellow ear-tufts; **red neck and flank**. NON-BREEDING black-and-white; **black cap stops at eye-level**, sharply defined against white face and foreneck. **IN FLIGHT**, **white trailing edge to wing** and **white 'shoulder' patch**.

VOICE Mostly silent but insignificant whinnies when nesting.

SLAVONIAN GREBE

sharply defined white cheek

N JUL–MAR

B MAR–JUL

Seabirds

Seabirds form a somewhat arbitrary collection of birds that rely on the marine environment for food year-round. Species in other groups, such as cormorants (*pp. 64–65*), divers (*pp. 66–67*), grebes (*pp. 68–69*), gulls (*pp. 82–100*), skuas (*pp. 101–103*), terns (*pp. 104–108*) and phalaropes (*p. 138*), may spend a considerable amount of the year at sea, but are not wholly dependent on the sea.

Auks (*pp. 72–75*)

Small–medium-sized, dumpy; more or less black-and-white; pointed or triangular bill; short legs set far back. Rather short, narrow wings.

GUILLEMOT

Shearwaters (*pp. 78–79*)

Medium–large-sized, black- or brown-and-white; slim bill; weak legs, unable to walk. Most often seen in flight: fairly long, narrow, stiff wings.

MANX SHEARWATER

Gannet (*pp. 80–81*)

Very large; largely white (juvenile brown); dagger-billed; short legs, does not walk. Most often seen in flight: long, angled wings.

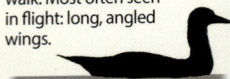

GANNET

Storm-petrels (*p. 76*)

Small; dark with white rump; small bill; weak legs, cannot walk. Usually seen in flight: short, broad, tapered wings.

NB only rarely sit on water

STORM PETREL

Fulmar (*p. 77*)

Large; pale, gull-like but rump/tail grey and no black on wingtip; short, thick, blunt bill; weak legs, cannot stand. Fairly long, narrow, stiff wings.

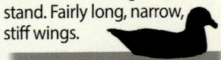

FULMAR

Plumages

Sexes look alike in **all species**, but seasonal differences in **Auks**. Juveniles look like adult except for **Gannet**, which develops from very dark to very white over several years (see *page 81*).

Seabird colonies, such as this Gannet colony in Shetland, are often in beautiful and dramatic locations.

Watching seabirds

The simplest way to see auks, Fulmar and Gannet is to watch them at well-known breeding sites. Seeing most petrels and shearwaters requires some planning, but dedication and a little luck are also needed. To maximise your chances, keep an eye on the weather: an onshore wind is helpful as many seabirds (as well as gulls, terns and skuas) may be blown closer to the shore, particularly during bad weather. Alternatively, ferries and dedicated wildlife boat trips also provide good opportunities at the right time of year.

GANNET

In flight

Auks fly fast and direct, with whirring wings low over the sea, either singly or in small flocks in line. **Shearwaters** and **Fulmar** fly with straight, stiff wings, usually a few beats between long glides, low over the sea, frequently banking or 'towering' in wind, shearwaters often in small to large flocks, in line. **Storm-petrels** flutter over the waves, dipping or pattering with feet and picking food from the surface. **Gannet** generally flies high over sea singly or in small flocks.

GUILLEMOT

ABOVE: **Auks** have a distinctive rapid, whirring flight action.
BELOW: **Shearwater** 'towering'.

SOOTY SHEARWATER

DIRECTION OF TRAVEL ⟶

Behaviour

All seabirds nest colonially. **Auks** and **shearwaters** swim on the surface and dive to feed, using their wings underwater. **Storm-petrels** and **shearwaters** visit their nest burrows/crevices after dark, shearwaters gathering in flocks offshore towards dusk. **Fulmar** breeds on open ledges and is easily seen. **Gannet** breeds in a few very large, dense colonies and feeds by plunge-diving.

Gannets, Fulmars and auks (such as these **Puffins**) are social and demonstrative.

71

Auks are seabirds that nest on the coast but are adapted to spend most of their lives far offshore, where they swim and dive for food. They may come close inshore after gales, but are only seen inland as storm-blown strays. In flight, they look small-winged and have rapid, whirring wingbeats.

IDENTIFY BY:
▶ bill shape
▶ head patterns
▶ body colour

WHERE sea cliffs and islands; on the sea	EAT fish and marine invertebrates

Guillemot and **Razorbill** fly low over the sea, swim buoyantly and dive for fish, and do not come to land except to breed. Guillemots nest on exposed ledges, Razorbills tend to nest inside deeper cavities. All auks can be seen from headlands especially in autumn gales.

To see breeding auks and other seabirds, visit colonies from March onwards. Some have easy viewing – such as Skomer Island and South Stack (Anglesey) in Wales; St Bees Head, Bempton Cliffs and the Farne Islands in north-east England; various east coast cliffs and the Northern Isles in Scotland; and west coast cliffs and islands such as Great Saltee and Rathlin in Ireland. In south-west England, isolated colonies can be seen at Portland Bill (Dorset) and Berry Head (Devon).

Locally common	Locally common
Look for blacker, blunter-billed auks in smaller numbers amongst numerous Guillemots.	Appears pale brown in bright light; look down from clifftop to see birds swimming underwater.

Razorbill *Alca torda*

L 38–43 cm | WS 60–69 cm

ID On ledge, upright on **pointed tail**. **Black-and-white**; bill **thick and blunt**, white line back to eye. NON-BREEDING **deep black cap**, whitish cheek with dark mark behind eye.

RAZORBILL

VOICE Guttural, growling "*goarrr*," harder, less whirring / musical than Guillemot.

Guillemot *Uria aalge*

L 38–46 cm | WS 61–73 cm

ID On ledge, upright on **square tail**. **Brown-and-white** bill **pointed**. Thin white 'spectacle' on minority 'bridled' form. NON-BREEDING **narrow dark cap** over broad white cheek, **black line** behind eye.

GUILLEMOT

VOICE Loud, whirring and growling calls at colonies.

B   'BRIDLED'

white band across bill and white line from bill to eye

thick bill

B FEB–AUG

pointed bill

B DEC–JUL

long, pointed tail

BREEDING AUKS **Guillemot** colonies, on flat offshore rocks or higher, sheer cliffs, are noisy, busy places in summer, becoming deserted as half-grown young leave the ledges in July. **Razorbills** tend to be fewer and **Puffins** often more separate on higher slopes.

Locally fairly common	Locally common
Scan large Scottish sea-lochs and harbours for isolated 'dots' with a telltale white wing patch, or look along the base of cliffs.	By far the best way to see Puffins is to visit a breeding colony from APR–JUL, where they can be remarkably confiding.

Black Guillemot
Cepphus grylle

L 32–38 cm | WS 49–58 cm

ID **Smoky-black** with large **white oval** on each wing; bright **red legs**. NON-BREEDING mottled grey, black and white; **white wing patches** still clear.

VOICE Thin, high-pitched whistle in summer: calls with open bill, bright red inside.

Usually small groups of 1–5, does not form large flocks offshore or on breeding ledges.

Puffin
Fratercula arctica

L 28–34 cm | WS 50–60 cm

ID Rotund, black-and-white with **orange legs**; stands and walks well. **Greyish-white face**, **colourful triangular bill**. NON-BREEDING grey-faced; bill duller, more greyish.

VOICE Low, hard cooing and "*arrk arrk;*" silent except when nesting.

Large flocks circle together above breeding colony in spring.

large white wing patch diagnostic

B FEB–AUG

red legs

colourful, triangular bill unique

B FEB–OCT

orange legs

Auks compared | in flight

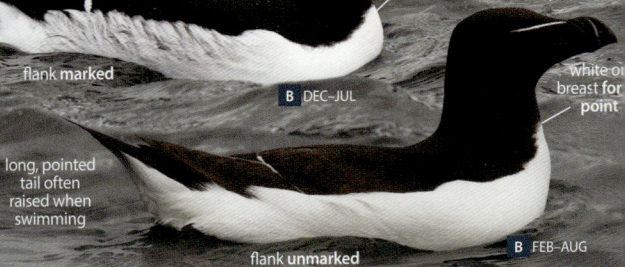

B FEB–AUG

clean
white flank

RAZORBILL
p.72

GUILLEMOT
p.72

marked
upper flank

B DEC–JUL

B

PUFFIN
p.73

B FEB–OCT

**BLACK
GUILLEMOT**
p.73

B FEB–AUG

BLACK GUILLEMOT
p.73

large white wing
patch diagnostic

B FEB–AUG

GUILLEMOT
p.72

white on breast
rounded

RAZORBILL
p.72

short tail

flank **marked**

B DEC–JUL

white on
breast **for
point**

long, pointed
tail often
raised when
swimming

flank **unmarked**

B FEB–AUG

PUFFIN
p.73

colourful, triangular bill unique

grey face

duller bill

B FEB–OCT

N JUL–MAR

74

RAZORBILL
p.72

AUG–MAY

clean
white flank

GUILLEMOT
p.72

AUG–JAN

marked
upper flank

AUG–FEB

**LITTLE
AUK**

SEP–APR

**BLACK
GUILLEMOT**
p.73

BLACK GUILLEMOT
p.73

SEP–APR

Juvenile **Razorbill** bill
shorter and thicker
than Guillemot's

OCT–MAY

GUILLEMOT
p.72

AUG–JAN

dark on side of neck
pointed

RAZORBILL
p.72

AUG–MAY

dark on side of neck
rounded

Rare, most late autumn OCT–MAR

Mostly N Sea coasts, rarely storm-driven inland.

Little Auk *Alle alle*

L 19–21 cm | WS 34–38 cm

ID Smallest auk; **black-and-white**; **small, stubby black bill**; **white streaks** on lower back. Usually swims low; dives with half-open wings. **IN FLIGHT**, quick, direct, low over water on slim wings; groups may look like small waders.

LITTLE AUK

AUG–FEB

LITTLE AUK

75

Storm Petrels flutter low over the sea when feeding, often pattering on the water surface, but have a more fluent, martin-like (*p. 188*) action in direct flight.

Petrels live predominantly at sea, only coming to land to breed (**Storm** and **Leach's Petrels** in burrows/stone walls, visited only at night; **Fulmar** on open ledges). They feed from the surface and are generally seen flying low over the water.

IDENTIFY BY:
▶ size and flight action ▶ tail shape
▶ upperwing and rump pattern
▶ underwing pattern

WHERE islands and coastal cliffs; at sea, offshore	EAT marine invertebrates, oily (mainly fish) offal

Storm Petrel is a quite widespread breeder on northern and western islands and headlands, with some birds present out to sea year-round. **Leach's Petrel** nests only on a few remote northern islands. **Fulmar** nests on cliffs, sometimes a little inland, ranging more widely around around the coast when not breeding.

Scarce, locally common, most APR–OCT

Best seen from ferry/boat far offshore, or during organized trips to breeding colonies at night.

Storm Petrel
Hydrobates pelagicus

L 15–16 cm | WS 37–41 cm
ID Tiny, blackish with **broad white band** around tail and **long white line under each wing**. Wings slightly rounded, curved back; tail broad. **IN FLIGHT** low over sea – House Martin-like (*p. 189*).

VOICE Soft purring, chuckling notes from nest burrow.

STORM PETREL

Scarce, local, most APR–NOV

Most likely to be seen inshore or from headlands in SEP–NOV after gales (when rarely also inland).

Leach's Petrel
Hydrobates leucorhoa

L 18–21 cm | WS 43–48 cm
ID Small but larger than Storm Petrel; **blackish** with **angled wings** and slight notch in tail; upperwing has broad **pale grey band**; underwing **all-dark**; white band above tail **narrow** and 'V'-shaped.

VOICE Whirring note with rising "*whuu*" from nest burrow and chattering flight calls nearby.

LEACH'S PETREL

square/round tail

plain upperwing

white bar on underwing

forked tail

pale upperwing band

dusky underwing

Fulmars have benefitted from a huge increase in discarded fish from trawlers and can now be found on most cliffs and rocky islands. From a distance, pairs on ledges dot slopes as 'white-spots'.

Fulmar

Grey rump/tail and lack of black on wingtip help to rule out gulls.

straight, narrow wings

The short, thick bill has 'tubular' nostrils that are used to help excrete excess salt and for the olfactory location of oily food.

rather thickset

pale patch on outerwing

Locally common

Look for birds sailing along clifftops near nesting colonies, especially from MAR–SEP; elsewhere, scan offshore, particularly from AUG–NOV.

Fulmar *Fulmarus glacialis*

L 43–52 cm | WS 101–117 cm

ID Grey-and-white; superficially gull-like (*p. 82*) but has very short legs (not able to stand or walk) and a different bill structure (see *above*). Broad, rounded white head, with bold **dark eye-patch. IN FLIGHT**, stiff flaps; glides low over sea in wind. Upperwing **grey** with pale patch towards wingtip (**no black**); **rump and short tail grey** above

VOICE Loud, harsh, cackling notes at breeding sites.

FULMAR

Buoyant on the sea, with high-tailed, big-headed, often forward-leaning shape and thick, blunt bill.

bulbous white head with bold black eye-patch

Shearwaters

are slim, long-winged seabirds; expert fliers low over the waves, rising higher in steep, banking glides in strong winds. **Manx Shearwater** breeds, the others are scarce or rare migrants seen from headlands or ships, mainly in autumn.

IDENTIFY BY:
► colour of upperparts
► colour of underside
► bill colour

WHERE at sea (Manx Shearwater breeds offshore islands)

EAT fish, squid, crustaceans

MANX SHEARWATERS

SHEARWATERS fly low over the sea, typically heading one way in loose flocks or lines; may rest in 'rafts' on the water.

Shearwaters cannot walk and come to land to visit their nest burrows only after dark, to avoid predatory gulls. Thousands of **Manx Shearwater** pairs calling to each other make an unearthly noise on remote islands in the north and west.

Locally abundant MAR–OCT	Rare and local, most JUL–OCT
At sea; breeds offshore islands; rarely inland after gale.	At sea; breeds Mediterranean, migrates north in summer.

Manx Shearwater
Puffinus puffinus

L 30–35 cm | WS 71–83 cm

ID **Black above**, **white below**; flies low over the sea with stiff-winged cross-shape. **Quick flaps between 'shearing' glides**, often **tilts onto wingtip**.

VOICE Strangled, nasal, four-syllable notes after dark at colonies.

Balearic Shearwater
Puffinus mauretanicus

34–39 cm | WS 78–90 cm

ID Small, stocky; **dull, brown above, dusky beneath** with pale brown belly and underwing. Rather heavy-bellied; wingbeats rapid between short glides.

MANX SHEARWATER

BALEARIC SHEARWATER

SOOTY SHEARWATER

GREAT SHEARWATER

CORY'S SHEARWATER

white flank

white 'hook' behind cheek

white belly

white under tail

blackish upperside

feet barely protrude

dark flank

dark under tail

pale brown underparts

rather heavily built and 'pot-bellied'

uniformly brown upperside

feet protrude

MANX SHEARWATER | BALEARIC SHEARWATER | SOOTY SHEARWATER | GREAT SHEARWATER | CORY'S SHEARWATER

Scarce JUL–SEP	Rare JUL–OCT	Rare JUL–OCT
At sea; breeds S hemisphere, migrates to north Atlantic.	At sea; breeds in S Atlantic, migrates to north Atlantic.	At sea; breeds E Atlantic islands, migrates north.

Sooty Shearwater
Ardenna grisea

L 40–50 cm | WS 93–106 cm

ID A heavy-bodied, slender-winged, **very dark** shearwater with **silvery underwing patches**. Resembles dark Arctic Skua (*p. 102*) but **short-tailed**, with **flap-flap-glide** flight.

Great Shearwater
Ardenna gravis

L 43–51 cm | WS 105–122 cm

ID Large dark brown and white shearwater; **sharply defined dark cap**, black bill, white face, **dark brown** upperparts; underside white, with smudgy **dark marks**.

Cory's Shearwater
Calonectris borealis

L 50–56 cm | WS 118–126 cm

ID Large **brown-and-white** shearwater (size of large gull). Steady, relaxed flight with low, curving glides; **brown** above, **pure white** below, with dusky head and **yellow bill**.

silvery patches on dark underwing

dark marks on underwing

all-white underwing

all-dark upperside

blackish cap and bill

pale head and bill

Shearwaters frequently dip a wingtip onto the water as they bank in flight.

WHERE breeds offshore
islands and a few mainland
cliffs; at sea
EATS fish

Locally common

Breeding sites occupied MAR–OCT; non-breeders and feeding birds widespread offshore, seen occasionally from most areas; locally frequent but erratic, depending on fish movements.

Gannet *Morus bassanus*

L 85–97 cm | WS 170–192 cm

ID Very large, usually far offshore flying steadily above the sea with occasional **headlong plunge**. ADULT **bright white** with **black tips** to long, straight wings. JUVENILE dark brown with fine white speckles. IMMATURES chequered, becoming increasingly white on head/neck, front edge of wing and rump. **IN FLIGHT**, see *opposite*.

VOICE Loud, rhythmic, mechanical calls, mostly at colony.

On water ADULTS are distinctive; JUVENILES are dark grey-brown – the wingtips are raised, unlike a Cormorant or a diver.

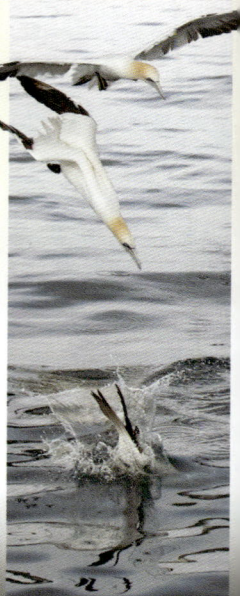

Gannets dive, angled from low level or more vertically from a height, wings pulled back into arrow-shape at last moment.

IN FLIGHT, pointed head and bill, held higher than the slender, pointed tail, together with long, straight or slightly angled wings make a distinctive shape, even at a very long range.

GANNET

A (4+ years old)

A

I (3 years old)

I (2–3 years old)

I (up to 1 year old)

I (1–2 years old)

Rate of progress from juvenile to adult varies individually.

New nesting colonies are small for several years but may increase rapidly once a certain threshold is reached; a few established sites number tens of thousands of pairs.

Gulls, Skuas & Terns

Gulls, Skuas & Terns are small to very large, short-necked, with long, pointed wings; all have webbed feet. Adult gulls have white neck, underparts and tail, browner immatures have whitish rump and dark tail-band; skuas always have a dark rump and tail; terns have white, grey or blackish underparts and white or grey rump and tail. Sexes look alike but seasonal and marked age differences.

Gulls (pp. 84–100)

Medium-sized to very large; rounded head; slightly hooked or rather pointed bill; medium-length legs. Two broad types: large, white-headed (when adult) and smaller, three with dark hoods when breeding; wide range of immature plumages. Equally likely on water, dry land or in flight; most walk freely.

Skuas (pp. 101–103)

Medium-sized to large; rounded head; short, slightly hooked bill; medium-length legs. Generally seen in flight, occasionally on water; on land only when breeding. All are long-distance migrants; most immatures remain in wintering areas.

Terns (pp. 104–108)

Small to medium-sized; very short neck; slim, pointed bill; short or very short legs. Generally seen in flight, or standing when roosting/breeding. All are summer migrants that take 2 years to mature, most birds in first year remain in wintering areas.

HERRING GULL

Broad-based wings; tail rounded or notched without projections.

ARCTIC SKUA

Broad-based or slim wings, with white 'flash'; tail rounded or with central projection.

ARCTIC TERN

Long, slim wings; tail notched or forked, some with long outer feathers.

BLACK-HEADED GULL

ARCTIC SKUA

ARCTIC TERN

In flight

Gulls can soar, glide long distances, or fly in long lines or 'V'-shapes with relaxed, steady beats of arched wings. Kittiwake use steep, banking glides in strong winds over the sea. Black-headed and Mediterranean Gulls may 'hawk' flying insects high in the air. **Skuas** are dynamic, like elegant birds of prey: streamlined and relaxed but fast, purposeful and acrobatic in pursuit of other birds. **Terns** are slender and far less robust, but Sandwich Tern is a strong, direct flier; most plunge-dive for food.

Behaviour

Gulls forage on beaches, follow boats, roost in sheltered bays or on beaches, and 'loaf', doing nothing for long periods. Although some are very bold on promenades, can be very wary inland, where they feed on fields and roost on lakes and reservoirs overnight.

Skuas breed on the Northern Isles and migrate along coasts, feeding as they go. Great Skuas take food from birds as large as a Gannet and kill smaller seabirds and gulls; others chase Kittiwakes and terns to force them to disgorge food, sometimes two together in a fast, twisting chase, their dark shapes identifiable as skuas at a great distance.

Terns are always around water, on the coast or inland; over reservoirs/rivers most dip to feed from the surface, but on the coast they plunge-dive from the air for fish.

GREAT SKUA

GANNET

Colonies

Most gulls and terns breed in noisy colonies, sometimes mixed. **Black-headed Gull** and **Common Tern** nest on marshes/islands inland as well as on the coast. **Kittiwake** typically nests in dense colonies on cliff ledges or coastal buildings. Tern colonies, such as **Little Tern** on shingle beaches and **Sandwich Tern** in dunes, are easily disturbed and may be deserted.

SANDWICH TERNS

Plumage progression

tail-band

no grey feathers

dark eye

grey feathers begin to appear

pale eye

J JUN–OCT

1Y SEP–APR

1Y MAR–OCT

2Y SEP–MAR

This sequence shows how a **Herring Gull's** plumage progresses from juvenile to adult over four years (see also pp. 88–91); smaller gulls and terns take two years to mature (see pp. 86–87), as do terns.

J   **1Y**   **2Y**   **A**

This sequence shows how a **Pomarine Skua's** plumage progresses from juvenile to adult plumage over a period of three years: most immatures remain in wintering areas all year.

Identification

Feather tracts shown here affect the appearance of all birds and are easiest to see on large, patterned ones such as immature gulls. It may not be necessary to learn the terms but knowing how a bird 'fits together' helps explain its appearance and lends extra precision to any description.

'mirror'

PRIMARIES
SECONDARIES

A

rump

tail-band

scapular

back

tertials

hindwing band

midwing (greater coverts)

innerwing
wing coverts and secondaries

outerwing
primary coverts and primaries

J/1Y

HERRING GULL

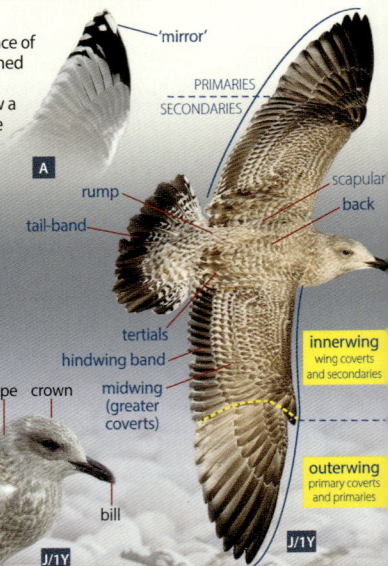

ear-spot

N

'eyelids'

hood

B

BLACK-HEADED GULL

wingtip (primaries)

scapulars

greater coverts

tertials

back

nape

crown

bill

tail

flank

J/1Y

tail white with some dark marks

tail increasingly white

tail white

ail-band

increasing extent of grey

white on wingtip

no brown feathers in wing

2Y FEB–OCT   **3Y** SEP–MAR   **3Y** MAR–OCT   **A** ALL YEAR

Skua plumages

Arctic Skua (shown here) and **Pomarine Skua** have pale, intermediate and dark forms in adult and juvenile plumages. The different forms interbreed freely and produce young of any form.

PALE   INTERMEDIATE   DARK

Watching gulls, terns and skuas

Swimming or standing gulls are best identified in even, flat light (bright/low sunlight creates contrasting light and shade). They face head-to-wind, so try to watch from the side: look for the upperpart tone, then bill/leg colours and wing patterns. As terns are often mobile over water, getting ideal views may be more difficult: watch for them settling on buoys, rafts, islets, *etc*.

In a mixed gull flock, a juvenile **Glaucous Gull** (*centre*) can be picked out from **Herring Gulls** by the creamy-buff wingtips (white on adults).

An unusual wingtip pattern draws attention to a two-year-old **Mediterranean Gull** (left of **Black-headed Gull**) – now check the head and bill.

Pomarine Skuas pass through the English Channel in April–May, often in small flocks.

Smaller gulls compared

KITTIWAKE
(*p. 95*)

LITTLE GULL
(*p. 93*)

NB moulting
from 1Y to A

BLACK-HEADED GULL
(*p. 92*)

MEDITERRANEAN GULL
(*p. 93*)

COMMON GULL
(*p. 94*)

SABINE'S GULL
(p. 95)

 N

 J

 B

KITTIWAKE
(p. 95)

 1Y

 N

 B

LITTLE GULL
(p. 93)

 1Y

 N

 B

**BLACK-HEADED
GULL**
(p. 92)

 1Y

 2Y

 B

**MEDITERRANEAN
GULL**
(p. 93)

 J/1Y

 1Y

 B

COMMON GULL
(p. 94)

87

Larger gulls compared

Progression from juvenile to adult takes several years…

GREAT BLACK-BACKED GULL
(p. 99)

1–2Y

0–1Y

LESSER BLACK-BACKED GULL
(p. 98)
Tertial pattern is a
good identification
feature – see p. 97

1–2Y Legs become yellow
from late 2nd-year.

0–1Y

YELLOW-LEGGED GULL
(p. 97)
Tertial pattern is a
good identification
feature – see p. 97

1–2Y Legs become yellow
from late 2nd-year.

0–1Y

HERRING GULL
(p. 96)

1–2Y

Tertial pattern is a
good identification
feature – see p. 97

0–1Y

ICELAND GULL (p. 100)
NB Glaucous Gull follows the
same progression – best
identified by structure
(see p. 100)

1–2Y Much like 1Y; both
fade to become very
pale.

0–1Y

REAT BLACK-BACKED GULL
(p. 99)

2–3Y

3Y+ (A)

ESSER BLACK-BACKED GULL
(p. 98)

2–3Y

3Y+ (A)

'ELLOW-LEGGED GULL
(p. 97)

2–3Y

3Y+ (A)

IERRING GULL
(p. 96)

2–3Y

3Y+ (A)

CELAND GULL *(p. 100)*

2–3Y

3Y+ (A)

Larger gulls in flight

Immature and adult plumages: progression from juvenile to adult takes several years; ageing is usually possible, but individuals mature at differing rates so some may not be aged with confidence.

GREAT BLACK-BACKED GULL (p. 99)

1–2Y

0–1Y

LESSER BLACK-BACKED GULL (p. 98)

0–1Y

1–2Y

YELLOW-LEGGED GULL (p. 97)

0–1Y

1–2Y

HERRING GULL (p. 96)

0–1Y

1–2Y

0–1Y

1–2Y

GLAUCOUS GULL (p. 100)
NB Iceland Gull follows the same progression – best identifed by structure (see p. 100)

2–3Y

3Y+ (A)

2–3Y

3Y+ (A)

2–3Y

3Y+ (A)

2–3Y

3Y+ (A)

2–3Y

3Y+ (A)

Smaller gulls: 'hooded'

Small–medium-sized; pale grey above, white below, with dark head markings that extend to a complete dark 'hood' in breeding plumage.

IDENTIFY BY:
► head patterns
► upperwing patterns
► bill and leg colour

Black-headed Gull is the common, small, 'white' gull; lively, quarrelsome, sociable, foraging for scraps on holiday beaches, catching flying ants high in the air, following the plough for worms, striding across playing fields or feeding around rivers and lakes. Migrants visit from N/E Europe, SEP–APR. **Mediterranean Gull** is a scarce resident, joined by migrants from central Europe AUG–APR. **Little Gull** is a passage and winter migrant from NE Europe, most JUL–MAY.

Locally common/abundant resident/migrant

Usually the commonest gull, often in flocks: look on coasts, pastures, playing fields, ploughed fields, *etc.*; winter roosts on lakes may number 1,000s, arriving in afternoon, departing at dawn.

BLACK-HEADED GULL	LITTLE GULL	MEDITERRANEAN GULL

WHERE widespread all year, up to high hilltops in summer; breeds pools, lakes, saltmarshes

EATS a wide range of items including scraps, offal, insects, worms

1Y ALL YEAR

IMMATURES show brown in the wings until they are a year old, after which they have 'adult' plumage.

Black-headed Gull *Larus ridibundus*

L 35–39 cm | WS 86–99 cm

ID Small, very pale; slender bill. ADULT wingtip black with **white stripe** along lower edge. BREEDING **dark brown hood**, white nape; white 'eyelids'; bill and legs dark purple-red. NON-BREEDING head white with black ear-spot; bill and legs bright red. JUVENILE (MAY–JUL) dark brown on head, neck and back. 1ST YEAR like adult but brown on wings; bill and legs orange-buff; dark tail-band.

IN FLIGHT, quick, agile; distinctive **white blaze** on outerwing, underwing blackish towards tip.

VOICE Whining, squealing calls; long "*kree-arrr*" and shorter "*kik*."

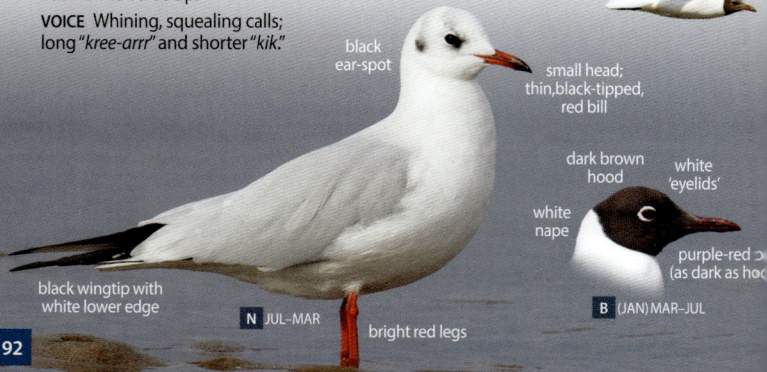

sharply pointed wings
white stripe
pale grey
pale grey underwing
blackish
1Y
N
tail-band
black edge
white blaze
B

black ear-spot
small head; thin, black-tipped, red bill
dark brown hood
white 'eyelids'
white nape
purple-red (as dark as hood)

black wingtip with white lower edge
N JUL–MAR
bright red legs
B (JAN) MAR–JUL

Look offshore, particularly on east coast, or scan large lakes during times of peak passage; in winter, check estuaries in the south and west.

Little Gull *Hydrocoloeus minutus*

L 24–28 cm | WS 62–69 cm

ID Very small, pale; fine, dark bill; short legs (rarely walks). ADULT wingtip white (black underside often visible). BREEDING **black hood**. NON-BREEDING head white with grey crown and black ear-spot. JUVENILE (MAY–JUN) dark brown above. 1ST YEAR dark crown, black ear-spot, black band on wing, black wingtip (incomplete hood FEB–JUL). 2ND YEAR like adult but wingtip has black streaks.

VOICE Squeaky "*kit-it*" or "*keek*."

WHERE lakes, reservoirs and coasts

EATS small aquatic and marine invertebrates

IN FLIGHT, buoyant, **dips to water surface.**

blackish 'W' across upperwings; hindwing darker than on juvenile Kittiwake (p. 95)

pale grey

white trailing edge and tip

white underwing

black tail-band

1Y

dark underwing

N AUG–MAR

B

black ear-spot

fine, black bill

black hood

1Y ALL YEAR

B FEB–JUL

Visit nesting colonies APR–JUL to see breeding adults, or look through gull flocks on the coast, particularly in AUG–MAR. Can be on busy beaches.

Mediterranean Gull *Larus melanocephalus*

L 37–40 cm | WS 94–102 cm

ID Small, very pale; thick bill. ADULT **wingtip white**. BREEDING **black head**; white 'eyelids'; bill and legs **bright red**. NON-BREEDING head white with **dusky 'mask'**; bill and legs **red or blackish**. JUVENILE brown and buff above; head whitish, grey smudge through eye; breast pale brown; wingtip black; bill and legs blackish. 1ST YEAR pale grey above, white below, wing fades browner MAR–JUN; blackish 'mask'; bill and legs buffish, reddish or black. 2ND YEAR like adult but has black streaks on wingtip.

VOICE Distinctive spring call, a loud, nasal "*ar-woww*."

WHERE beaches, marshes, lakes, sometimes ploughed fields, pig farms, mainly coastal

EATS fish, molluscs, worms, insects, *etc.*

IN FLIGHT, quick, rather stiff.

black streaks

pale grey 'panel'

white streaks (1Y Common Gull plain (p. 94))

black tail-band

1Y ALL YEAR

2Y ALL YEAR

greyish nape

dusky 'mask'

white wings

large head; thick bill

B

black hood (extends onto nape)

white 'eyelids'

bright red bill contrasts with hood

white wingtip

N JUN–MAR

B FEB–JUL

Smaller gulls: 'white-headed'

Medium-sized; white head in breeding plumage, otherwise streaked/dingy. Immature plumages distinct for a year, less obvious the following year, then fully adult.

IDENTIFY BY:
► **head patterns**   ► **upperwing patterns**
► **bill and leg colour**

COMMON GULL   KITTIWAKE   SABINE'S GULL

Kittiwake is declining but still numerous on some coasts in the N and W; nests on sheer cliffs (a few on buildings) and spends the winter at sea. **Common Gull** breeds mostly in N, rare in England and Wales, but is widespread SEP–MAR with migrants from N Europe and Iceland. **Sabine's Gull** is an Arctic breeder that winters off the African coast; it is rare in Britain and Ireland, passing through on migration.

Locally common; widespread winter migrant	WHERE coasts, lakes, rivers, moors, short grass	EATS worms, other invertebrates, some fish
Search for nesting pairs around sheltered coastal bays; at other times, look on beaches, pastures and playing fields, and at evening roosts on lakes.		

Common Gull *Larus canus*

L 40–46 cm | WS 100–115 cm

ID Medium-sized; rounded head, small bill, **dark eye**. ADULT mid-grey above; wingtip black with **large** white spots. BREEDING head bright white; bill and legs **bright yellow-green**. NON-BREEDING head/neck streaked grey-brown; bill **greenish**, often with dark band; legs **grey-green** (Herring Gull (*p. 96*) is larger, has red on the bill and a paler back). JUVENILE chequered brown and buff above; wingtip black-brown. 1ST YEAR back grey; rows of brown spots across wing; bill buff with black tip; legs orange.

IN FLIGHT, rather slow, relaxed action.

VOICE Various short, squabbling notes; adults' calls are **higher, more squealing** than those of Herring Gulls.

J/1Y

well-defined black tail-band

broad white trailing edge

B

grey-brown

uniform black wingtip

black wingtip with two broad white spots (often joined)

streaked head

greyish-green bill, dark tip

greenish bill, paler yellow tip

2Y

N AUG–MAR

bold, dark eye

slim yellow (no re...

pale buff bill, dark tip

J/1Y ALL YEAR

white patch (bolder than on Herring Gull)

2ND YEAR as adult but more black, less white, on wingtip.

black wingtip with white spots

B FEB–JUL

! Ring-billed Gull (*p. 258*)

long, yellow-green legs

Beware: black diagonal across innerwing of one-year-old **Kittiwake** fades, so can resemble Sabine's Gull of same age – but hindwing triangle not as white.

Rare, most AUG–NOV, very rare inland after storms

Look out to sea especially from western headlands after gales.

Sabine's Gull *Xema sabini*

L 30–36 cm | WS 80–87 cm

ID Small; well-defined **triangles of, black, white and grey** on upperwing; underwing white with a **grey bar**. Bill and legs **dark grey**. ADULT BREEDING dark grey hood; yellow bill tip. NON-BREEDING white head with blackish cap/nape. JUVENILE **grey-brown** above and on neck; black tail tip.

Kittiwakes bank over in steep, high arcs in strong winds.

Locally common when breeding; scarce OCT–FEB

Easy to see when nesting, MAR–SEP; otherwise look offshore, particularly when windy, and around fishing harbours.

WHERE most coasts; rare inland (some migrate overland in spring)

EATS mostly marine fish, particularly sandeels, sprats

IN FLIGHT, light, buoyant, with shallow beats.

Kittiwake *Rissa tridactyla*

L 37–42 cm | WS 93–105 cm

ID Medium-sized; slim bill; short legs, cannot walk far; a 'sea' gull. ADULT mid-grey above, **black wingtip**; black eye; **green-yellow bill**; **black legs**. JUVENILE distinct **black collar** (lost during 1st winter, JAN) and ear-spot; **black bill**; **blackish band along wing**.

VOICE Loud "*kitti-a-wa-ake*" and mewing notes at the colony; otherwise silent.

blackish 'W' across upperwing

J

uniformly white underwing

short, notched tail

narrow white trailing edge,

B

triangular black wingtip

dusky-grey ear-spot

J JUN–JAN

blackish band

black collar

black bill

yellow-tipped, grey bill

dark grey hood

black, white and grey triangles

B FEB–JUL

grey bar on underwing

dark grey bill

I/N ALL YEAR

grey crown

dusky ear-spot

N OCT–MAR

dark eye

slim green-yellow bill (no red)

B FEB–OCT

Nests on narrow ledges, either on sea cliffs or buildings.

2ND YEAR as adult but with some black spots near bend of wing.

black wingtip

short, black legs

Larger gulls all walk, swim and fly well. Brown juveniles with black bill and pink legs change to adult colours over four years; intermediate stages increasingly grey/black above (see *pages 88–91*). Adults have a white head, body, rump and tail, pale eyes, a thick **yellow bill with a red spot** and **black wingtips spotted with white**.

IDENTIFY BY:
▶ back colour   ▶ leg colour
▶ upper and underwing patterns

Adults are easier to identify than juveniles: **Herring Gull**, the typical large, pale 'seaside' gull, but also found inland, is the palest and has pink legs. **Yellow-legged Gull** is much scarcer and has yellow legs. **Lesser Black-backed Gull**, darker above, with yellow legs, is widespread in winter, more local in summer. Less abundant but widespread, **Great Black-backed Gull** has the blackest back (except for a few equally dark NW European Lesser Black-backed Gulls, OCT–MAR) and pale pinkish legs.

Common, locally abundant; disperses SEP–MAR, when darker N European birds also appear

Tame in coastal areas; occurs almost anywhere inland but more wary. Roosts form, SEP–MAR, and are worth scanning for other gull species.

WHERE beaches, islands, cliffs, rooftops; forages on rubbish tips, fields; roosts on lakes or sea

EATS mostly fish, marine invertebrates, food waste, edible refuse from tips

Herring Gull
Larus argentatus

L 54–60 cm | WS 123–148 cm

ID The 'benchmark' for comparison. ADULT **pale grey** above; wingtip black with white spots. (Common Gull (*p. 94*) is smaller, has an all yellow bill and a darker back). Eye 'staring', pale yellow, eyering **yellow**. **Legs pink**. Head **heavily streaked** grey-brown AUG–MAR. JUVENILE/1ST YEAR evenly mottled brown and buff, some darker, others paler overall.

VOICE Whining, crying and laughing notes; pairs call loud, ringing "*kee-yow, kyow, kyow-kow-kow-kowkowkow.*"

A
pale grey above
black wingtip with white spots
pale grey
pink legs

prominent pale patch
1Y
no dark midwing band

brown-barred rump and tail
brown tail-band

1Y ALL YEAR
pale grey upperparts

pale yellow eye, yellow eyering (rather 'staring')

B (JAN) FEB–SEP
pink legs

N European migrants have a darker grey back, duller bill and less black on wingtip

❗ Caspian Gull (*p. 258*)

Tertials compared

Juvenile/1st year larger gulls can be very difficult to identify; one feature that can be useful is the patterning on the **tertial feathers**.

brown, with wavy buff fringes ('oakleaf' pattern)

HERRING GULL

dark base in solid crescent; pale fringes only at tip

YELLOW-LEGGED GULL

dark brown, finely edged white

LESSER BLACK-BACKED GULL

blackish, with buff fringes and notches

GREAT BLACK-BACKED GULL

Very rare breeder, scarce migrant from continental Europe, mostly AUG–APR

Look amongst Herring Gull flocks anywhere, especially for white-headed adults OCT–JAN

WHERE lakes, reservoirs, coasts

EATS mostly fish, crustaceans molluscs, other invertebrates

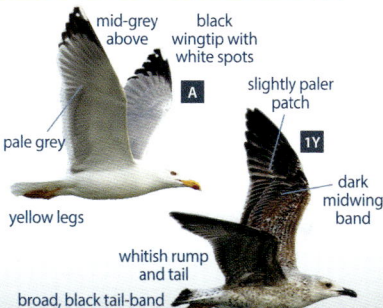

Yellow-legged Gull
Larus michahellis

L 52–58 cm | WS 120–140 cm

ID ADULT **darker grey** above than Herring Gull, **paler** than Lesser Black-backed Gull (*p.98*), with more bulbous head; wingtip black with white spots. Eye pale yellow, eyering red, may appear **dark-eyed**. Legs **yellow**. Head **white all year** with slight grey streaks JUL–NOV. JUVENILE/1ST YEAR mottled brown, buff and blackish, greyer hindneck, often more rufous on body; **whitish head with smudgy dark 'mask'**.

VOICE Barking notes, squeals and deep, full-throated "*kow, kow, ow-ow-ow*" (closer to Lesser Black-backed Gull, lower pitched than Herring Gull).

YELLOW-LEGGED GULL

mid-grey above

black wingtip with white spots

pale grey

A

yellow legs

slightly paler patch

1Y

dark midwing band

whitish rump and tail

broad, black tail-band

whitish head with slight smudgy 'mask'

greyish hindneck

rather thick bill

pale yellow eye, red eyering (dark-eyed at distance)

1Y ALL YEAR

mid-grey upperparts (darker than most Herring Gulls)

yellow legs

A ALL YEAR

Features are intermediate between Herring and Lesser Black-backed Gulls.

! Caspian Gull (*p.258*)

97

WHERE beaches, islands, cliffs, moors, rooftops;
forages on tips, fields, roosts on lakes

EATS fish, small mammals, small birds, edible
refuse from tips

Common resident, migrant from Africa APR–
AUG, and visitor from NW Europe SEP–MAR

From SEP–APR (outside breeding season) watch
roosts, particularly from the Midlands south,
which may contain thousands. Listen for calling
migrants overhead APR–MAY.

Lesser Black-backed Gull
Larus fuscus

L 48–56 cm | WS 117–134 cm

ID Slightly slimmer, longer-
winged, shorter-legged
than Herring Gull (p. 96).
ADULT **dark grey** above;
wingtip black with white
spots. Eye pale yellow,
eyering red. **Legs yellow**. Head **heavily
streaked** grey-brown AUG–MAR. JUVENILE/1ST
YEAR dark, heavily mottled grey-brown and
buff, dusky around eye.

VOICE Whining and laughing notes; loud,
deep, throaty *"kee-yow, kyow, kyow-kow-kow-
kowkow."*

LESSER BLACK-
BACKED GULL

black wingtip with white spot
('mirror') on outermost feather

dark grey

dark grey
above

yellow legs

A

white rump
and tail
barred brown

1Y

broad,
black
tail-band

dark hindwing band

dark midwing
band

no pale patch

1Y ALL YEAR

fairly
slender bill

pale yellow eye
red eyering

small head,
slim neck

dark grey
upperparts

white spots on
wingtip wear away
MAR–AUG

B FEB–AUG

bright yellow legs

black wingtip with long white tip on outermost feather, and white spot ('mirror') and tip on next

WHERE coasts and inland waters, tips

EATS fish, dead animals, small mammals, small birds, edible refuse from tips

Common resident, disperses more widely AUG–MAR, when migrants arrive from N Europe

Scan around open beaches, harbours and fishing boats offshore; look for pairs on tall stacks/exposed rocks MAR–AUG. Inland, search through mixed winter roosts.

Great Black-backed Gull
Larus marinus

L 61–74 cm | WS 144–166 cm

ID **Biggest gull** with **very large bill**, broad, **bulbous head** and rather long legs. ADULT **almost black above**; wingtip black with white spots. Eye pale yellow, eyering red. Legs **pale pinkish** or whitish. Head **white all year**, lightly streaked grey OCT–FEB. JUVENILE/1ST YEAR best told by **large size**, **heavy bill**, boldly **chequered** look, with buffish-white head.

VOICE Deep, throaty barking notes and loud "*kow kow kow*."

GREAT BLACK-BACKED GULL

blackish

black above

pink legs

A

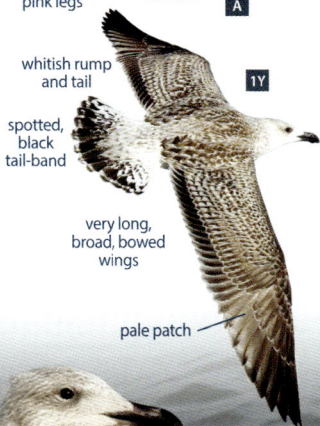

whitish rump and tail

1Y

spotted, black tail-band

very long, broad, bowed wings

pale patch

relatively pale head

boldly chequered

1Y ALL YEAR

very large bill

bulbous head

pale yellow eye, red eyering

almost black upperparts

B FEB–SEP

pink legs

Large 'white-winged' gulls

Glaucous and **Iceland Gulls** have all-pale wingtips (see also the very different looking Mediterranean Gull (*p. 93*)). Winter visitors from Greenland and Iceland, some remain faithful to sites and can linger into spring in the north; farther south, most often in winter roosts on reservoirs. Plumages alike.

IDENTIFY BY:
▶ at all ages best separated by head shape, bill size and wing length; bill pattern helpful in one-year-old birds.

EAT fish, offal, waste/scraps

WHERE mostly northern Britain and western Ireland, often around harbours; rare inland and farther south where most often seen in mixed winter gull roosts

GLAUCOUS GULL

ICELAND GULL

ADULT head and body white, upperparts pale grey; **wingtip white**; in winter, head streaked brown. JUVENILE buff-brown; **wingtip pale buff**; IMMATURES bill pale with black band; amount of pale grey on upperparts increases with age (see *pages 88–91*).

GLAUCOUS GULL

ADULT: white wingtips

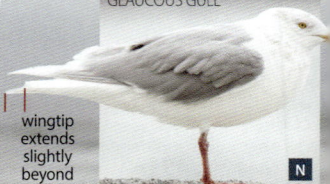

ICELAND GULL

wingtip extends slightly beyond tail

wingtip extends well beyond tail

GLAUCOUS GULL

ICELAND GULL

Rare OCT–APR

Glaucous Gull
Larus hyperboreus

L 63–68 cm | WS 138–158 cm
ID Very large; **wingtip extends slightly beyond tail**; head and bill heavy, forehead sloping, crown rounded; **bill long, heavy**; legs quite long. ADULT head and body white, upperparts pale grey; **wingtip white**; in winter, head streaked brown. JUVENILE/1ST YEAR **bill pink with sharply defined black tip**.

1ST YEAR: buff wingtips

'heavy' head

sloping forehead

GLAUCOUS GULL

long bill, long chin

rounded forehead

Rare NOV–APR

Iceland Gull
Larus glaucoides

L 52–60 cm | WS 123–139 cm
ID Large; **wingtip extends well beyond tail**; head and bill dainty, forehead steep, **crown domed**; bill **rather short**; legs short. JUVENILE/1ST YEAR bill dark pink with **extensive black tip**.

sho bill sho chi

ICELAND GULL

A pale gull with whitish wingtip in a gull roost will be a **Glaucous Gull** or **Iceland Gull** which are best separated by noting structural differences detailed on this page.

ARCTIC SKUA

SKUAS have a distinctive profile in direct flight.

Skuas

Skuas are sleek, predatory and superficially gull-like (*p. 86*) – but darker, with a dark or barred rump, dark tail and a white 'flash' on the outerwing. Juveniles of the three smaller species are more or less barred and spotted. **Great Skua** is very large, brown, streaked with buff and has a crescent-shaped white wing patch. **Pomarine Skua** and **Arctic Skua** have both pale and dark forms, **Long-tailed Skua** is typically of the pale type. Away from breeding areas they are predominantly seen over the sea, particularly during their spring (APR–MAY) and autumn (JUL–NOV) migration periods.

IDENTIFY BY: ▶ size   ▶ tail shape

WHERE coasts and islands; rare inland, chiefly after storms

EAT fish, small mammals, birds; food stolen from other seabirds

GREAT SKUA

ARCTIC SKUA

POMARINE SKUA

LONG-TAILED SKUA

Note: DARK FORM also occurs (plumage as Arctic Skua), but extremely rare

LONG-TAILED SKUA
(*p. 103*)

white breast, dusky belly

INTERMEDIATE FORM

dark breast-band or underparts

PALE FORM

white underparts

ARCTIC SKUA (*p. 102*)

entirely black-brown

DARK FORM

POMARINE SKUA (*p. 103*)

PALE FORM

dark breast-band

pale yellowish underparts

Note: DARK and INTERMEDIATE FORMS also occur (plumages as Arctic Skua)

GREAT SKUA (*p. 102*)

no distinct forms, some paler/buffer than others

Great and **Arctic Skuas** return from S Atlantic in APR–MAY to breed on northern islands and, rarely, moors. Arctic Skuas have high-flying, diving display flights and wild calls; Great Skuas display on the ground with raised wings. **Pomarine** and **Long-tailed Skuas** pass Britain and Ireland en route between southern seas and NE Europe in APR–MAY and JUL–NOV. All chase other seabirds in a fast, twisting pursuit, to steal food.

Note: in "Length", the term 'tail' refers to the tail projection of smaller skuas.

Scarce, local breeder; scarce migrant APR–NOV

Breeding adults can be seen around islands off N and W Scotland and Ireland from APR–AUG. Otherwise, look offshore from headlands for migrating birds in APR–MAY and JUL–NOV.

Great Skua *Catharacta (Stercorarius) skua*

L 50–58 cm | WS 125–140 cm

ID Large (size of Herring Gull (*p. 96*)), heavily built; broad-based wings taper to point. Brown with pale buff streaks, prominent **crescent-shaped white 'flash'** on outerwing above and below. Rump and tail always dark, unlike immature gulls. JUVENILE/IMMATURE less streaked: dark brown above, dark or rufous below.

VOICE Short, barking calls at colony.

Scarce, local breeder; scarce migrant MAR–NOV

Breeding adults can be seen around islands off N and W Scotland from APR–JUL. Otherwise, watch along coast, especially from headlands or in bays with fishing terns in APR–MAY and JUL–NOV.

Arctic Skua *Stercorarius parasiticus*

L 38–41 cm (+ 'tail' up to 7 cm) | WS 107–125 cm

ID Medium-sized, round-bodied; elegant in flight, with **spike-like** tail projection and pale 'flash' on outerwing. PALE FORM black cap; brown above, neck and **underparts white**, sometimes with greyish breast-band. INTERMEDIATE FORM brown with paler cheeks and belly. DARK FORM dark brown. JUVENILE rusty brown, barred paler; pale wing 'flash'; tail with **short central projection**. Underwing has broad whitish crescent towards wingtip.

VOICE Loud, nasal "*ya-wow*" calls when breeding, otherwise silent.

prominent white 'flash' on outerwing

streaked buff and brown

short tail, no long projection

large and bulky

brown underparts

DARK FORM

spike-like tail projection

rather 'flat-chest

some ha a breas band

uniform white underpa

PALE FORM

white 'flash' on outerwing, more extensive beneath

Juvenile/immature

skuas are more or less barred; PALE, INTERMEDIATE and DARK forms intergrade and species can be very difficult to identify; most immatures stay south for their first year.

LONG-TAILED SKUA

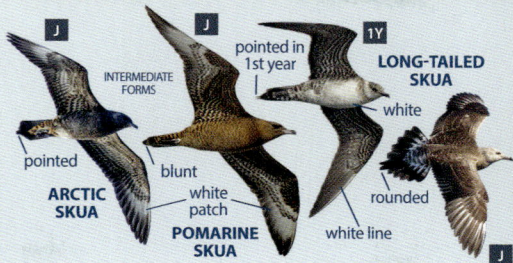

INTERMEDIATE FORMS

J

J

pointed

ARCTIC SKUA

blunt

white patch

pointed in 1st year

POMARINE SKUA

1Y

LONG-TAILED SKUA

white

rounded

white line

J

Scarce APR–NOV

Look offshore in APR–MAY, when small flocks pass through, and JUL–NOV, often close by in wind/rain.

Pomarine Skua *Stercorarius pomarinus*

L 38–57 cm (+ 'tail' up to 10 cm) | WS 110–138 cm
ID Large, heavy, rather broad-winged; long, **'spoon-shaped'** tail projection (often broken by autumn) and pale 'flash' on outerwing. PALE FORM black cap; brown above; neck yellowish and underparts whitish, with **dusky breast-band**; flank slightly or strongly **barred**. INTERMEDIATE FORM brown with paler cheeks and belly. DARK FORM dark brown. JUVENILE brown to blackish; **tail rounded without central projection**. Underwing has two whitish crescents towards wingtip.

Rare APR–OCT

Best chance is to look offshore from NW Britain in MAY, or E coast in AUG–SEP after onshore winds.

Long-tailed Skua *Stercorarius longicaudus*

L 35–43 cm (+ 'tail' up to 15 cm) | WS 102–117 cm
ID Small. ADULT like pale form Arctic Skua but **no breast-band**, **darker belly**; paler upperwing with dark hindwing band, outerwing 'flash' restricted to thin, white streaks above and below; **very long**, flexible tail projection. JUVENILE **greyish**, with whiter belly and nape, or darker overall; short blunt tail projection.

two whitish crescents

large and deep-chested

long, pointed tail projection

small and slender

pale breast, dark belly

no breast-band

whitish underparts, flanks barred brown

always has a breast-band

PALE FORM

pale greyish-brown upperside

blunt ('spoon-shaped') tail projection (often broken by autumn)

white 'flash' on outerwing

dark hindwing band

faint white 'flash' on outerwing

103

Terns are more slender and smaller than most gulls, with a sharply pointed bill; all except Black Tern are pale grey and white with a dark cap in breeding plumage. They typically feed by diving, or dipping to the surface. All are summer migrants that winter in Africa or farther south.

IDENTIFY BY:
▶ size and shape   ▶ bill and leg colour
▶ wing pattern and translucency

EAT fish, small aquatic/marine invertebrates

SANDWICH TERN	BLACK TERN	LITTLE TERN

Locally common MAR–OCT; rare in winter, when most have migrated to Africa

Listen for the distinctive rasping call and look for birds flying offshore, or in wide-open bays; groups often rest on islands and spits in shallow lagoons or on shingle beaches or low sandbanks.

WHERE sand dunes, beaches, offshore islands, and offshore; rare inland

Sandwich Tern *Thalasseus sandvicensis*

L 37–43 cm | WS 85–97 cm

ID The **biggest and whitest** tern; long wings and long bill give distinctive silhouette, powerful appearance in flight. ADULT silvery-grey above, **white** below; black cap with ragged crest, forehead white by JUN/JUL. Long wings whiter towards tip, increasingly streaked black during summer. Bill **black with pale tip**, **legs black**. JUVENILE has brown bars above; dark tip to tail; black bill.

VOICE Highly distinctive, loud, rhythmic, abrupt, short, tearing "*kierr-ik, ki-rink*" or "*ko-yok.*" Young have high, whining "*srreee-i*".

Sandwich Terns dive for fish from a greater height and make a larger splash than other terns.

dark on wingtip (increases from very faint streaks, MAR–APR, to black, SEP–OCT)

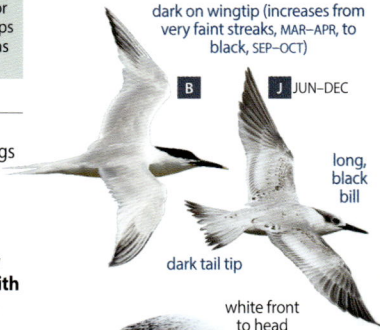

B   J JUN–DEC

long, black bill

dark tail tip

white front to head

N JUN–FEB

black cap

spiky crest   long, back bill with pale tip

B MAR–JUL

black legs

Scan large inland lakes particularly in APR–MAY for adults in breeding plumage, and again in JUL–SEP for juveniles and moulting adults, when small groups may feed briefly before moving on.

WHERE coasts and inland lakes/reservoirs

J JUN–SEP
dark mark

Juvenile has same head/breast pattern as non-breeding adult, but is browner on the back.

Black Tern *Chlidonias niger*

L 22–26 cm | WS 56–62 cm

ID Small; dips to feed from surface (so do Common Terns (*p. 106*), inland). ADULT BREEDING **smoky grey above**, including short, notched tail; **sooty-black below**. Bill black, legs dark reddish. NON-BREEDING **mid-grey above**, white below; black cap, extends down onto cheeks and nape; **dark mark** on side of breast ('blotchy 'in-between' plumages during moult). JUVENILE like non-breeding adult but a little browner above, forewing darker.

VOICE Call insignificant, slightly squeaky, "*ki-ki-ki*" or "*kyeh*."

white under tail **B**
short, notched tail **J**

smoky grey back and wings
short, black bill
sooty-black **B**
dark reddish legs

Scarce APR–SEP; migrates to W Africa

Look just offshore near sand and shingle beaches and on adjacent coastal lagoons: watch for quick dive and splash, even in rolling surf.

WHERE almost entirely coastal: undisturbed beaches or offshore; very rare inland

Little Tern *Sternula albifrons*

L 21–25 cm | WS 41–47 cm

ID Smallest, quickest tern. ADULT pale grey above, white below, with black crown, nape and eyestripe and white forehead all year; **yellow bill** and orange legs; outerwing has blackish leading edge. JUVENILE has fine dark bars above, forewing and outerwing dark brownish-grey; bill blackish, legs yellowish.

VOICE Quick, rasping "*kreet*" and fast, rhythmic chatter "*kiereet kiereet kiereet*."

blackish leading edge **B**
black crown and nape
white forehead and black eyestripe
slim, yellow bill (often with black tip)
B APR–SEP
orange legs

105

EAT fish, small aquatic invertebrates

Common, Arctic and Roseate Terns are medium-sized terns that are difficult to identify. Adults in breeding plumage are pale grey above, paler below, with a **black cap** and elongated outer tail feathers ('streamers'). All are summer migrants.

IDENTIFY BY:
▶ bill length and colour ▶ leg length
▶ overall structure ▶ wing details

Common Tern nests around the coast and inland, especially on flooded gravel pits; **Arctic Tern** is a coastal nester, mostly farther north, but appears inland on migration. **Roseate Tern** is rare everywhere and nests at just a few locations.

COMMON TERN ROSEATE TERN ARCTIC TERN

WHERE coasts, lakes, reservoirs, flooded pits, rivers

Locally common APR–OCT; migrates to W Africa

Look offshore and on adjacent lagoons, saltmarsh pools, sandbanks; the commonest tern inland, nesting on artificial rafts/islets in large lakes and often seen feeding along rivers.

Common Tern *Sterna hirundo*

L 34–37 cm | WS 70–80 cm

ID ADULT pale grey above, greyish-white below, black cap; tail streamers **relatively short**; closed wingtip dark grey with **shortest feathers contrastingly pale grey**. Bill rather long, **scarlet with black tip**; legs **long**, red. From SEP, forehead and underparts white, 'shoulder' blackish; bill and legs blackish.

VOICE Calls sharp "*kit*," squabbling "*kit-it-it-it*," long-drawn, nasal "*kierri-kierri*."

COMMON TERN

dark streaks towards tip on upperwing

broad dark band

translucent patch

flattish head

long neck

upperwing uniform

thin dark trailing edge

translucent white flight feathers

rounded head

short neck

ARCTIC TERN

Common/Arctic Terns in flight

Common Tern has a longish bill; flattish head; long head/neck; relatively short tail; a long innerwing with a relatively broad outerwing.
Arctic Tern has a short bill; rounded head; short head/neck; long tail; a short innerwing with a long, finely tapered outerwing.

J JUN–OCT

blackish 'shoulder'

JUVENILE head flattish; forehead white, tinged buff; blackish 'shoulder'; reddish bill and legs relatively long. **IN FLIGHT** (see p. 108) dark forewing contrasts with **pale midwing** and darker **grey band** on hindwing; rump **pale grey**; underwing as adult.

rather long, black-tipped scarlet bill

white underparts

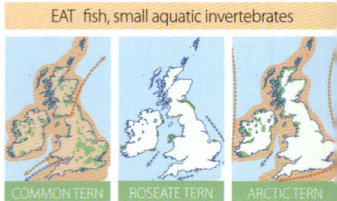

rather short tail streamers

contrastingly pale patch

long, red legs

B APR–SEP

Regular only on a handful of islands in Ireland, Wales and north-east England; otherwise unpredictable, check flocks of terns on the coast.

WHERE offshore islands, beaches; unusual away from a few breeding sites

Roseate Tern *Sterna dougallii*

L 33–36 cm | WS 67–76 cm

ID ADULT **very pale** grey above, white below with **pink tinge**, black cap; tail streamers **very long**; closed wingtip **pale grey**. Bill long, **slim**, **black with red base** in APR–MAY, red becoming increasingly extensive by AUG; legs **quite long**, red. **IN FLIGHT**, blackish front edge to outerwing, **no dark trailing edge** beneath; quick flight action, relatively short wings.

VOICE Calls include distinct double "*chivik.*"

B

blackish leading edge to outerwing

JUVENILE similar to Common/Arctic Terns but has a darker forehead, black bill and black legs.

J JUN–OCT

very pale grey upperparts

very long tail streamers

white underparts with pink tinge

long, slim black bill (becomes redder at base during summer)

longish, red legs

B APR–AUG

Look on any coast or scan inland lakes in APR–MAY and JUL–OCT when migrants are passing through and flocks may pause briefly to feed.

WHERE coasts, islands, sea; migrants inland

J JUN–OCT

Arctic Tern *Sterna paradisaea*

L 33–39 cm | WS 66–77 cm

ID ADULT pale grey above, greyish below, black cap with contrastingly white cheek and throat; tail streamers **very long**; closed wingtip **uniformly silvery-grey**. Bill quite short, **blood-red**; legs **very short**, red. Has complete black cap until OCT, when forehead starts to become white. **IN FLIGHT**, see *opposite*.

VOICE Calls sharp "*kiki-kit-it,*" whistling "*kee-a,*" rasping "*kair-airrr,*" "*kair-kek.*"

JUVENILE generally 'cleaner' and greyer than Common Tern; head rounded; forehead white; diffuse blackish 'shoulder'; reddish bill and legs relatively short. **IN FLIGHT** (see *p. 108*) dark forewing blends back into **pale hindwing**; rump **white**; underwing as adult.

short, blood-red bill

cheek distinctly white

greyish underparts

very long tail streamers

wingtip uniformly silvery-grey

short, red legs

B APR–OCT

107

Terns in flight

Little, **Black** and **Sandwich Terns** are distinctive, but **Common**, **Arctic** and **Roseate Terns** are difficult unless they are seen well enough for subtle details of the plumage and general structure to be appreciated (see *p.106*)

ARCTIC TERN
(p.107)

B APR–OCT

COMMON TERN
(p.106)

B APR–SEP

B APR–SEP

LITTLE TERN
(p.105)

B APR–AUG

ROSEATE TERN
(p.107)

B MAR–JUL

SANDWICH TERN
(p.104)

B APR–AUG

BLACK TERN
(p.105)

J JUN–OCT

COMMON TERN
(p.106)

J JUN–SEP

J JUN–OCT

ARCTIC TERN
(p.107)

Waders

Waders include 32 regular species (and many rare ones, with seven shown on *p.257*), 18 of which breed regularly. They range in size from very small (size of a Chaffinch (*p.242*)) to large (about the size of a Buzzard (*p.164*)) and can conveniently be divided into ten 'types', four of which are represented by single species (see *page 111*).

Plumage variations

Differences according to age and season must be appreciated for correct identifications of some waders. Sequences shown by small sandpipers are illustrated here by the plumages of **Sanderling** (*p.126*). Breeding, non-breeding and juvenile plumages look quite different, but the change from one to the next takes a few weeks – so intermediate stages are commonly seen, too. Plumage changes come about through moult (replacing old feathers with new ones), bleaching (old feathers becoming paler or losing their colour) and wear (the typically pale edges of fresh feathers abrade, exposing the underlying, usually darker, feather areas).

[NB dates in square brackets are the month in which the photo was taken]

NON-BREEDING (AUG–MAR) plumage is grey-and-white.

[NOV]

JUVENILE (JUL–OCT) has strong upperpart pattern and a hint of breeding colours (rufous-buff neck)

[AUG]

During MAR–MAY, breeding colours are obscured by pale feather edges…

[MAY]

…that quickly wear off to reveal…

DEC

SEP

MAR

JUN

During JUL–AUG, patches of faded breeding colours remain amongst new winter feathers.

[AUG]

…the rich, mottled breeding plumage MAY–JUL.

[MAY]

A mixed flock of mostly **Bar-tailed Godwits** (*p.135*) in various plumages, with **Oystercatchers** (*p.114*) in the foreground and **Grey Plovers** (*p.119*), also in various plumages, intermingled, plus a few **Avocets** (*p.115*) and **Black-headed Gulls** (*p.92*).

Many waders habitually fly in flocks, sometimes comprising more than one species, such as these **Golden Plover** with Dulnin (smaller birds).

no wingbar

LITTLE RINGED PLOVER

TAIL: dark; **RUMP:** dark with white sides

wingbar

CURLEW SANDPIPER

TAIL: white with dark tail-band; **RUMP:** white 'square'

no wingbar

GREENSHANK

TAIL: barred; **RUMP:** white, merging with back to form a white 'triangle'

In flight

Wing and tail patterns revealed in flight may be crucial to identification, or provide the easiest clues. Check if wings are plain, have wingbars or other markings; check the rump – plain; dark with white sides; contrastingly white as a band above the tail; or extending as a long, white triangle up onto the back. These patterns may distinguish individuals of one species within a mixed flock.

Bills and behaviour

Most waders are more or less long-legged, but the bill ranges from short to very long and can be straight, upswept or downcurved. Focus on the length and shape of the bill: the main kinds are shown here. The way in which waders feed also provides a vital identification clue: some, particularly long-billed species, probe deep into soft mud, damp soil or long grass for worms; others, such as small sandpipers and plovers pick from the surface; and phalaropes pick from the water's surface.

LONG, EVENLY DOWNCURVED
Curlews

CURLEW

LONG, SLIGHTLY DOWNCURVE
Sandpipers

SHORT, STOUT, POINTED
Plovers, Turnstone

GREY PLOVER

GREENSHANK

LONG, SLIM, SLIGHTLY UPCURVED
'Shanks', sandpipers, godwits

CURLEW SANDPIPER

BLACK-TAILED GODWIT

LONG, STRAIGHT, TAPERED
Godwits, 'Shanks', Snipes/Woodcock

The types of wader

Stocky; short-bill; rather short legs; stop-and-tilt feeding action. Three distinct sub-types (see *p. 116*), dry land, freshwater or coastal.

GOLDEN PLOVER

RINGED PLOVER

Plovers (larger) (*p. 118*)   **Plovers** (small) (*p. 117*)

Thickset; short, pointed bill; short, orange legs; shoreline sandpiper with bright white underparts.

Turnstone (*p. 115*)

Medium-sized; straight or slightly upcurved bill; long legs.

Small; slightly downcurved bill; short to medium-length legs.

DUNLIN

REDSHANK

GREEN SANDPIPER

'Shanks' (*p. 132*)   **Small sandpipers** (*p. 122*)

Uniquely black-and-white with an upturned bill.

Avocet (*p. 115*)

Large, brown; long, downcurved bill.

CURLEW

Curlews (*p. 136*)

Large, reddish or brown; long, straight or upcurved bill.

BAR-TAILED GODWIT

Godwits (*p. 134*)

Large, brown; short, yellow-based bill; long, yellow legs; dry-land, plover-like.

Stone-curlew (*p. 122*)

Small to medium-sized, brown, well-camouflaged; very long, straight bill; not seen on open beaches.

SNIPE

Snipes/Woodcock (*p. 120*)

Small; longish thin, straight bill; mainly marine, habitually swim well offshore.

RED-NECKED PHALAROPE

Phalaropes (*p. 138*)

Large, black-and-white; long, straight, orange bill.

Oystercatcher (*p. 114*)

Waders in flight

CURLEW SANDPIPER
(p. 125)

DUNLIN
(p. 124)

PURPLE SANDPIPER
(p. 128)

LITTLE STINT
(p. 125)

SANDERLING
(p. 126)

GREY PHALAROP
(p. 138)

RINGED PLOVER
(p. 117)

KNOT
(p. 127)

RUFF
(p. 129)

LITTLE RINGED PLOVER
(p. 117)

TURNSTONE
(p. 115)

RED-NECKED PHALAROPE
(p. 138)

REDSHANK
(p. 133)

DOTTEREL
(p. 118)

SPOTTED REDSHANK
(p. 132)

LAPWING
(p. 116)

GREENSHANK
(p. 133)

GOLDEN PLOVER
(p. 119)

GREY PLOVER
(p. 119)

Many waders are nondescript at rest but reveal patterns on their wings, rump and tail in flight: these can be important for identification.

WHIMBREL
(p. 137)

CURLEW
(p. 136)

BAR-TAILED GODWIT
(p. 135)

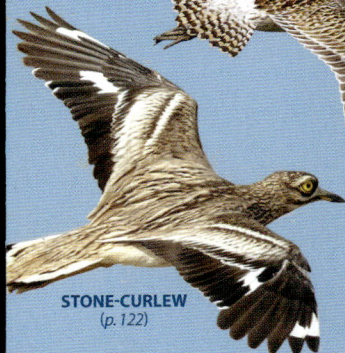

STONE-CURLEW
(p. 122)

BLACK-TAILED GODWIT
(p. 134)

AVOCET
(p. 115)

OYSTERCATCHER
(p. 114)

WOOD SANDPIPER
(p. 131)

JACK SNIPE
(p. 121)

SNIPE
(p. 120)

WOODCOCK
(p. 121)

COMMON SANDPIPER
(p. 130)

GREEN SANDPIPER
(p. 131)

Oystercatchers often fly to roost in flocks, in lines or 'V'-shapes, usually keeping low over the water. Larger flocks create a 'dazzle' effect, perhaps confusing potential predators.

Common resident/migrant from N Europe

Eyecatching and easily seen, often in flocks and particulary around the coast, where the distinctive piping call is is a frequent sound.

WHERE estuaries, mussel beds, low rocky shores, shingle beaches, upland pastures, gravel pits

EATS insects, shellfish, crustaceans, arthropods

Oystercatchers breed on shingle or grass on coasts and in upland pastures.

Oystercatcher *Haematopus ostralegus*

L 39–44 cm | WS 72–83 cm

ID Unmistakable large black-and-white wader with angular head, bright **orange bill** and rather short, thick, **pink legs**; red eye and eyering. NON-BREEDING white collar. JUVENILE/IMMATURE white collar; upperparts tinged brown, bill tip blackish. **IN FLIGHT**, strikingly **black and white**: long, **broad** white wingbar and **triangular** white rump.

VOICE Shrill, **piping, penetrating** notes, such as "*peep*," "*k-peep*," "*kip-kip-kip*" and fast, bubbling, ecstatic piping from small groups.

white rump

broad white wingbar in black wing

B

OYSTERCATCHER

white collar

N AUG–MAY

vivid orange bill

B DEC–SEP

pink legs

114

Look for small groups feeding amongst seaweed along the sea shore; check for dark shapes in high tide wader roosts; sometimes very approachable along the seafront in ports and coastal towns.

WHERE coasts: pebbly beaches, rocky shores, muddy creeks; uncommon inland

EATS insects, shellfish, crustaceans, arthropods

Turnstone *Arenaria interpres*

L 21–24 cm | WS 43–49 cm

ID Fairly small, stocky; dark brown above, white below, **black breast**; rather short, **pointed bill**; **orange legs**. BREEDING black-and-**chestnut** above; **head largely white**. **IN FLIGHT**, bold white wingbar and white back/rump.

VOICE Fast, abrupt, rather low-pitched, or strung into quick trill – "*kew*," "*tuk-a-tuk*."

bold black-and-white pattern

N/I SEP–MAY

chestnut on back/wings

black-and-white head/breast

B APR–SEP

short orange legs

TURNSTONE

Look on coastal nature reserves in East Anglia, where breeds; often in large flocks on muddy estuaries in the SE and SW (OCT–MAR).

WHERE shallow, brackish lagoons; in winter, estuaries

EATS shrimps, worms, other small aquatic invertbrates

Avocet *Recurvirostra avosetta*

L 42–46 cm | WS 67–77 cm

ID Unmistakable large, black-and-white wader; round body, slender head; long, **upcurved bill**; long **grey** legs. JUVENILE mottled brown on head and upperparts. **IN FLIGHT**, white with **black wingtips** and **diagonal band** across innerwing.

VOICE Calls ringing, piping, "*klute*" or "*krup krup krup*."

unique black-and-white pattern

upswept bill

long grey legs

AVOCET

Sweeps bill sideways through shallow water when feeding.

115

Plovers have a short, stubby bill, medium-length legs and distinctive 'run-stop-look-and-tilt' feeding action. The six regular species can be divided into three distinct groups: the large Lapwing, two small ('ringed') and three medium-sized ('round-headed') plovers.

IDENTIFY BY:
► bill and leg colour
► head pattern
► pattern on spread wing and rump

EAT molluscs, worms and other small aquatic invertebrates

LAPWING | RINGED PLOVER | LITTLE RINGED PLOVER

Lapwing is a widespread breeder in grassy areas but joined in the winter by many migrants from N Europe. **Ringed Plover** is present year-round and typically found on sandy or pebbly beaches, whereas **Little Ringed Plover** is a summer migrant only and prefers pebbly or sandy ground inland.

Lapwing *Vanellus vanellus*

L 28–31 cm | WS 82–87 cm

ID Large plover; green above, white below (but buff under tail), broad **black breast-band** and black cap that extends into a long, wispy, **upswept crest**. BREEDING glossy **green** above, iridescent purple on wing. BREEDING MALE has broader wings with more white at tip, longer crest and more solidly black face than FEMALE. NON-BREEDING/JUVENILE shorter crest, buff fringes to feathers on upperparts.

IN FLIGHT, broad, **rounded wings**, strikingly **black-and-white below**.

VOICE Calls creaky, nasal "*pee-wit*," "*wheet*" and emphatic, shrill "*pwee-y-weet*." Song wheezy, rasping; ripping, throbbing wing noise in display.

WHERE breeds on lowland fields, damp moors, edges of marshes; winters, on fields

Common resident/migrant from N Europe

Large flocks can be seen around wetlands and on open fields (JUL–MAR); tumbling display flights are exciting to watch (MAR–JUN).

broad, rounded, black-and-white wings

short crest

MB FEB–JUN

J/I APR–FEB

long, upswept crest

Lapwing flocks 'flicker' black and white in the air, drifting slowly over open spaces.

N JUN–MAR

buff fringes on green back and wings (lost by MAR, when uniform glossy green)

Ringed Plover *Charadrius hiaticula*

L 17–19·5 cm | WS 35–41 cm

ID Small, rounded; short bill; brown above, white below; **orange** legs; no yellow eyering. BREEDING black, white and brown head; black breast-band; **orange-and-black** bill. NON-BREEDING (SEP–MAR) brown breast-band. JUVENILE brown breast-band/band through eye, **whitish line over eye**; blackish bill. **IN FLIGHT, white wingbar**.

VOICE Loud, musical "*too-ee*" with **upward** inflection. Song quick, rhythmic "*too looee*" notes, in low, straight-winged flight.

WHERE shorelines, from coasts to inland lakes and reservoirs; breeds on open, stony ground

Common resident/migrant to/from N Europe

Easiest to see in winter when loose flocks feed out on muddy estuaries.

prominent white wingbar

black-tipped, orange bill

whitish line above/behind eye

no eyering

J MAY–MAR

orange legs

B MAR–SEP

Little Ringed Plover *Charadrius dubius*

L 15·5–18 cm | WS 32–35 cm

ID Small, slim; short bill; brown above, white below; **dull**, grey-pink legs. ADULT black, white and brown head; black breast-band; **yellow eyering**; blackish bill. JUVENILE brown breast-band/band through eye, very little whitish-buff over eye; thin yellow eyering. **IN FLIGHT,** upperwing **plain brown**.

VOICE Call **distinctive**: **abrupt** "*tew*" or "*te-u*" with downward inflection. Song a hard, rolling "*crree-a crree-a*" in bat-like display flight.

WHERE gravel pits, lake shores; breeds on rough, bare places near water

Scarce and local MAR–OCT; winters in Africa

Listen for the distinctive calls and scan nearby rough, gravelly ground inland, from mid-March.

plain upperwing

J

B

brownish/buff above/behind eye

thin yellow eyering

yellow eyering

black bill

J MAY–OCT

A MAR–JUL

dull, grey-pink legs

The three medium-sized plovers are **Golden Plover**, **Grey Plover** and **Dotterel**. **Golden Plover** is present year-round, breeding in the north and very widespread in winter when joined by large numbers of birds from Iceland and N Europe, often at traditional sites inland. **Grey Plover** is a winter visitor only and a common sight on muddy estuaries right around the coast. **Dotterel** is a rare summer migrant, breeding on high peaks in Scottish mountains.

EAT molluscs, worms and other small invertebrates

GOLDEN PLOVER | DOTTEREL | GREY PLOVER

Dotterels migrate in small flocks (known as 'trips') and stop over for a few days, often at traditional sites.

Rare and local APR–OCT; winters in Africa

Can be seen fairly reliably by visiting Scottish mountains such as Cairngorm in the summer, but essential to take care not to cause disturbance.

WHERE breeds on high, stony plateaux; migrants on hills, open fields or coast

FB APR–AUG

black cap | white 'face' and breast-band

bold white stripe over eye (forms 'V' seen from rear)

Dotterel *Eudromias morinellus*

L 20·5–24 cm | WS 57–64 cm

ID Round-bodied but looks slender when active; short, slim bill; pale **yellow legs**. BREEDING rather uniform brown with **black belly**, **pale breast-band**, **black cap**, **broad white stripe over eye**. NON-BREEDING white below. JUVENILE pale grey-brown, spotted buff above; **broad buff-white stripe over eye**. **IN FLIGHT**, plain upperwing; dark rump.

VOICE Call abrupt "*pi-urr*," "*pew*" or purring note.

round-bodied and round-headed waders with medium-length legs

BREEDING: MALE less boldly patterned than FEMALE.

MB APR–AUG

plain upperwing

dark rump

bold buff-white stripe over eye

J

A

hint of pale breast-band

J JUN–OCT

buff belly

pale yellow legs

Locally common resident and winter visitor from N Europe SEP–APR

In winter, look for flocks of 'yellow' birds on open fields or in flight, often with Lapwing (p. 116).

Locally common AUG–APR **from Arctic tundra**

Look for rounded grey shapes scattered across mudflats, or bunched up in mixed flocks of roosting waders at high tide.

Golden Plover *Pluvialis apricaria*

L 25–28 cm | WS 53–59 cm

ID Round body, rather dainty; short, slim bill. BREEDING brown spangled **yellow** above; broad **white band** around **black face, foreneck** and **breast**. NON-BREEDING/JUVENILE **yellow-brown** above (spotted yellow/greyish); breast yellowish, bright white belly. **IN FLIGHT**, weak whitish wingbar; dark rump; plain white underwing.

VOICE Call loud, piping, mournful whistle, "*peeuw*;" rhythmic song given in flight over moors, a repeated "*poo-peeee-oo*."

Grey Plover *Pluvialis squatarola*

L 26–29 cm | WS 56–63 cm

ID Stout body; largish head, **thick, black bill**. BREEDING silver-grey, spangled **black** above; **broad white band** around **black face and foreneck** ends as **patch beside breast** NON-BREEDING/JUVENILE **grey** above; dull whitish below. **IN FLIGHT**, white wingbar; **white rump**; distinctive **black 'wingpits'**.

VOICE A frequent estuary sound: relaxed, plaintive whistle, trisyllabic with a downslur in middle – "*tee-yoo-eee*."

N/J

dark rump

white underwing

white rump

N/J

black 'wingpit'

spangled yellow

white band

B FEB–AUG

British/Irish breeders (*above*) have less black on face/breast than N European migrants in APR.

spangled silver-grey

white patch

B MAR–SEP

Pristine in spring, but by AUG returning migrants have irregular patches of black and white below.

JUVENILE is yellower than NON-BREEDING ADULT

spangled yellow/brown

short, slim bill

N/J JUN–MAR

bright white belly

greyish legs

spangled white/grey-black

thick bill

stout body

N/J JUN–MAR

dull whitish underparts

greyish legs

! American Golden Plover (p. 257)

119

JACK SNIPE

SNIPE

WOODCOCK

Snipes & Woodcock are small to medium-sized waders with a long, straight bill. They have well-camouflaged plumage patterns of brown, black and cream, with a striped or barred head.

IDENTIFY BY:
► bill length ► head pattern
► habitat ► voice

EAT worms, other small wetland invertebrates

SNIPE   WOODCOCK   JACK SNIPE

WHERE breeds lowland fields, damp moors, marshes; winters on fields

Common resident, summer migrant and winter visitor from N/E Europe, Iceland/Faeroes

Look for long-billed birds probing into wet mud along rushy edges of pools/marshes, and in flooded grassland; in APR–JUN, listen for 'drumming' especially at dusk over wet habitats.

Snipe *Gallinago gallinago*

L 23–28 cm | WS 39–45 cm

ID Medium-sized; remarkably **long bill**. Dark brown with buff lines above; head striped black and buff, crown black with **pale central stripe**; flank **barred** dark brown. **IN FLIGHT**, long bill; pale trailing edge to narrow wing; rufous and white marks on rounded tail.

VOICE Loud, harsh "*skaarch*;" in spring (mainly MAR–JUN), rhythmically repeated "*chip-per chip-per*;" often from post or wire; harsh "*chip*." Switchback display flight, loud, vibrant, buzzing "*h'h'hhhhhhh'h*" made by tail in dives.

The long bill and cream lines create excellent camouflage when feeding among grasses.

If flushed flies off high, with **harsh calls**, in **fast zigzag**.

pale, rounded tail

pale trailing edge

narrow, pointed wings

buff lines along back and wings

pale central crown stripe

barred flank

extremely long bill

! Long-billed Dowitcher (p. 257)

Woodcock *Scolopax rusticola*

L 33–38 cm | **WS** 55–65 cm

ID Medium-sized, most often seen in flight. 'Dead-leaf' brown, black and grey pattern; **black bands across back of head**. **IN FLIGHT**, dove-sized, stocky, short-tailed, broad wings tapering to a point; long, straight bill points slightly down. If flushed during day, looks **rufous-brown**.

VOICE Alternate sharp, whistled "*tsiwik!*," low, croaking grunt, "*rorrk-rorrk*" during display flight (termed roding).

Common resident and winter visitor from N/E Europe; mainly nocturnal, rarely seen

Best seen by visiting areas of woodland with small valleys or clearings at dusk in MAY–JUN: listen for distinctive call and look for a displaying ('roding') bird flying slowly over canopy.

If flushed, flies off **fast and straight**, **without calling**.

WHERE woodland of all kinds; feed in adjacent fields at night

broad-based wings

bill points slightly down

black bands across back of head

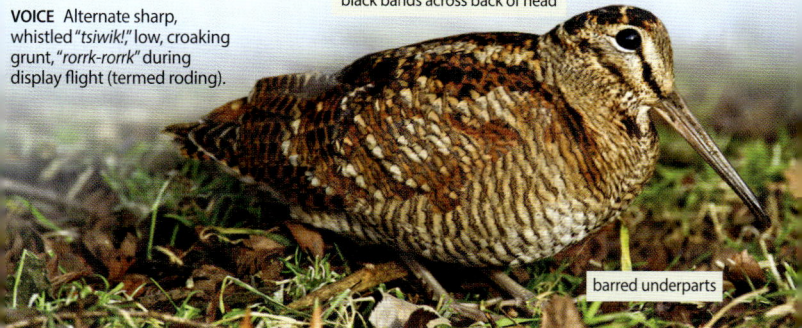

barred underparts

WHERE wet bogs and grassy or muddy places, reedbeds

Scarce migrant OCT–MAR (from Scandinavia eastward)

Hard to see: scan gaps in vegetation along muddy, reedy shores, where may be seen feeding with a curious springy, bouncing action.

Snipe (*left*) have very long bill, pale central crown stripe.
Jack Snipe (*right*) are smaller, darker, with shorter bill, black crown.

Jack Snipe
Lymnocryptes minimus

L 18–20 cm | **WS** 33–36 cm

ID **Small**; **short bill**. Dark brown with long, buff lines beside darker panel above; head striped black and buff; **crown black**, no pale stripe; flank **streaked** dark brown. **IN FLIGHT**, short bill; weak pale trailing edge to narrow wing; dark, pointed tail.

VOICE Usually silent; sometimes a quiet croak.

If flushed, rises **silently**, **without zigzag**, often turning back to settle close by.

long buff stripes along body

black crown

dark, pointed tail

faint pale trailing edge

narrow, pointed wings

streaked flank

relatively short bill

Stone-curlew
Burhinus oedicnemus

L 38–45 cm | WS 76–88 cm

ID Large, **pale brown**; plover-like (*p. 116*), with yellow-and-black bill, **long, yellow legs** and long tail. **Pale stripes** on head more obvious than **yellow eye**; black and buff lines along wing. **IN FLIGHT**, blackish wings with white patches.

VOICE Loud, Oystercatcher-like (*p. 114*) pipes and sharp "*ki-vi-vi*," and Curlew-like (*p. 136*) whistles.

WHERE grassy/sandy heaths and stony fields

EATS insects, molluscs, small lizards, seeds

Rare MAR–SEP; winters Africa

Scan grassy heathland in East Anglia and flinty arable fields on southern downland; listen for calls at dusk.

white patches on blackish wings

large, yellow eye

black-tipped yellow bill

dark-bordered buff stripe across wing

long, yellow legs

STONE-CURLEW

The elusive **Stone-curlew** is most active and noisy at dusk. It blends into pale backgrounds as its pale underparts cancel out the effect of light-and-shade.

Small sandpipers

Sandpipers in the genus *Calidris* are sparrow- to thrush-sized, but with a longer bill and legs. Breeding adults are usually easily identified but juveniles may be more difficult. They feed in and around shallow water, often in flocks, probing with the bill while standing or walking forward. They may wade, walk or run short distances. Sandpipers in the genera *Actitis* and *Tringa* have an exaggerated head-bobbing and 'tail-pumping' action; they are rather solitary.

EAT molluscs, worms, insects and other small aquatic invertebrates

IDENTIFY BY:
▶ size ▶ bill shape ▶ rump pattern
▶ colour of underparts

Flying sandpipers form co-ordinated flocks, often of mixed species, such as these **Sanderling** (TOP), **Turnstone** (MIDDLE) and **Dunlin** (BOTTOM), flashing white underwings as they turn, then settle down in a rush to feed, or to join a roost.

Calidrids compared

JUVENILE plumages have a hint of adult breeding colours.

J JUL–OCT

B MAR–AUG

SANDERLING
(p. 126)

J JUL–OCT

B FEB–SEP

KNOT
(p. 127)

J JUL–OCT

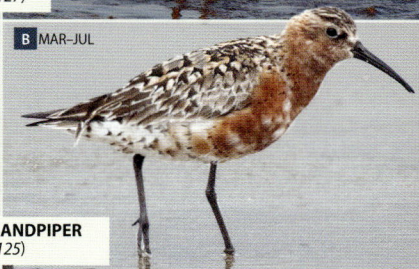

B MAR–JUL

CURLEW SANDPIPER
(p. 125)

J JUL–OCT

B APR–AUG

LITTLE STINT
(p. 125)

J JUN–OCT

B MAR–SEP

DUNLIN
(p. 124)

Dunlin feed in or around the water's edge, with a quick, probing action; they tend to look rather round-shouldered and quite short-legged.

Common summer and passage migrant, and winter visitor from Scandinavia eastwards

The commonest small wader on muddy estuaries and coastal lagoons, where easy to see, often in large flocks, particularly in winter.

Dunlin *Calidris alpina*

L 17–21 cm | WS 32–36 cm

ID Small, round-shouldered; medium to long, slightly downcurved, '**droop-tipped**' black bill; rather short, blackish legs. BREEDING red-brown, streaked black and cream above; **black belly patch**. NON-BREEDING mouse-brown above, white below. JUVENILE bright buff-brown with cream stripes above; breast **streaked grey**. IN FLIGHT, white wingbar and white sides to dark rump.

VOICE In spring on beaches, and in nesting areas, sings long, thin, bubbly trill. Call is a thin, slightly vibrant "*trr-eeee*."

WHERE breeds high moors on the Northern Isles; otherwise beaches, estuaries, inland lakes

DUNLIN

N JUN–MAR

Non-breeding Dunlin look mouse-brown in sunlight but greyer on dull days.

dark rump with white sides

white wingbar

J

creamy-buff over eye

bill, tends to look 'droop-tipped'

J

bill length very variable

B MAR–SEP

grey feathers appear on back by SEP

J

black belly patch

rather short, blackish legs

dark streaks on breast extend to flank

J JUN–OCT

! Pectoral Sandpiper (p. 257)

Scarce: most JUL–OCT, few APR–MAY, migrating between Arctic and Africa; rare in winter

Look amongst Dunlin in autumn for tiny waders feeding rapidly.

WHERE lakes, coasts

Little Stint *Calidris minuta*

L 14–15·5 cm | WS 28–31 cm

ID Tiny; short, straight, black bill; long, black legs. BREEDING (see *inset image*). NON-BREEDING pale grey above, white below. JUVENILE bright rusty-brown with black spots above and **white line along side of back**; breast **buff** with a few smudgy streaks. **IN FLIGHT**, white wingbar, white sides to dark rump.

VOICE A short, ticking "*tip*" or "*tip-ip-it*."

LITTLE STINT

B APR–AUG

bright white underparts

Breeding ADULTS are scarcer than autumn migrants: richer chestnut and black above.

dark rump with white sides

J JUL–OCT

white line each side of back forms 'V' seen from above

short, straight black bill

white wingbar

J

unstreaked flank

long, black legs

J

buff breast

! Temminck's Stint (*p.257*)

Scarce: most AUG–OCT, few APR–MAY, on migration between Arctic tundra and Africa

Look amongst Dunlin in autumn for birds wading more deeply.

WHERE coasts, coastal pools, inland lakes

Curlew Sandpiper *Calidris ferruginea*

L 19–22 cm | WS 37–42 cm

ID Small, with **smoothly downcurved bill** and **white rump**. ADULT NON-BREEDING pale grey, blotched pale red in autumn moult. JUVENILE grey-brown above with crescentic buff feather edges; pale stripe over eye; **peachy-buff** beneath, flank and belly plain white. **IN FLIGHT**, white wingbar and **band of white** above tail.

VOICE Call a throaty, rippled "*chirr-up*."

CURLEW SANDPIPER

B MAR–JUL

Breeding ADULTS (rare) are red with a white chin and eyering.

white rump

scaly effect above

white wingbar

J

long white stripe over eye

unstreaked flank

Often wades deeply when feeding.

long, blackish legs

peachy-buff tinge to breast

J JUL–OCT

very long, smoothly downcurved, black bill

Sanderling are a little bit quicker and more active than **Dunlin** (*p. 124*), more likely to be following the waves washing across a sandy beach with a twinkling, to-and-fro, 'clockwork' run.

WHERE coasts, mostly sand or small shingle but also mudflats

Locally common JUL–MAY (from the Arctic); scarce passage migrant inland, most often appearing briefly in MAY

Look for flocks of strikingly white small waders running along the tideline on sandy beaches in autumn/winter; mingles with other waders and roosts in large mixed flocks at high tide.

Sanderling *Calidris alba*

L 18–21 cm | WS 35–39 cm

ID Small; straight, rather stout black bill; **black legs (no hind toe)**. BREEDING head, back and breast marbled rusty-brown and cream; underparts pure white (see *inset images*). NON-BREEDING pearl **grey above, white below**. JUVENILE grey, spangled with complex **black spots** above; **blackish 'shoulder'**; neck/side of breast bright buff, rest of underparts unmarked bright white. IN FLIGHT, wings **dark; broad white stripe**. **VOICE** Call short, sharp *"kwit."*

SANDERLING

B MAR–AUG

[JUN]

[AUG]

Moults in August from full breeding plumage (top) to non-breeding plumage (bottom)

broad white wingbar

straight, rather stout black bill

N AUG–MAR

blackish 'shoulder'

unmarked bright white underparts

grey, spangled black above

J JUL–OCT

black legs

no hind toe (diagnostic)

buff on neck/breast side

Knot are medium-sized, with medium-length legs and bill, and in winter are drab grey; they are bigger, more thickset than **Dunlin** (p. 124), smaller and paler than browner **Redshank** (p. 133).

WHERE estuaries; a few on rocks, shingle beaches; occasional migrants inland

Locally common JUL–MAY (from the Arctic)

Look for waders a little larger and greyer than Dunlin walking slowly in tightly bunched groups as they feed.

Knot *Calidris canutus*

L 23–26 cm | WS 45–54 cm

ID Medium-sized, dumpy; rather **short, thick, straight**, black bill; short, **dull grey-green legs**. BREEDING bright **pale orange-red**. NON-BREEDING **drab, grey**. JUVENILE greyish above with fine buff/white feather edges (**lacy effect**); underparts **pale peach** with fine grey streaks. **IN FLIGHT**, pale; narrow white wingbar and **plain grey rump**.
VOICE Low "*nut*" in quiet chorus from flock.

KNOT

B FEB–SEP

[AUG]

Breeding ADULTS gain bright colours quite quickly in FEB–MAR, but lose them gradually and look more patchy in JUL–AUG.

narrow white wingbar

J

plain grey rump

short, thick, straight, black bill

grey above and rather dull white below (not conspicuous on mud)

N AUG–MAR

lacy effect above

pale peach underparts with fine grey streaks

J JUL–OCT

short, grey-green legs

! Long-billed Dowitcher (p. 257)

127

Purple Sandpipers are well camouflaged and unobtrusive when feeding on weed-strewn tidelines.

Scarce and local, small numbers AUG–APR (from Iceland and Scandinavia)

Look for small, dark waders leaping between splashing waves on seaweed-covered rocks/groynes/piers, often with Turnstone (p. 115).

Purple Sandpiper
Calidris maritima

L 19–22 cm | WS 37–42 cm

ID Small, thickset; slightly downcurved bill **orange-yellow** at base; short, **orange-yellow legs**. NON-BREEDING **dark** greyish above, with pale feather edges giving scaly effect; whitish, mottled grey below; head plain except for **white ring around eye**. IN FLIGHT, narrow white wingbar; **broad black stripe on rump**.

VOICE Call weak, sharp "*quit*" or "*quit-it*."

PURPLE SANDPIPER

WHERE sea coasts, mostly rocky shores

B MAY–AUG

Birds in BREEDING plumage in late spring/summer are chequered black and rufous above and have a mostly black bill.

If encountered on its own, a Purple Sandpiper can be very confiding.

narrow white wingbar

N

broad black stripe on rump

plain head

white ring around eye

orange-yellow base to bill

N OCT–APR

orange-yellow legs

Scarce summer migrant (APR–JUL) and winter visitor; more frequent AUG–OCT on migration between N/E Europe and Africa

Look along muddy margins for birds feeding, particularly in autumn; breeding plumage males are most likely as passage migrants in MAY.

WHERE freshwater/coastal pools; winters saltmarshes, wet meadows; occasionally on fields

Ruff *Calidris pugnax*

MALE L 29–32 cm | WS 54–60 cm
FEMALE L 22–26 cm | WS 46–49 cm

ID Medium-sized (MALE larger than FEMALE); small head, long wingtip; short, **slightly downcurved** bill; long, **pale legs**. BREEDING MALE chestnut or blackish, with broad black/rufous/white ruff. FEMALE/NON-BREEDING MALE grey-brown above; **plain head**; **buff breast** (MALE may be whiter on head). Legs **yellow-ochre** (red on NON-BREEDING MALE). JUVENILE dark above with well-defined **pale buff fringes**; underparts **plain buff**. IN FLIGHT, narrow white wingbar; white sides to dark rump may join in 'V'.

VOICE Usually silent, unlike most waders.

RUFF

M

[MAR]

MB APR–JUN

[APR]

MALES in breeding plumage have multi-coloured ruffs, but moulting birds (such as the above bird from March) are more frequently seen.

[MAY]

MB

J

narrow white wingbar

white sides to dark rump

A

slightly downcurved bill

dark above with pale buff fringes

long wings

long neck, small, plain head

J JUL–OCT

plain buff underparts

long, pale legs (colour from greenish-ochre to red)

MN JUN–APR

! Buff-breasted Sandpiper (p. 257)

These three sandpipers are solitary or occur only in very small groups, never in large flocks.

Common Sandpiper is a summer migrant, breeding near upland lakes and streams. **Green Sandpiper** is a passage migrant and winter visitor to lakes and slow streams, but tiny numbers breed in trees in north Scotland. **Wood Sandpiper** is a rare passage migrant, occurring in small numbers in spring and particularly autumn, but also breeds in tiny numbers in north Scotland.

EAT worms, other small wetland invertebrates

COMMON SANDPIPER   GREEN SANDPIPER   WOOD SANDPIPER

Common Sandpiper is characteristic of rivers and lakes in upland valleys, where its rhythmic songs draw attention APR–JUL.

Common summer/passage migrant APR–OCT; rare and local in winter, when most in Africa

Listen for song beside stony lakes and rivers in APR–JUL, and look for migrants by inland lakes APR–MAY and JUL–SEP, usually 1–5 (never large flocks). Almost always calls as flies away.

WHERE rivers/lakesides, sheltered shorelines; coasts in winter (not on open estuary)

Common Sandpiper *Actitis hypoleucos*

L 18–20·5 cm | WS 32–35 cm

ID Small; **long tail** (past wingtip); **mid-brown**, barred darker above; brown breast, white below extending as **white 'hook'** in front of 'shoulder'; white stripe over eye; legs dull, pale. **IN FLIGHT**, **stiff, bowed wings**; long, white stripe; dark tail tip.

VOICE Call distinctive, ringing, with slight melancholy **fall in pitch** and volume – "*swee-wee-wee-wee.*" Song varied fast, rhythmic trills.

white wingbar

plain brown above

characteristic stiff downward wing-flick

long tail

plain, mid-brown above

white stripe over eye

dull pale legs

white 'hook' between wing and fairly well-demarcated brown breast

Rare, mainly JUL–SEP on migration between N Europe and Africa; rare breeder in N Scotland

Look along the muddy margins of freshwater pools or coastal lagoons, particularly near clumps of rushes and reeds.

WHERE mostly freshwater margins, coastal pools/ditches

Wood Sandpiper *Tringa glareola*

L 18·5–21 cm | WS 35–39 cm

ID Small; long wings (equal to tail); brown above, **spotted with buff**; streaked buff breast, white below; **long white stripe over eye**; legs **long, yellowish**. **IN FLIGHT**, brown-and-white: **white rump**, barred tail, **grey-brown underwings**.

VOICE Thin, high, quick, "*chiff-if-if*" on even pitch.

white rump

grey-brown wings

long white stripe over eye

brown above, boldy spotted buff

streaked buff breast

long, yellow legs

Very rare breeder; mostly migrant between N Europe and Africa, or winter visitor, AUG–APR

Listen for the distinctive call and scan the mud along the water's edge for birds feeding inconspicuously, in ones and twos.

WHERE mostly freshwater margins, coastal pools/ditches (not on open estuary/beach)

Green Sandpiper *Tringa ochropus*

L 20–24 cm | WS 39–44 cm

ID Fairly small; long wings (equal to tail); **dark** green-brown above, finely spotted white; dark breast, white below; **short white stripe from bill to eye**; legs dull greenish. **IN FLIGHT**, almost **black-and-white**: all-dark wings, square **white rump** and **black underwings**.

VOICE Loud, fluty, yodelling "*tluee-wee-wee*."

prominent white rump

blackish wings

dark green-brown above, finely speckled white

short white stripe between bill and eye

dark breast

especially bright white below

dull greenish legs

131

'Shanks' medium-sized; long bill and legs.

IDENTIFY BY:
► bill and leg colour ► head/body pattern
► wing pattern in flight ► call

'Shank' calls at-a-glance

Redshank	bright "teu" or sad "teu-hu"
Greenshank	ringing, loud "tyew-tyew-tyew"
Spotted Redshank	clear "chew-it"

EAT invertebrates, such as worms and molluscs

REDSHANK   GREENSHANK   SPOTTED REDSHANK

Reshank is a widespread breeder, common in winter when joined by European migrants. **Greenshank** breeds in N Scotland and small numbers winter around the coast. **Spotted Redshank** is mainly a scarce passage migrant.

GREENSHANK

REDSHANK

REDSHANK

GREENSHANK

Outside the breeding season, 'shanks' often form mixed flocks

SPOTTED REDSHANK

Scarce, mainly APR–MAY, AUG–OCT, on migration between N Europe and Africa; rare in winter

Look for long-legged, medium-sized waders (sometimes 5–10) dashing about, swimming or upending like ducks in shallow water along muddy edges of reservoirs or coastal pools.

WHERE muddy edges and pools, mainly near the coast

white oval on back

J

Spotted Redshank *Tringa erythropus*

L 29–33 cm | WS 61–67 cm

ID Medium-sized, long-necked, elegant; **long, fine** bill, fractionally **tapered downwards to tip**, with **streak of red at base**; **long, red legs**. BREEDING **blackish** (see *inset*). NON-BREEDING **pale grey above**, white below, with long **whitish stripe above eye**. JUVENILE browner, with barred underparts. **IN FLIGHT**, **plain** grey wings; thin **white oval** on back.

VOICE A distinct, clear "*chew-it.*"

B MAR–MAY

J JUN–SEP

pale grey above

distinct white stripe from bill to beyond eye

bill fine, slightly droop-tipped; red on lower edge only

long, bright red legs

greyish, more striped on head and whiter on breast than Redshank

N JUL–MAR

BREEDING **blackish** with pale spots (rare). JUVENILE browner than non-breeding adult but head and bill patterns similar.

Scarce breeder MAR–JUL; winter migrant from N Europe JUL–MAR

Listen for the distinctive three-note call from estuaries or shallow pools on the coast, and look along muddy creeks or scan the margins for single birds or small groups.

WHERE breeds moorland; winters lakes, reservoirs, estuaries

Greenshank *Tringa nebularia*
L 30–34 cm | WS 55–62 cm

ID Large, tall; **greyish above**, white below, bill long, very **slightly upturned**, greyish (no red); **greenish** legs. BREEDING grey and white (see *inset*). NON-BREEDING/JUVENILE head whiter. **IN FLIGHT**, **dark wings** and long **triangle of white** up back.

VOICE Loud, **distinct**: ringing, powerful "*tyew-tyew-tyew*" on same note.

long white triangle up back

dark wings

J

bill faintly upturned; greyish

greyish overall (paler on head and whiter on breast than Redshank)

greenish legs

J JUN–NOV

B MAR–JUL

BREEDING **grey-and-white**; blackish spots above and on white underparts; legs yellow-green.

Locally common resident, migrant/winter visitor from N Europe and Iceland AUG–MAR

Noisy and easy to see feeding on estuaries and in saltmarsh creeks. Breeding birds often perch on fence posts, calling loudly MAR–JUN.

WHERE estuaries, freshwater edges, marshes

Redshank *Tringa totanus*
L 24–27 cm | WS 47–53 cm

ID Medium-sized; slim, straight bill with **red at base**; **bright orange-red legs**. BREEDING **brown** (see *inset*). NON-BREEDING/JUVENILE **brown** with white belly. **IN FLIGHT**, **white triangle** up back; **broad white band along rear edge of wings**.

VOICE Musical "*teu*," "*teu-hu*" or "*teu-huhu*." Frenetic "*pit-u-pit-u-pit-u*" or "*kyip*" in alarm; rhythmic "*t'leeo-t'leeo-t'leeo*" song.

white triangle up back

broad white patch

B

B MAR–OCT

BREEDING **largely brown** with blackish spots above; whitish, blotched and barred dark brown below; legs vivid red.

'weak' head pattern; white stripe above eye indistinct

bright orange-red legs

bill straight; whole of base red

N JUL–MAR

! Lesser Yellowlegs (*p.257*)

133

Godwits are tall, upstanding waterside birds, a little like small Curlews with a straight bill; they are often seen in flocks.

IDENTIFY BY:
▶ leg length ▶ bill shape ▶ back/tail pattern
▶ wing/tail pattern in flight

EAT invertebrates, particularly worms

BLACK-TAILED GODWIT

BAR-TAILED GODWIT

A few **Black-tailed Godwit** breed in Britain, but **Bar-tailed Godwit** is an Arctic breeder and purely a winter visitor to our estuaries. Both are most easily seen on mud- and sand-flats or marshes from August to April, tending to remain in separate flocks.

Black-tailed Godwit *Limosa limosa*

L 37–42 cm | WS 63–74 cm

ID Large; very long, **straight** bill, pink at base; **long** legs, **long above joint**. BREEDING head/breast rich **coppery-orange** or rusty-red, **white on belly**. NON-BREEDING **plain** grey-brown above, white below. JUVENILE bright, **rusty**, with dark spots above. IN FLIGHT, **broad white band** along wing (underwing white with black edges) and **white band** above **black tail**.

VOICE Quick, nasal notes; mechanical/metallic bickering when feeding/quarrelling.

WHERE breeds wet fields, marshes; winters on and around muddy estuaries

Rare breeder; locally common winter visitor from central/N Europe and Iceland AUG–APR

Most easily seen in winter feeding on estuaries, especially in SW England and SW Ireland, often in enclosed, muddy creeks rather than on open mudflats.

upperparts **plain**

N JUN–MAR

legs **long** above joint

bill **straight**

J MAY–OCT

coppery-orange head and breast; white on belly

B FEB–JUL

underwing white edged black

square white rump; black tail

white triangle up back; brown tail

underwing uniformly pale

BLACK-TAILED GODWIT

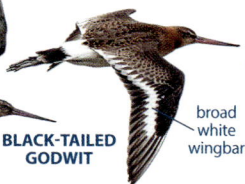

broad white wingbar

plain wings

BAR-TAILED GODWIT

Bar-tailed Godwit *Limosa lapponica*

33–41 cm | WS 62–72 cm

○ Large; very long, **slightly upcurved** bill, pink at base; **medium-length** legs, **short above joint**. BREEDING head/underparts orange to **rich red**. NON-BREEDING **grey-brown, streaked grey-black** above, white below. JUVENILE even more streaked black and brown above; plain buff beneath. **IN FLIGHT, plain wings**; **white triangle** on back; **barred tail**.

VOICE Nasal, whickering "*ki-wee ki-wee*" or "*ik-ik-ik.*"

WHERE mostly muddy coastlines; rare inland

Locally common AUG–APR (from Scandinavia)

Scan mud for large, straight-billed waders at low tide; watch for distinctive lines or 'V's if disturbed or flying to roost, flashing brown/white as they rise and fall in acrobatic, twisting flight.

upperparts **streaked**

N SEP–MAY

legs **short** above joint

bill slightly **upcurved**

FB FEB–AUG

FEMALES are longer billed than MALES and paler, more orange in breeding plumage.

J JUN–OCT

rich red underparts

MB FEB–AUG

Curlew look pale against a dark heather moor, but darker against dead grass or on open mudflats.

Curlews are large, long-legged, long-striding waders with long, downcurved bill; no significant sex, age or seasonal differences in streaked buff-brown plumages.

IDENTIFY BY: ▶ **head pattern** ▶ **bill shape** ▶ **call**

EAT worms, insects, molluscs, crustaceans, shellfish

CURLEW   WHIMBREL

Locally fairly common resident/migrant from N Europe SEP–MAR

Although breeding birds lost from most areas, listen for the unmistakable bubbling song on higher moors. On the coast, in mixed roosts at high tide, look for lines (10s or 100s) of noticeably bigger, darker birds than godwits and Redshanks.

Curlew *Numenius arquata*

L 48–57 cm | WS 89–106 cm

ID Large; rather heavy and sedate; **streaky brown**, no obvious pattern; **long, smoothly downcurved bill** with **pink at base**. **IN FLIGHT**, steady, rather gull-like (*p. 82*) with pale innerwing; **white triangle** on rump.

VOICE Hoarse or barking notes; loud "*vi-vi-vi*" of alarm; clear, fluty "*cur-lee*" and "*cue-cue-cue*." Song loud, mournful, accelerating into mesmeric bubbling trill.

white triangle on rump/lower back

A very long bill indicates a FEMALE, very short a JUVENILE or MALE, but bill lengths overlap considerably.

sometimes has dark cap but never a strong stripe through the eye

J/M

bill blackish with pink base, long and smoothly downcurved

plain face

closely streaked/ barred/chequered

brighter and more buffy than Whimbrel

F

WHERE breeds moors/wet heaths; most of year on coast, from rocky shores to muddy estuaries and coastal pools

plain 'face'

pale band over eye

pale crown stripe

A few **Whimbrel** breed in mainland Scotland but most are on the Northern Isles, where they behave much like Curlews on open moorland.

Rare breeder; scarce passage migrant APR–MAY and JUL–OCT rare in winter when most in Africa

Easiest to see on migration when small flocks regularly appear on the coast (and sometimes inland), their presence usually revealed by the distinctive far-carrying, trilling call.

Curlew (*left*) large, boldly streaked and blotched, with weak head pattern, smoothly downcurved, pink-based bill; **Whimbrel** (*right*) more closely streaked, with bold head pattern and more angled, blackish bill.

Whimbrel *Numenius phaeopus*

L 37–45 cm | WS 78–88 cm

ID A little smaller and darker than Curlew; bill **blacker**, slightly shorter and more angled towards tip. Head with **dark brown stripe** through eye and on each side of crown, **central pale line on top** (similar but much weaker on some Curlews).
IN FLIGHT, rather deep-chested; dark with **white triangle** on rump.

VOICE Call diagnostic: quick, even repetition of short whistle in rippling trill: "*pipipipipipipip*." Song long whistles developing into even, sad trill.

On Whimbrel and Curlew, pale spots on feather edges wear away more quickly than dark areas, giving a plainer, darker look by MAY–JUN.

white triangle on rump/lower back

bill blackish, downcurved and distinctly angled towards tip

head distinctly striped

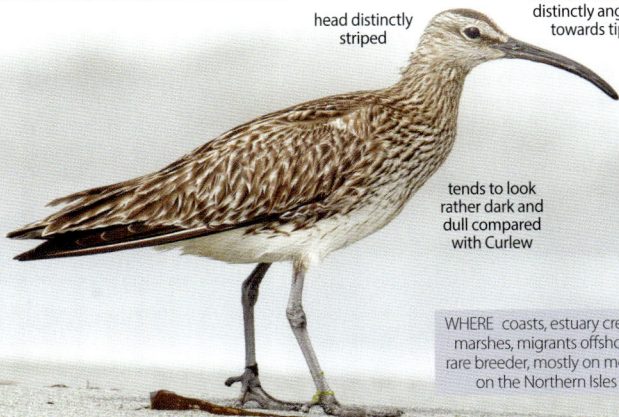

tends to look rather dark and dull compared with Curlew

WHERE coasts, estuary creeks, marshes, migrants offshore; rare breeder, mostly on moors on the Northern Isles

137

► WADERS IN FLIGHT p. 112

Phalaropes are small, fine-billed waders that **swim** most of the time, with high shoulders, sloping back; winters out at sea.
IDENTIFY BY: ► bill shape ► head pattern

Apart from making a special trip to Shetland, where **Red-necked Phalarope** breeds in small numbers, seeing phalaropes is mostly a matter of luck. The great majority of sightings, both inland and coastal, are of **Grey Phalarope** – particularly after an autumn gale.

EAT small invertebrates, mostly taken from surface

GREY PHALAROPE   RED-NECKED PHALAROPE

Grey Phalarope
Phalaropus fulicarius

L 20–22 cm | WS 36–41 cm
ID Small, swims, occasionally on shoreline. Bill thin, **yellow at base.** BREEDING rarely seen (see *inset*). NON-BREEDING pale grey above; white below, black cap and 'mask'. JUVENILE **blotched black-brown** above, increasingly grey SEP–OCT. **IN FLIGHT,** dark wings, white stripe, like Sanderling (*p. 126*). **VOICE** Simple "*tik*" notes.

WHERE at sea, occasionally storm-blown inland

Rare migrant from Iceland to S Atlantic AUG–NOV

Most likely offshore as an individual (occasionally small flocks); sometimes on inland waters after a gale SEP–NOV.

rather broad white wingbar

J/N

black 'mask'

bill relatively thick (but hard to judge in isolation)

yellow base to bill

grey back

J/N JUL–APR

FB APR–AUG

BREEDING ADULT a very rare sight in spring: **orange-red** body, **white face,** mostly **yellow bill;** FEMALE brighter than MALE.

Red-necked Phalarope
Phalaropus lobatus

L 17–19 cm | WS 30–34 cm
ID Small, rather elongated; swims. **Bill very fine, all-black.** BREEDING **dark grey** with **buff stripes above, grey breast, white chin, red on neck** (brightest on FEMALE). NON-BREEDING pale grey above, white below, black cap and mask. JUVENILE **dark grey** above, **striped buff;** white below. **IN FLIGHT,** dark wings with white stripe. **VOICE** Short, sharp "*kwit*" call.

WHERE freshwater/coastal pools; breeds ponds/marshes

Rare breeder and passage migrant from N Europe APR–OCT; winters Atlantic/E Pacific

Can be very confiding when feeding actively.

narrow white wingbar

FB

MB APR–AUG

needle-fine bill, all-black

J JUN–OCT

black 'mask'

buff stripes

FB APR–AUG

JUVENILE best told by back pattern and black 'mask' turning down at rear.

Large Waterside Birds

are tall, upstanding birds from crow- to swan-sized, with long legs, large feet and a medium or long bill. They wade in shallow water, feed in marshy ground or damp pastures, or are secretive in reedbeds. There is one main group (Herons and Egrets) plus three more distinctive species.

Herons & Egrets
(pp. 141–142)

Large or very large; grey (Heron) or white (egrets); long, thin neck and dagger-like bill.

Bittern
(p. 140)

Large, brown, thickset; dagger-like bill.

Spoonbill
(p. 143)

Large, white; bill long, thick at base, flattening into broad, rounded tip.

Crane (p. 143)

Huge, grey; long-necked but quite short-billed, lower neck much thicker than herons'; bunch of bushy feathers over short tail.

Plumages

Sexes are alike and there are just small seasonal differences, with long plumes or brighter facial skin, bill and legs colours early in the breeding season. Juveniles are duller or little different from adults.

In flight

Herons, egrets and Bittern fly with bowed wings and neck coiled back or withdrawn (but extend neck when landing). Spoonbill and Crane fly with flat wings and neck outstretched. Grey Heron may migrate in loose flocks; smaller egrets form flocks or tight packs flying to roost; Crane and Spoonbill fly in lines or 'V's.

Behaviour

Herons and egrets generally use 'wait-and-see' feeding technique, standing at water's edge. Bittern is a reedbed bird, feeding within dense wetland vegetation; when alarmed, points bill upwards and very well camouflaged. Spoonbill feeds by slow, steady, long-striding walk in shallow water. Crane feeds in open marshes.

GREY HERONS

CATTLE EGRETS

GREY HERONS

GREY HERONS

LITTLE EGRETS

Large waterside birds in flight

GREY HERON

CRANE
(p. 143)

BITTERN

GREAT WHITE EGRET
(p. 142)

LITTLE EGRET
(p. 142)

CATTLE EGRET
(p. 142)

SPOONBILL
(p. 143)

Bitterns, Herons & Egrets
solitary or in small groups; herons and egrets colonial when nesting. All have coiled neck and bowed wings in flight.

IDENTIFY BY: ▶ overall colour ▶ colour of bill, legs and feet

EAT fish, amphibians, occasional small mammals and birds, insects

Rare, local breeder, more widespread in winter from NW Europe

Requires reeds or tall, dense grasses in standing water, with hidden ditches and pools where feeds. Search repeatedly with binoculars, as easily overlooked due to amazing camouflage; watch for one moving in a low crouch lifting its big feet over the vegetation.

WHERE reedbeds and fenland

Bittern *Botaurus stellaris*

L 69–81 cm | WS 100–130 cm

ID Large, superbly camouflaged **buff and brown**, mottled and streaked with black and rufous. Thick, dagger-like bill; green legs.

IN FLIGHT **broad wings**, **thick neck** and big, **trailing feet**; pale band across innerwing.

VOICE In spring, a remarkable deep, booming, 'foghorn'-like *"whoo-ump!"*

BITTERN

Bitterns are easy to overlook as their plumage blends in with their reedy habitat.

black crown

tawny neck

Grey Herons may line the banks of a river or lake, or gather to rest on nearby fields.

Single birds or small numbers easy to see in almost any wetland area: often at the margins, standing still or wading slowly, neck outstretched, ready to take a fish with rapid lunge; when resting, stands hunched on ground nearby.

Grey Heron *Ardea cinerea*

L 84–102 cm | WS 155–175 cm

ID Very large, tall, elegant; **grey-and-white**. ADULT white head with black eyestripe extending into long plume; bill and legs yellowish to brown. JUVENILE grey head, dark cap; grey-and-yellow bill. **IN FLIGHT**, heavy, with **neck coiled back**, feet trailed and **wings deeply bowed**. Wing pale grey with **dull black outer half**, pale patch on leading edge; tip **rounded**.

VOICE A shouted *"fraank"* if disturbed; various noisy bill-rattling sounds and rhythmic calls from young birds at the nest.

GREY HERON

WHERE from seaweedy, rocky or muddy coasts to inland lakes, rivers and marshes

B FEB–MAY

Bill of breeding adult pink, red or orange for brief period in spring.

dark, bowed wings

trailing feet

head/neck coiled back

immature drab grey for first year

J

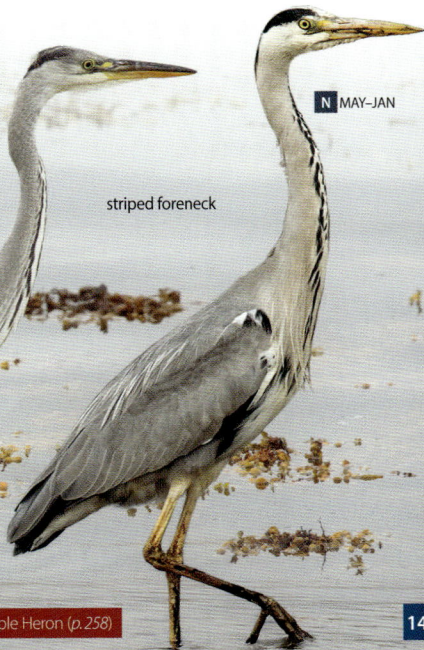

N MAY–JAN

striped foreneck

! Purple Heron (*p.258*)

EAT fish, amphibians, small mammals, birds, insects

Usually obvious, white, waterside birds, although can be hidden when resting (or nesting) in trees. **Little Egret** are widespread, on still and flowing water, wet pastures, and at many coastal sites; others rare but look on extensive marshes especially in SW England and check egrets in fields for **Cattle Egret**. Numbers are swelled by birds from Europe in spring.

LITTLE EGRET

GREAT WHITE EGRET

CATTLE EGRET

Rare, but increasing	Generally uncommon, local	Rare, increasing, now breeds
WHERE freshwater lakes, marshes, reedbeds, riversides	WHERE estuaries, saltmarsh, riversides, lakes, meadows	WHERE marshy grasslands, fields with livestock

Great White Egret
Ardea alba

L 85–105 cm | WS 140–170 cm

ID Large; as tall as Grey Heron (p. 141) and even longer-necked; **dark legs and feet; yellow bill.** BREEDING (MAR–JUL) **black bill** and a cloak of very long, wispy plumes. **IN FLIGHT**, heavy; long, broad wings; long legs; dark feet.

VOICE Hoarse croaks.

Little Egret
Egretta garzetta

L 55–65 cm | WS 88–106 cm

ID Small; **black legs; yellow feet.** Slender, **grey-black** bill; long, slender plumes from back of head: BREEDING long, wispy plumes on back. JUVENILE legs greenish. **IN FLIGHT**, broad wings; legs trail; yellow feet.

VOICE Deep, croaking calls.

Cattle Egret
Bubulcus ibis

L 45–52 cm | WS 82–95 cm

ID Small; **brownish legs and feet**; thick **yellow bill.** Feeds in fields with livestock (as do some Little Egrets). BREEDING buff on crown, breast and back. **IN FLIGHT**, quick beats, short legs and dark feet.

VOICE Occasional croaks.

head/neck coiled back

GREAT WHITE EGRET

N head/neck coiled back

LITTLE EGRET   CATTLE EGRET

B FEB–JUN

bill never yellow

B FEB–JUN

B MAR–JUN

bill never black

N MAY–FEB

N MAY–FEB

N

yellow feet

black feet

legs and feet black-brown to yellowish

Spoonbill
Platalea leucorodia

L 80–93 cm | WS 120–135 cm

ID Large, white, with long, **thick, black legs**; bill long, **flat**, black with broad yellow tip; bushy crest on nape. Stands rather horizontal.

BREEDING buff on neck. JUVENILE/IMMATURE pink bill, flight feathers tipped black.

VOICE Normally silent.

SPOONBILL

Crane *Grus grus*

L 96–119 cm | WS 180–240 cm

ID Huge; grey, with **blacker flight feathers** and blackish feathers bunched above and drooping over tail. Head and neck **black** with **white band** behind eye; red crown. JUVENILE head grey. **IN FLIGHT, head outstretched**, wings very long, broad, **tips slightly 'fingered'**.

VOICE Flight call deep, trumpeting "*crr-rr-ouk*."

CRANE

A

head/neck outstretched

Juvenile/immature has black wingtips

J/I

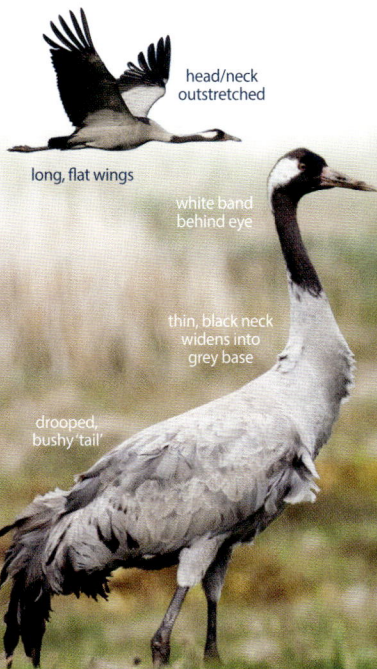

head/neck outstretched

long, flat wings

white band behind eye

thin, black neck widens into grey base

drooped, bushy 'tail'

bushy crest

thick neck

unique flat-tipped bill

B FEB–JUN

143

Rails & Crakes
are round-bodied, mostly short-billed but long-legged birds, with a very short tail. Toes are slim or broadly lobed (in **Coot**), but not webbed. Sexes are similar, with no seasonal variations, but juveniles are typically duller than adults. **Corncrake** is a dry-land bird, the others inhabit freshwater wetlands.

IDENTIFY BY:
▶ **overall plumage**
▶ **bill shape and colour**

MOORHEN

COOT

EAT invertebrates, seeds, berries, shoots and roots

WHERE open water, marshes, reedbeds, riversides

Common resident/winter visitor from N Europe

Frequent sight on standing and flowing waters; may feed close to water's edge on *e.g.* lawns, but often skulks in vegetation.

Moorhen *Gallinula chloropus*

L 30–38 cm | WS 55–60 cm

ID Medium-sized, dark; on water, **tail held up** and **head bobbed** rhythmically. ADULT **red-and-yellow bill**, white streaks along side and large **white patch under tail**. JUVENILE overall brown, with dull bill but with same white marks as adult. **IN FLIGHT**, usually low and short, wings lifted high on upbeat, legs dangling; not usually seen in full flight by day.

VOICE Loud, ringing "*kuttuk*," explosive "*kurrt*;" abrupt "*ki-yek*" and "*krek-krek-krek*." Gives nasal "*kit-it*" call during high territorial flights at night.

A
Toes not lobed; rarely dives.

pointed wingtip; tail raised when swimming
red-and-yellow bill
white streaks along side

C APR–AUG

J MAY–OCT

Downy CHICK blackish; red and blue on head but no colourful, wispy down; bill red and yellow. JUVENILE pale brown but white beside tail and white flank stripes distinctive.

Coot fly well, but often simply skitter across the water surface, sometimes splashing up water to deter predatory gulls or harriers.

Common resident/winter visitor from N and NE Europe

Generally easy to see amongst ducks on lakes/reservoirs or feeding on adjacent grassland.

WHERE lakes, reservoirs, ponds, marshes, riversides; rarely on sea

Coot *Fulica atra*

📏 36–39 cm | WS 70–80 cm

ID Duck-like on open water, sometimes in flocks. Swims buoyantly, back **rounded** and **tail down**; **dives** from surface, reappearing in horizontal, swimming position. ADULT blackish with large **white facial shield and bill**. JUVENILE whitish on face and breast. **IN FLIGHT**, heavy, clumsy, lacks manoeuvrability; broad wing has **pale trailing edge**; disturbed flocks may rise and circle over lakes.

VOICE Loud, sudden "*kowk!*," various sharp, metallic notes. Young have feeble but far-carrying whistles.

Broad-lobed toes; dives repeatedly.

flies more readily than Moorhen

white bill

rounded wingtip; tail held low when swimming

entirely black plumage

C APR–AUG

J MAY–OCT

Downy CHICK black with wispy red and orange down on head and neck; red on bill. JUVENILE has white on face and breast, bill dark, but round-backed shape distinctive

145

Rare APR–SEP; winters Africa

WHERE grassland, riverside thickets

EATS small insects and other invertebrates, seeds

Rare APR–SEP; winters Africa

Elusive and far more often heard than seen: a distinctive rasping call. May be seen dashing across an open gap in a fast, crouched run. Most likely in the Northern and Western Isles of Scotland and some remote areas of north-west Ireland.

stubby, pink bill

Usually near-invisible in thick vegetation but may come into the open when singing.

rusty wings

Corncrake *Crex crex*

L 27–30 cm | WS 42–53 cm

ID Small, pale; **streaky brown** with **rusty wings**. **IN FLIGHT**, rusty wings conspicuous; legs trail beneath short tail.

VOICE Key feature is a **repeated double rasp**, "*crrek crrek*," light and scratchy at a distance but loud, heavy and resonant at close range.

CORNCRAKE

Locally common resident/ migrant from NW Europe

WHERE marshes and swamps with tall vegetation

EATS mainly invertebrates but also larger animals and carrion

Listen for distinctive squealing call and wait quietly; usually hidden in dense vegetation but sometimes ventures into the open along reedy wetland margins, creeping on flexed legs and long toes.

white leading edge to wing

short wings raised high in flight

head/neck outstretched, feet dangled

WATER RAIL

Water Rail *Rallus aquaticus*

L 23–26 cm | WS 38–45 cm

ID Small, slender, but deep-bodied. Brown above, streaked black; **grey** below, **barred black-and-white** on flank; **buff patch** under raised tail. Bill long and pointed, mostly **red**; legs pinkish. JUVENILE breast/flank barred buff; bill blackish. **IN FLIGHT**, slender head/bill; short wings, white leading edge beneath; legs trail.

VOICE Pig-like squealing and loud, sharp "*pik-pik-pik*" calls.

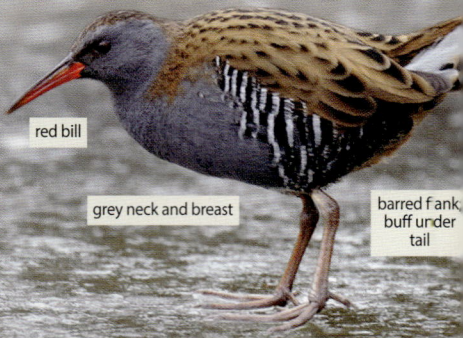

red bill

grey neck and breast

barred flank buff under tail

'Gamebirds'

'Gamebirds' are small to large, rotund and small-headed with a short, arched or hooked bill, short, bare or feathered legs and a springy or creeping walk. In flight, usually fast and direct, with bursts of wingbeats before long glides on short, broad, stiff wings. Most species are terrestrial, but some also feed or roost in trees.

Quail
Thrush-sized, slim-winged summer visitor; elusive in grass or crops. Not social. No seasonal changes; male and female look slightly different.

Pheasant & Partridges
(pp. 148–149)

Medium to large; run with head raised. Legs bare. Social. No seasonal changes. Pheasant heavy-bodied; very long tail; sexes look very different. Partridges short-tailed; sexes look alike or differ slightly.

Grouse
(pp. 150–153)

Medium to very large; tend to fly rather than run. Legs feathered. Slight or marked seasonal changes; male and female/juvenile look very or slightly different.

GREY PARTRIDGE

BROWN HARE

Scarce and local APR–OCT; winters in Africa

In some years quite widespread in large cereal fields and rolling downland, in others rare; distinctive call is far-carrying. Elusive and very hard to see: best chance is a bird crossing open space or vehicle track in grass or crops.

QUAIL

WHERE large cereal fields, extensive grassland

EATS seeds, insects and other small invertebrates

Quail *Coturnix coturnix*

L 16–18 cm | WS 32–35 cm

ID Tiny, rounded; streaked brown and buff. MALE has **striped black-and-buff head**, white on throat. **IN FLIGHT**, quick, direct on long, narrow wings.

VOICE A bright, liquid, rhythmic *"quik, quik-ik,"* repeated from within thick grass or cereal crops, especially at dusk.

slender wingtip

cream stripes on back and flank

white throat band

M

F

FEMALE throat brown and white.

147

Pheasant & Partridges

Pheasant & Partridges are secretive in low vegetation, or easily visible on bare fields. They run if mildly disturbed but fly fast and low; **Pheasants** may 'erupt' almost underfoot with loud call and clattering wings. Juvenile Pheasants can fly when half-grown, but have longer, more pointed tail than **partridges**.

IDENTIFY BY:
▶ size ▶ tail shape ▶ head pattern

EAT seeds/grain, leaves, insects and other invertebrates

PHEASANT | GREY PARTRIDGE | RED-LEGGED PARTRIDGE

Common (introduced)

Familiar and numerous, millions are released each year, some of which subsequently breed.

WHERE arable land, woodland, scrub, reedbeds and damp thickets, drier heaths

Pheasant *Phasianus colchicus*

L MALE 70–90 cm (incl. tail 35–45 cm); FEMALE 55–70 cm (incl. tail 20–25 cm) | WS 70–90 cm

ID Large, various colour forms. MALE **green/blue-black head** with broad, **scarlet wattle**; **long, pointed tail**. Most have white collar. Typically coppery-red, flank spotted black; pale wing patch; rump rufous, buff or blue-green. Minority darker, a few blackish overall. FEMALE smaller, shorter-tailed; **pale brown** with cream and black spots and streaks. IN FLIGHT, fast, rather low, but straight and direct without agility, soon drops exhausted into cover.

VOICE MALE calls loud "*cor-kok*" followed by a loud flurry of wings; discordant "*ku-cha, kuch-a, kuchok, ok ok.*"

glides on stiff, 'fingered' wings
M

M

evenly spotted black on pale beige-brown

F

long tail

M

Characteristic calls draw attention: often near hedges/bushy downland thickets, or hidden in long grass. More likely to fly than run if flushed.

Grey Partridge *Perdix perdix*

L 28–32 cm | WS 45–48 cm

ID Rounded; **grey-and-brown** with **pale orange face; streaks of cream and black** above. Beneath, grey with **rufous bars** on flank and **dark brown 'horseshoe'-shaped** mark on belly (largest on MALE). Bill grey, legs pale brownish. **IN FLIGHT**, rufous tail sides; pale brown wings; **streaked back**.

VOICE A repeated, slightly creaking or squeaky "*kier-vit*" or "*cheevit*."

WHERE grassland, farmland, arable fields with hedgerows

barred wings

rufous tail, bright buff rump

orange face

grey bill

back streaked and barred

flank barred rufous and grey

short tail

dark brown patch on belly

brownish legs

Usually seen on open ground but often perches on e.g. straw bales or barn roofs to call; may wander into gardens. More likely to run than fly if disturbed.

Red-legged Partridge *Alectoris rufa*

L 34–38 cm | WS 47–50 cm

ID Rounded; **unstreaked** pale **sandy-brown and grey; white throat** edged black above streaked black 'necklace'. **Black, rufous and grey/white bars** on flank. Bill and legs red. **IN FLIGHT**, rufous tail sides; pale brown wings; **plain back**.

VOICE Curious mechanical, chuffing sounds, soft or loud, often "*chu chu chu chu ka-chekchek ca-chekchek cachekchek….*"

WHERE sandy or stony arable fields and downland, heaths

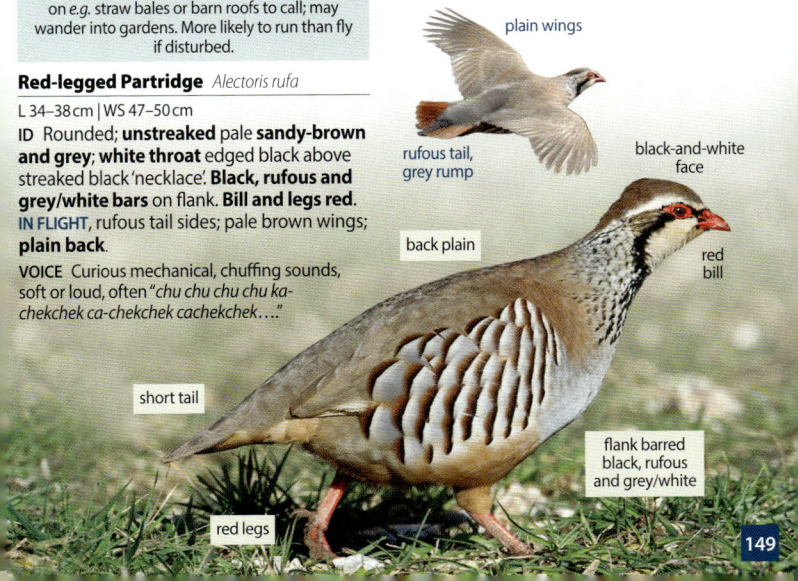

plain wings

rufous tail, grey rump

black-and-white face

back plain

red bill

short tail

flank barred black, rufous and grey/white

red legs

149

Red Grouse need heather moors but have declined with changing climate and moorland conditions, especially in Ireland, south-west England and Wales.

Grouse are medium–large, round-bodied, small-headed birds, that fly strongly, sometimes quite high. **Black Grouse** and **Red Grouse** have far-carrying calls over moorland; **Capercaillie** is elusive in forest; **Ptarmigan** is a high-altitude specialist.

IDENTIFY BY:
▶ body colour ▶ tail shape
▶ calls ▶ wing colour

EAT heather shoots, seeds, some small invertebrates

RED GROUSE   PTARMIGAN

WHERE heather moorland, boggy moorland slopes

Locally common
Easily seen and heard on suitable moors: look for dark birds perched on hillocks or flying over high ridges. Family groups sit tight until disturbed at close range, flying off rapidly.

Red Grouse *Lagopus lagopus*

L 33–38 cm | WS 55–66 cm

ID Heavier and much darker than partridges. White, feathered legs and feet. MALE marbled **dark rufous and blackish**. FEMALE browner, mottled with yellowish-buff. **IN FLIGHT**, tail and upperwing plain **blackish** (unlike partridges), with white patches on underwing.

VOICE Crowing calls and distinctive, staccato "*korrr-rr-ack-go-back, ack, go-bak go bak bak.*"

tail and upperwing blackish

M

underwing dark with white patches (extent varies)

less evenly barred than FEMALE Black Grouse (p. 152)

mottled brown, no strong face or flank pattern

F

dark red-brown

M

no strong flank pattern

Ptarmigan face a difficult future, as mountain habitats are likely to contract in response to climate change.

Elusive and supremely well camouflaged on lichen-covered rocks; unlikely to fly, even if approached closely. Restricted to northern mountain tops, such as the Cairngorms massif.

WHERE mountain tops

F AUG–NOV/MAR–APR

In spring and autumn, patchy intermediate stages show a lot of white.

Ptarmigan *Lagopus muta*

L 31–35 cm | WS 55–65 cm

ID Similar to Red Grouse; **white wings** all-year. NON-BREEDING white, except for black tail; MALE has black face patch. BREEDING MALE greyish with 'pepper-and-salt' speckling of black and buff. BREEDING FEMALE browner with yellower marks. **IN FLIGHT**, instantly identifiable by white wings, black tail.

VOICE Short, low grunts and croaks; more rhythmic series in short, high display flight.

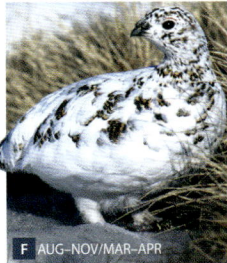

M OCT–NOV/MAR–APR

wings white all-year

yellower/browner, more barred than MALE

F APR–JUL

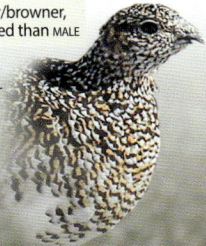

more uniformly white in colder winters

M NOV–FEB

black between eye and bill on MALE

M APR–JUL

greyer, less barred than FEMALE

WHERE bushy heaths, woodland edge and moors; adjacent fields, trees	EATS shoots, berries, fruit of heather, bilberry and dwarf shrubs, birch catkins, pine cones

Scarce and local

Once widespread but now restricted to more remote moorland and heath. Easiest to see in organized watches but males on grassy pastures in spring can be conspicuous.

Black Grouse *Lyrurus tetrix*

L MALE 49–58 cm; FEMALE 40–45 cm | WS 65–80 cm
ID Large, heavy-bodied. MALE large, round; **glossy black** with **red wattle**; thick, steely-blue neck; broad **white bar** on each wing; and puffy **white patch** beneath **long, curled tail**. FEMALE brown, like a large Red Grouse (*p. 150*) but paler, and browner colour and much more **closely barred**; tail grey-brown, notched. **IN FLIGHT**, long profile, long tail: MALE **broad, white wingbar**, FEMALE thin, white wingbar and notched, **brown tail** without black sides.

VOICE Displaying male has rolling, crooning "*crrroo-crrroo*" calls interspersed with sudden, wheezy, 'sneezing' notes.

BLACK GROUSE

MALES gather to display at a 'lek' with ritualized postures and calls: tail raised and spread, long outer feathers curving round and down at the tip.

F

white wingbar

F   M

male patched pale brown in 'eclipse', JUL–SEP

large red wattle

black bill

M

F

more evenly barred than Red Grouse (*p. 150*)

barred breast

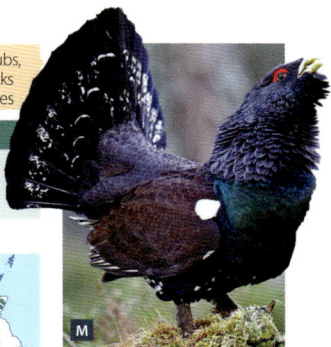

Rare, very local and declining

Extinct in Britain *ca.* 1785; reintroduced from 1837. Sensitive to disturbance, best seen on an organized watch APR–MAY, when males are displaying, or SEP–OCT.

Capercaillie *Tetrao urogallus*

L MALE 74–90 cm; FEMALE 54–63 cm | WS 87–125 cm

ID MALE huge forest grouse, with **broad, rounded tail**. **Dark brown** above, **dark grey** on head, neck and rump, with red facial wattle. Breast glossed green; white 'shoulder' spot and flank stripe; underwing white. FEMALE large, **red-brown**; white below, with bold **black bars and spots** and broadly **rounded tail**; distinctive **patch of clear orange** across breast. **IN FLIGHT**, very large: MALE **plain wings**; FEMALE greyish rump, rounded pale **rusty-brown tail**.

VOICE Quiet unless the male is displaying with peculiar croaks, hisses and cork-popping sounds.

CAPERCAILLIE

MALES display alone or at a 'lek', with spread tail and making hissing and 'popping' calls.

pale bill

white on flank

orange breast

Pigeons & Doves

are more or less interchangeable terms for this group of medium-sized to large birds. They have a rounded head; a small bill with a fleshy patch ('cere') at the base; and short legs. Flight, after a quick, clattering take-off, is steady and powerful, with deep, regular or flicked wingbeats and occasional glides. The wings can produce a loud whistle in flight and can be used to make loud 'claps' or clatter. They can be identified by their cooing or purring songs. The sexes look almost alike and there are no seasonal changes, but juveniles are duller, less colourful, than adults.

IDENTIFY BY:
▶ neck markings ▶ song
▶ wing/tail patterns in flight

Pigeons and Doves in flight

COLLARED DOVE (p. 157)

pale grey

TURTLE DOVE (p. 157)

ashy grey

broad, white

WOODPIGEON (p. 156)

broad white tips

narrow white tips

white bar

pale grey

white

no white

narrow, pale grey

STOCK DOVE (p. 156)

AT DISTANCE, Woodpigeons and Stock Doves often fly together and are similar. Look for a Woodpigeon's **white band on the wing** which differs from Stock Dove's **wholly pale grey midwing**.

pale grey

WOODPIGEON

STOCK DOVE

lower back white

ROCK DOVE

broad black bars

Feral Pigeons often fly in flocks 10–100 strong or more, whether over fields, around quarries or in urban areas. They tend to be quick, more or less coordinated but with individuals often rolling or twisting within the flock, frequently with wings raised in a deep 'V'.

Common

Wild Rock Doves are restricted to cliffs, dunes and fields in N Scotland and W Ireland. Feral Pigeon much more widespread, as often seen on arable fields, cliffs and beaches as in towns.

WHERE **Rock Dove**: coastal cliffs; **Feral Pigeon**: urban areas and around farms, *etc.*

EAT **Rock Dove**: grain and weed seeds; **Feral Pigeon**: scraps and grain

Rock Dove / Feral Pigeon
Columba livia

. 30–35 cm | WS 62–68 cm

ID Medium-sized. Wild Rock Dove is pale blue-grey with a glossy green neck patch, **two broad, black bars** across wing and a **small** pale patch (cere) on dark bill; orange eye. **IN FLIGHT**, **square white patch** on lower back; grey upperwing with broad, black bars; **white underwing** contrasts with **dark body**, narrow dark trailing edge and all-dark tail.

FERAL (OR TOWN) PIGEONS and domestic variants (racing/ homing and 'fancy' pigeons) range from all-dark through sandy-brown to all-white, with a variety of chequered and pied patterns in between; they have a **large** pale patch (cere) on bill; orange eye. **IN FLIGHT**, fast, erratic; tight groups dive around sea cliffs/caves, Feral Pigeon around piers, buildings.

VOICE Deep, rolling "*coo*" and long "*crrrroo-rroo*" notes.

Although **Feral Pigeon** typically looks very different to Rock Dove, such as this 'chequered' bird (*left*), some are similar (*right*). Populations on sea cliffs tend to revert to the ancestral Rock Dove 'type' but usually have a larger pale patch (cere) on the bill than their wild cousins.

bill all-dark with pale cere

orange eye

glossy green neck patch

ROCK DOVE

two dark bars across closed wing

ROCK DOVE / FERAL PIGEON

Common, often abundant

One of the commonest large birds, increasingly confiding in towns and gardens. In autumn, thousands migrate near coasts.

WHERE farmland, woodland, towns, gardens

EATS grain, seeds, leaves, berries, fruit, buds, shoots

Woodpigeon *Columba palumbus*

L 38–43 cm | WS 68–77 cm

ID Large, long-winged, long-tailed. ADULT **white neck patch**, pink breast; pale eye; red-and-yellow bill; dull pink legs. JUVENILE dull, no white neck patch. **IN FLIGHT**, grey with **white band across midwing**, underwing darker than body; **white band** across blackish tail beneath.

VOICE Loud, rhythmic "*coo, crroo-crroo, cu-coo, cuk crroo- crroo, cuk.*" Strained cooing, grunting notes close to nest. Wings may whistle loudly; **clattered in alarm** or display flight.

white wing band

J

A

frequently rises and 'stalls' in flight

pale eye

white neck patch

A

WOODPIGEON

Common

Generally shy but often feeds with other pigeons, Jackdaws (*p.237*) and Rooks (*p.234*); look for compact, rounded pigeons in flight.

EATS grain, seeds, leaves, buds, small invertebrates

WHERE woods, parkland with old trees, farmland, moorland cliffs, quarries

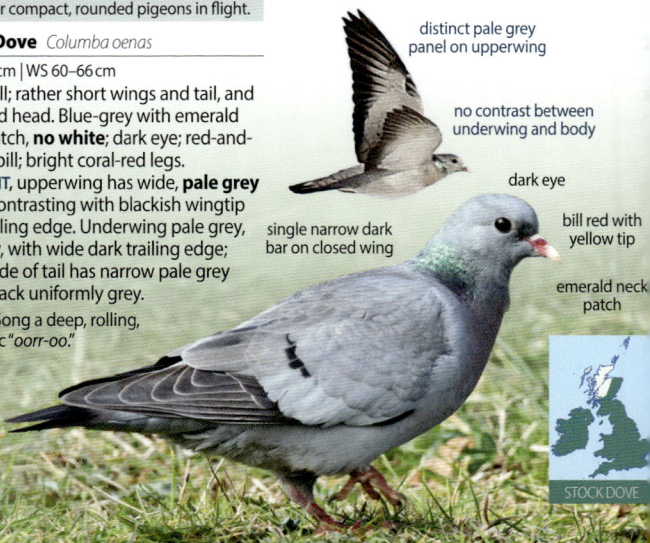

Stock Dove *Columba oenas*

L 28–32 cm | WS 60–66 cm

ID Small; rather short wings and tail, and rounded head. Blue-grey with emerald neck patch, **no white**; dark eye; red-and-yellow bill; bright coral-red legs. **IN FLIGHT**, upperwing has wide, **pale grey** panel contrasting with blackish wingtip and trailing edge. Underwing pale grey, as body, with wide dark trailing edge; underside of tail has narrow pale grey band. Back uniformly grey.

VOICE Song a deep, rolling, rhythmic "*oorr-oo.*"

distinct pale grey panel on upperwing

no contrast between underwing and body

dark eye

single narrow dark bar on closed wing

bill red with yellow tip

emerald neck patch

STOCK DOVE

Increasingly difficult to find – a purring song in May–July from a thicket edge or a tall tree beside open fields is likely to be a Turtle Dove.

WHERE woodland, farmland, downland thickets

EATS grain and small seeds

Turtle Dove *Streptopelia turtur*

L 25–26 cm | WS 45–50 cm

ID Small, neat; **chequered orange-brown above; streaked neck patch; pink breast contrasts with white belly**. JUVENILE paler rufous, broad pale feather edges above; no neck patch. **IN FLIGHT**, agile, quick, tilting/rolling action, narrow-tipped wings often swept back; **ashy grey** underwing; dark tail with **broad white tip** (narrower than Collared Dove's). Display flight high, often in long, soaring glide and descent with tail widely fanned.

VOICE A prolonged, purring, soporific coo, "*currr-urrurrr-curr.*" No flight call.

TURTLE DOVE

upperside of tail grey with a dark band and white tip

wings often swept back

ashy underwing; contrast between breast and belly

chequered orange-brown above

streaked neck patch

pink breast

white belly

A familiar bird in many towns and villages, often perched on aerials/roofs, and frequently seen around docks, farms, horse paddocks. Present all year.

WHERE farmland, gardens, places with grain

EATS grain, seeds, buds, small invertebrates

Collared Dove *Streptopelia decaocto*

L 29–33 cm | WS 48–53 cm

ID Slim; almost **uniformly pale buff-brown** with **black collar**. JUVENILE lacks black collar. **IN FLIGHT**, strong, direct (less agile than Turtle Dove); **pale grey** underwing; longish dark tail **with very broad white tip** below. Display flight has steep rise followed by long, arcing descent.

VOICE Three-note "*cu-coo-cuk,*" middle note strongest but slightly varying emphasis. Flight call nasal, slurred "*kwurrrr.*" Wings clatter less than pigeons, but can make loud whistles in flight.

COLLARED DOVE

upperside of tail with dark base and broad white tip

pale grey underwing; little contrast between breast and belly

uniformly pale buff-brown

black collar

157

Birds of Prey are small to very large diurnal predatory birds with a
hooked bill for tearing/manipulating food and sharp, curved claws for capturing, killing and carrying prey. Their wings may be long, with wide, 'fingered' tips (outermost feathers slightly separated), long and slim with more pointed tips, or rather short with blunter tips. The 15 species include four summer migrants that winter in Africa, and can be conveniently divided into seven groups (as opposite).

In flight

Appearance changes with flight action and intent. **Direct flight** ('**travelling**') involves flaps and **glides**; larger species '**sail**' in long glides. Most '**soar**' to gain height, with wings raised or flat. Hunting falcons, hawks and eagles may '**stoop**', diving with folded wings; harriers glide on raised wings between occasional flaps. A few **hover** in a fixed point relative to the ground. Territorial/courtship **display** may be simply a long glide between exposed perches, or 'bounding' undulations and dives; Honey-buzzard flutters wings above its back; harriers have Lapwing-like (p. 116) 'tumbling' display.

hover

direct flight

soaring

Birds of prey, such as these **Buzzards**, adopt many different profiles in flight, even within the various flight actions outlined above; the shape can also appear different depending on the angle of view.

Identification

The features that are particularly important in the identification of birds of prey are shown in the annotated image here.

wingtip
outer primaries are abruptly narrowed towards their tip, forming separate 'fingers'

'wrist' patch
'wrist' (carpal) joint

PRIMARIES
SECONDARIES

hindwing

tail

belly

BUZZARD

Plumages

Sexes look alike except in **harriers**, **hawks** and **falcons** (but females typically larger than males). Juveniles differ from adult, or look like female. **Eagles** mature over 8–9 years (1–2-year-old, immature and adult can be told apart but accurate ageing of immatures is often impossible). **Kite**, **buzzards**, **Osprey** and **hawks** look like adult by second year, but **harriers** and some **falcons** may have intermediate immature plumage.

Eagles (pp. 162–163)
Very large, dark; protruding head; long broad wings.

WHITE-TAILED EAGLE

Kites (p. 167)
Large, rufous; long, angled wings; forked tail.

RED KITE

Buzzards (pp. 164–165)
Large, dark, underparts and underwing boldly patterned; short, bulky head; broad wings.

BUZZARD

Osprey (p. 166)
Large, boldly contrasted; small, pale head with black band; angled wings.

OSPREY

Harriers (pp. 168–169)
Large, slim, long-tailed; with slim wings.

HEN HARRIER

Hawks (pp. 170–171)
Small to large, secretive; eyes pale; wings broad.

SPARROWHAWK

Falcons (pp. 172–175)
Small to large, long-winged; eyes dark; tail slim or rather short and broad; most have strong head pattern.

HOBBY

GOSHAWK

159

Birds of Prey in flight

WHITE-TAILED
EAGLE
(p. 163)

J

GOLDEN
EAGLE
(p. 162)

I

RED KITE
(p. 167)

BUZZARD
(p. 164)

HONEY-
BUZZARD
(p. 165)

J

F

A

CARRION
CROW
(p. 235)
(for scale)

F/J

M

MARSH HARRIER
(p. 168)

KESTREL
(p. 173)

M

F

SPARROWHAWK
(p. 170)

M

F

MERLIN
(p. 172)

F

PEREGRINE
(p. 175)

A

A

GOSHAWK
(p. 171)

HOBBY
(p. 174)

A

OSPREY
(p. 166)

A

J

HEN HARRIER
(p. 169)

M

**MONTAGU'S
HARRIER**
(p. 169)

M

F

F

▶ BIRDS OF PREY IN FLIGHT *p. 160*

Eagles are huge and impressive. They are mostly dark brown with long wings and a heavy bill. Females look similar to males, but are larger. Juveniles differ in wing and tail colour and develop adult plumage over several years.

IDENTIFY BY:
▶ **tail colour and pattern** ▶ **flight shape**
▶ **angle of wings when soaring**

GOLDEN EAGLE

WHITE-TAILED EAGLE

WHERE	mature forest, mountains, coastal cliffs, crags
EATS	mammals, birds, dead animals

Scarce

Most likely at long range over mountainsides, peaks, coastal cliffs; sometimes over extensive forest and lower valleys.

Golden Eagle *Aquila chrysaetos*

L 80–93 cm | WS 190–227 cm

ID Huge, long-winged. ADULT brown; spiky golden-buff 'shawl'. New feathers blackish, but fade to pale straw, giving **blotchy** effect; bill grey. JUVENILE blacker; eyes dark brown.

IN FLIGHT, longer head, wings and tail than Buzzard (*p. 164*); longer tail than White-tailed Eagle. ADULT no strong pattern; buffish band on upperwing, flight feathers and tail barred. JUVENILE flight feathers unbarred; **white wing patches** (small above, large below); **tail white with black band**. White reduces over 6–7 years. SOARING very long wings raised in 'V'. TRAVELLING wings hunched, slightly angled in glide. DISPLAY bounding, twisting undulations.

VOICE Various yapping, yelping notes.

Overall bulk quite unlike Buzzard, which is often over-optimistically mistaken for an eagle.

very long 'reach' when soaring

white tail, black tail-band

long, broad tail

soars on raised wings

wings hunched inwards in glide

white wing patches

eye yellowish to golden-brown

spiky pale golden-buff 'shawl'

greyish bill

heavily feathered legs

A **White-tailed Eagle** on the ground sits more upright than a Golden Eagle (this bird is a JUVENILE).

WHERE marshes, lakes, inland and coastal cliffs, islands

EATS fish, mammals, birds, dead animals

Rare

Most in NW Scotland; try visiting the coasts of Mull or going on an organized boat trip to see feeding birds, often close by.

White-tailed Eagle
Haliaeetus albicilla

L 76–92 cm | WS 200–244 cm

ID Huge, broad-winged. ADULT pale brown, with **paler head and neck; huge yellow bill.** Tail **white**, often stained or worn duller. JUVENILE has black teardrop spots above, black lines and 'V's on buff breast; some blacker with rufous tinge.

IN FLIGHT, clearly very large; **long head, short tail**, long, wide, 'barn door' wings. ADULT brown with paler head, **white tail**. JUVENILE tail dark with paler streaks. IMMATURES dark head, pale breast; tail whiter with age. SOARING wings held **flat** or drooped (not in a 'V'). TRAVELLING deep, powerful wingbeats often in longer series between glides than Golden Eagle's.

VOICE Powerful "*kik-rik-rik*" and "*kee-kee-kee.*"

A massive, heavy eagle, less graceful than Golden Eagle in flight.

2Y very broad-winged

A

protruding head

short, wedge-shaped tail

white tail

yellow eye

A

soars on flat wings

pale head and neck

huge yellow bill

A

bare legs

short tail

▶ BIRDS OF PREY IN FLIGHT p. 160

Buzzards

Buzzards are large, mostly brown, broad-winged and short-headed; more barred and closely patterned than the much larger eagles. **Buzzard** frequently soars with wings raised, but **Honey-buzzard**, which is longer-tailed and has a longer, slender head, soars on flat wings. The sexes look alike in **Buzzard**; and differ slightly in **Honey-buzzard**; juveniles differ slightly from adults.

IDENTIFY BY:
▶ tail pattern   ▶ underpart/underwing colour/pattern
▶ head shape   ▶ shape in flight

BUZZARD

HONEY-BUZZARD

WHERE woodland, wooded mountain slopes, heaths and moors, farmland

EATS mammals, amphibians, birds, insects, worms

Locally common

Look for birds circling over woodland and crags; often seen in fields and on roadside perches (even suburban lamp-posts). Distinctive calls draw attention.

Buzzard *Buteo buteo*

L 48–56 cm | WS 113–128 cm

ID Large, broad-winged, often soars; can look surprisingly eagle-like (p. 162) but is much smaller. Most are **mottled brown** with a **pale 'U' below brown breast**; dark eye. ADULT belly typically barred. JUVENILE belly streaked.

IN FLIGHT, head **short and broad**; wings broad; tail short and wide. Underwing strongly patterned, **whitish beyond** dark 'wrist'; hindwing and tail narrowly barred. SOARING usually (not always) with **wings raised in a 'V'**, wingtips fingered. TRAVELLING stiff wingbeats; glides with wings hunched in slight kink. HOVERING occasional. DISPLAY steep switchbacks, fast plunge-dives.

VOICE Loud, nasal, "*pi-yaaa*," explosive close-up. Flatter 'squealing' "*pair pair pair*" from JUVENILES.

broad-winged

rather 'chunky' profile

TAIL finely barred

HEAD shor broa

WINGS usually raised in a 'V' when soaring

TAIL relatively short, broad

JUVENILE has narrower wings/ longer tail and less well-defined dark trailing edge and tail-band than ADULT

most show pale 'U' below dark breast

dark eye

bare legs

! Rough-legged Buzzard (p. 258)

Buzzards compared

Buzzard and Honey-buzzard can be difficult to tell apart: focus on the overall shape and flight action. Study the pictures on these pages to understand different characters of this often tricky pair.

long, narrow

short, broad

BUZZARD

wings raised

F

'chunky' overall

slender overall

long

short

BUZZARD

HONEY-BUZZARD

wings flat or drooped

HONEY-BUZZARD

WHERE broadleaved and coniferous woodland, wooded parkland

EATS small reptiles and amphibians, insects, especially bees, wasps and their larvae dug out from nests with the feet

Rare MAY–OCT; winters in Africa

Only in summer; hard to find and best looked for from established watchpoints: may soar over wood or glide, often high up, between feeding areas.

Honey-buzzard *Pernis apivorus*

L 52–59cm | WS 135–150cm

ID Large, Buzzard-like. ADULT **yellow eye**. JUVENILE dark eye.

IN FLIGHT, head long and **narrow**; wings broad, may appear more 'pinched-in' at body than Buzzard; tail long, **slim** or widely fanned. Underwing strongly patterned with **dark 'wrist'**. Tail pale with **dark tip** and **two/three dark bands at base**, weaker on FEMALE. MALE upperwing greyish with black trailing edge; underwing white with black 'wrist', hindwing plain except bold blackish trailing edge. FEMALE browner, pale patch near tip on upperwing; underwing like Buzzard but hindwing less barred. SOARING wings held **flat or slightly raised**, wingtips broad. TRAVELLING relaxed wingbeats, glides with wings **smoothly downcurved**. DISPLAY flutters wings vertically over back between upward sweeps.

VOICE Melodious "*whee-ooo*" or "*whi-whee- oo.*"

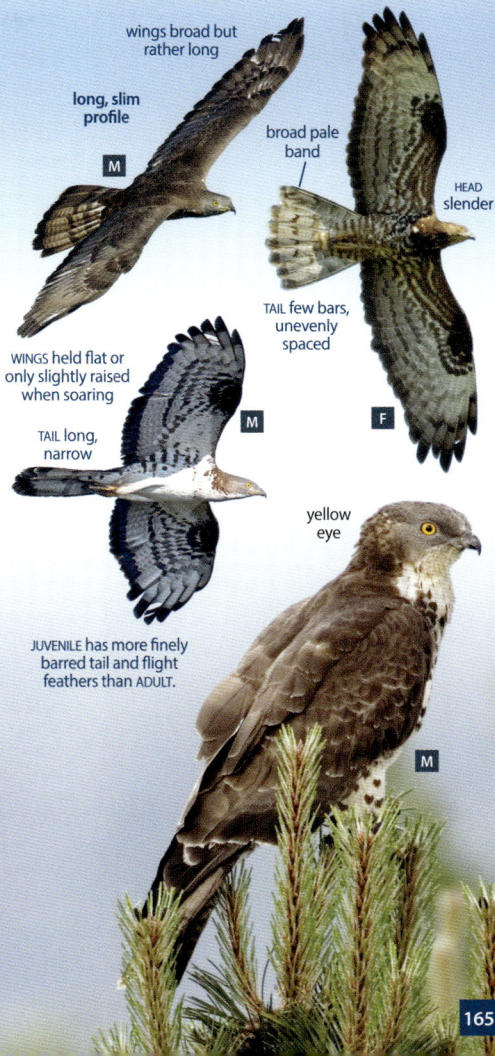

wings broad but rather long

long, slim profile

M

broad pale band

HEAD slender

WINGS held flat or only slightly raised when soaring

TAIL few bars, unevenly spaced

M

F

TAIL long, narrow

yellow eye

JUVENILE has more finely barred tail and flight feathers than ADULT.

M

Osprey

uniform brown
upperwing

short, pale tail

white
crown

black 'wrist'
patch

white
underwing

dark band

white below

WHERE forested lakes, well-wooded moors;
migrants on estuaries, rivers, reservoirs

EATS fish

white head with blackish
band through yellow eye;
black bill

uniform
brown
above

white
below

long wings, short tail

A

Scarce MAR–OCT; winters in Africa

Easily seen at nest-watch schemes – otherwise
best looked for at large lakes in spring
and autumn; despite being a fish-eater, its
appearance causes most wetland birds to panic.

Osprey *Pandion haliaetus*

L 52–60 cm | WS 150–180 cm

OSPREY

ID Very large; long-winged,
often upright on perch
or circling over open
water. ADULT brown above,
white below with dusky
breast-band; **head white
with blackish band**. JUVENILE has 'scaly', buff
fringes over upperparts.

IN FLIGHT, short, pale, barred tail; **white
crown** and white underwing with a central
dark band and **black 'wrist' patch**. SOARING
wings **bowed or angled**, resembles a large
gull but with wider, upcurved wingtips.
TRAVELLING steady, slow beats of slightly
bowed wings. HOVERING **frequent** over water.
DISPLAY steep rise before twisting 'stall' and
steep, gliding descent.

VOICE High, whistling *"weilp weilp weilp"* or
"kew kew kew."

Kites

Kites seem deceptively slow and graceful in flight but they have real agility and power.

sharp corners to tail

white patch on outerwing

pale band on upperwing

tail rufous above; triangular, notched when closed

angled wings pushed well forward

Locally common

Gathers locally at feeding stations; increasingly suburban, visiting gardens following widespread introductions, but generally seen over well-wooded farmland and hills.

WHERE woodland edge, farmland, moors, villages

EATS invertebrates, dead animals and refuse

Red Kite *Milvus milvus*
L 61–72 cm | WS 175–195 cm

ID Large; long wings and long, deeply notched tail. ADULT **reddish-brown** with paler feather edges; head greyish; eye and bill yellow. JUVENILE paler feather fringes.

IN FLIGHT, long, flexible wings with **white patch near dark wingtips** on underwing and pale band across innerwing above; long, **rusty-red, triangular/notched** tail. JUVENILE shallower tail fork. GLIDING/HUNTING flat profile, long wings and tail, and slow, fluent action recognizable at long range. TRAVELLING curved wings held well forward, tail often twisted over. SOARING on **flat or bowed wings** to great height.

VOICE Wailing, screaming versions of Buzzard-like (*p. 164*) notes.

RED KITE

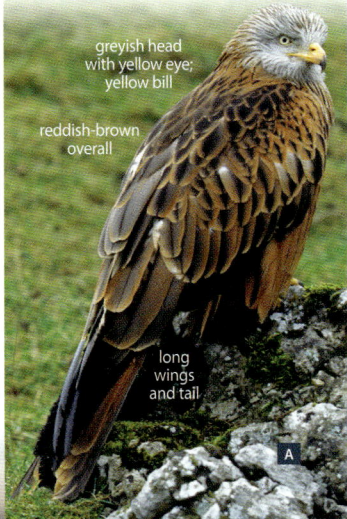

greyish head with yellow eye; yellow bill

reddish-brown overall

long wings and tail

A

► BIRDS OF PREY IN FLIGHT p. 160

Harriers are medium- to large-sized; slim, long-winged, small-headed and long-tailed. **May soar, but typically fly in a low glide with wings raised in a 'V'.** Males and females look very different; juveniles much like adult females.

IDENTIFY BY:
► wing and tail patterns
► rump colour
► wingtip shape and structure

Harriers' spring display flights include acrobatic tumbling, rolling undulations and 'food passing' between pairs. **Marsh Harrier** (all year) breeds in reedbeds, but is more widespread in winter. **Hen Harrier** (all year) breeds on moors (rare), seen mostly in winter (including some from NE and W Europe). **Montagu's Harrier** (rare summer visitor) most likely seen on spring/autumn migration.

WHERE **Marsh**: reedbeds, reedy marshes, ditches, floods, saltmarshes. **Hen**: moors, especially patchy heather, northern islands; in winter, wanders widely over heaths, marshes, flooded meadows, downland. **Montagu's**: heaths, cereal fields and downland; on migration wanders widely e.g. coastal marshes.

EAT **All**: small birds, small mammals (on the ground). **Marsh Harrier**: also amphibians

| MARSH HARRIER | HEN HARRIER | MONTAGU'S HARRIER |

Rare, local resident/migrant from NW Europe

Look over reedbeds and reedy waterways and ditches; from OCT–MAR scan low-lying coasts with reeds, saltmarshes, but also check wet grassland.

Marsh Harrier *Circus aeruginosus*

L 43–55 cm | WS 120–135 cm

ID Large, heavy, FEMALE noticeably bigger than MALE. MALE back/forewing brown, head pale grey-brown, underparts rufous; wingtip black; tail grey. FEMALE/JUVENILE **dark brown** with **cream cap and throat**.

IN FLIGHT, MALE **wing brown and grey** with black tip; tail grey. IMMATURE MALE duller with dark trailing edge to wing. FEMALE/JUVENILE **dark brown** with **cream head and forewing**. SOARING on flat wings pushed forward (rather Buzzard-like (*p. 164*)). TRAVELLING/HUNTING steady, relaxed beats between glides on raised wings.

VOICE Silent except high chatter over nest.

cream on head and forewing

upperwing grey with black tip and brown forewing

dark brown overall

brown head/ body

cream cap and throat

brown back

grey tail

In winter look for bird flying slowly, low over open or wet ground, flushing small birds. In summer, scan areas of moorland.

Hen Harrier *Circus cyaneus*

L 45–55 cm | WS 99–121 cm

ID Large, long-tailed, short wingtip. MALE **light grey**; black wingtip; white belly. IMMATURE MALE browner-backed. FEMALE/JUVENILE brown; underparts buff, streaked black: FEMALE dark cheek, white marks around dark eye-patch; JUVENILE more rufous below, dark cheek and face, narrow pale collar.

IN FLIGHT, MALE grey above with **white rump**, black wingtip; **underwing white** with black tip, **dark trailing edge**; tail grey. FEMALE/JUVENILE **broad white rump**, tail barred cream and brown. SOARING rare. TRAVELLING/HUNTING relaxed beats between glides on raised wings.

VOICE Calls when breeding, chattering "*chet-et-et-et-it-it-et,*" otherwise silent.

WINGTIP broad (4 long feathers)

F

black trailing edge

M

white rump

broad white rump

white belly and underwing

F

short wingtip

M

Usually a chance encounter of a migrant bird flying low over open fields or coastal dunes and marshes.

Montagu's Harrier *Circus pygargus*

L 39–50 cm | WS 97–115 cm

ID Large, slim, long-tailed, very long wingtip. MALE grey with black wingtip; white belly **streaked rufous**. FEMALE brown above, buff with black streaks below; dark cheek behind white eye-crescents. JUVENILE underparts bright, plain **buffy-orange**; bold dark cheek, white around eye, weak pale collar.

IN FLIGHT, MALE slender, elegant. MALE grey above with **grey rump, black midwing bar**. Underwing white with **black bar** and chestnut **spots**; outer tail barred. FEMALE/JUVENILE **thin white rump**, tail barred cream and brown. FLIGHT ACTIONS as Hen Harrier.

VOICE Calls "*kekekek*" and "*jik-jik-jik*" near nest.

WINGTIP long, slim (3 long feathers)

M

F

black bar

grey rump

thin white rump

dark markings on belly and underwing

F

M

rufous streaks

black bar

very long wingtip

169

► BIRDS OF PREY IN FLIGHT p. 160

Hawks

Hawks are medium–large-sized, broad-shouldered, long-tailed and fast. They fly with a quick flap-and-glide action on broad wings with rounded tips but also soar and can stoop at great speed. Eyes yellow or orange (falcons dark). Females much larger than males with some slight plumage differences; juveniles differ quite markedly.

IDENTIFY BY:
► size ► underside pattern ► flight profile

SPARROWHAWK   GOSHAWK

Sparrowhawk is a 'smash-and-grab' hunter, but will also sit still to 'ambush' prey; never hovers. Look for **long, slim tail**; wing broad-based, **outer half short**, spreads to wide tip, or swept back to short point. MALE is smaller, more agile, with faster wing action, than Kestrel-sized FEMALE. **Goshawk** is rare and elusive but displays over woods in early spring. In display, both hawks have a slow, patrolling flight, high soaring with white undertail coverts fanned, steep undulations and headlong plunges at high speed.

Common

Listen for alarm calls of tits and Starlings and look up for a passing hawk; otherwise, look over woodland for soaring birds and, in MAR–MAY, for dramatic display flights.

Sparrowhawk *Accipiter nisus*

MALE L 29–34 cm | WS 58–65 cm
FEMALE L 35–41 cm | WS 68–77 cm

ID Small–medium-sized. MALE bluish-grey, variably bright pink-orange below. FEMALE dull grey, fades browner; pale stripe over eye and pale nape. Underparts **dull white** with **grey bars**.

IN FLIGHT, see *opposite*. SOARING wings flat, broad tips slightly 'fingered'. TRAVELLING quick, level; quick flaps between glides, wingtips curved back. HUNTING long, slanting dive or short dash.

VOICE Call a chattering "*kewkewkewkewkewkew*" near nest, otherwise silent.

WHERE woods, farmland, marshes, parks and gardens
EATS birds

wings broad-based, shorter-tipped than falcons

M

F

J

JUVENILE browner with rusty-buff feather fringes.

Both sexes may show large white spots above.

yellow/orange eye rules out falcons

Kestrel-sized
(p.173)

F

no larger than Mistle Thrush
(p.206)

M

bluish-grey above

barred underparts

pinkish/orange below

Hawks compared

Female Sparrowhawk pigeon-sized, male Goshawk crow-sized but can be difficult to tell apart: focus on the overall shape and flight action. Female Goshawk much bigger, long-winged.

GOSHAWK
shortish wings
long wings (bulging innerwing, narrower tip)
J
long head
broad rump
short head
SPARROWHAWK
slender rear body
square tail
rounded tail
SPARROWHAWK
GOSHAWK

A

Scarce and rather local

Elusive in forest, but also hunts over open farmland and wetlands close by; listen for loud calls in FEB–APR and look from a vantage point for birds circling over forest.

WHERE woodland, forest clearings, heath and moor

EATS birds, mammals

Goshawk *Accipiter gentilis*

MALE L 49–56 cm | WS 90–105 cm
FEMALE L 58–64 cm | WS 108–127 cm

ID Large, long-winged, round-tailed, large-headed; FEMALE Buzzard-sized (*p. 164*), MALE crow-sized. (*p. 232*) ADULT blue-grey above (FEMALE browner), pale below with grey bars, broad white patch under tail; dark face-band.

IN FLIGHT, see *above*. SOARING wings straight, slightly upswept. TRAVELLING more, slower flaps than Sparrowhawk; short glides with wings swept-back, pointed (looks like Peregrine (*p. 175*) head-on). HUNTING may soar at height and stoop with closed wings onto prey, or straight, fast pursuit.

VOICE Call near nest a repeated, shouted "*cha-cha-cha-cha-cha*" (resembles Green Woodpecker (*p. 186*)), and high whine.

M

JUVENILE brown, plain-faced; underparts **streaked black on bright buff**.

FJ

broad, dark cheek patch

FEMALE fades to brownish above

grey bars on white underparts

M

Falcons have a small head, dark eyes, hooked bill, long, pointed wings, long tail and slender body. Some age/sex plumage differences.

IDENTIFY BY:
► upperpart pattern   ► head pattern
► tail pattern   ► flight action

KESTREL

WHERE wooded slopes, moors, dunes, saltmarshes

EATS birds (caught in flight)

Scarce; migrants from N Europe OCT–MAR

Mostly a chance encounter, perched on or near the ground, or dashing low across open space, often flushing larks/pipits/finches.

Merlin *Falco columbarius*

L 24–32 cm | WS 58–73 cm

ID Dove-sized; square-head, short tail. MALE **blue-grey** above, orange-buff with dark streaks below. Tail grey with black band. FEMALE/JUVENILE **dark brown** above, tail **barred cream and brown**; underparts streaked buff/barred brown.

IN FLIGHT, shortish wings are **wide-based but sharply pointed**. TRAVELLING fast, low, with quick, whippy beats and **few glides**. SOARING rare, does not hover. HUNTING low, fast, approaches prey with thrush-like (*p. 205*) **flicked in-out wing action**, before **fast, twisting chase**.

VOICE Sharp "*ki-ki-ki-ki;*" "*week-week-week-week-week*".

FEMALES and JUVENILES very similar

J

TAIL 3 or 4 bars

F

pointed wingtip

A fast-flying male **Sparrowhawk** (*p. 170*) and Merlin can be confused if not seen well

TAIL barred

EYES yellow

BREAST barred

TAIL single band

M

EYES dark

streaked

orange-buff head

M

dark brown

blue-grey

F

M

MERLIN

hovers, looking for small mammals: vision is sensitive to ultra-violet light and able to detect the urine trails of voles.

WHERE farmland, moors, heaths, marshes, crags

EATS small mammals, insects, occasionally lizards

Locally common

Easily seen perched upright on pole or wire, or when hovering (as if suspended on a string); often hunts over roadside verges, but this is becoming a much less frequent sight.

Kestrel *Falco tinnunculus*

L 31–37 cm | WS 65–82 cm

ID Pigeon-sized, with long, slim tail. MALE back rufous with black spots; head grey; tail grey with black band. FEMALE/JUVENILE **ginger-brown**, barred dark.

IN FLIGHT, two-tone upperparts: rufous with black-brown outerwing. TRAVELLING/GLIDING relaxed, loose beats on angled-back, pointed wings. SOARING on blunt-tipped, straight wings, tail often fanned. HOVERING **frequent** and prolonged. DISPLAY quick, flickering, rolling from side to side.

VOICE Sharp, whining "*kee-kee-kee-kee.*"

grey with black tip

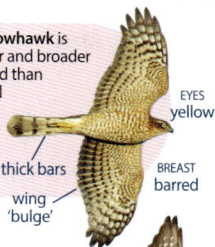

Sparrowhawk is bulkier and broader winged than Kestrel

EYES yellow

thick bars

BREAST barred

wing 'bulge'

barred

rather blunt wingtip

thin bars

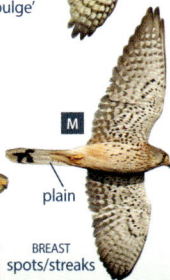

plain

BREAST spots/streaks

grey head

ginger-brown with dark bars

rufous, with black spots

KESTREL

173

Hobbies frequently feed over water, chasing hirundines or catching large insects such as dragonflies.

WHERE wooded farmland, heaths, marshes, lakesides	EATS small birds, insects (caught in flight)

Scarce APR–SEP; winters in Africa

Look over areas with many dragonflies or flocks of Swallows and martins, especially in autumn; may also gather LATE APR–JUN to feed on St Mark's Flies and over fields with chafers emerging in summer.

Hobby *Falco subbuteo*

L 29–35 cm | WS 68–84 cm

ID Dark grey above; white below, **thickly streaked black**; **rusty-red under tail** (on ADULT); dark hood; **narrow** black 'moustache'. **IN FLIGHT**, uniformly dark above. Elegant; **small head**; **narrow rump** and base to longish tail; **long, pointed wings**. TRAVELLING quick or meandering, wingbeats deep and supple with short glides. SOARING on flat, slightly angled wings. HUNTING hawks for large insects; **changes pace** on flat or bowed wings, deep, whippy beats before upward glide or stall, catching prey in feet; chases birds with long, slanting approach.

VOICE Rather ringing, bright "*kew-kew-kew-kew*."

narrow rump

heavily streaked

rusty-red

uniformly dark grey

HOBBY

narrow black 'moustache'

streaked below

JUVENILE browner above; feather edges and cheek buff; underparts streaked black, **pale red or no red under tail**.

174

Peregrines sometimes hunt low over water, usually trying to flush waders or wildfowl.

| WHERE cliffs, crags, lakes and coastal areas, towns and cities | EATS birds (caught in flight) |

Scarce; winter migrants from N Europe SEP–MAR

Can be watched at nest sites in urban areas from organized viewpoints, but lakes, marshes and estuaries with large numbers of waders and wildfowl are also good places to look.

Peregrine *Falco peregrinus*

MALE L 38–45 cm | WS 87–100 cm
FEMALE L 46–51 cm | WS 104–114 cm

ID Blue-grey above; white below, belly **barred grey**; dark hood; **broad** black 'moustache'. **IN FLIGHT**, rump subtly paler than back and tail. Muscular; **large head**; **broad** across rump and base of **short** tail; wing **broad** but pointed. TRAVELLING wings tapered; deep, whippy beats, few or no glides. SOARING high, drifting on flat or upswept wings. HUNTING fast, direct; rolls over to catch prey from beneath, or circles before stoop with closed wings.

VOICE Around the nest, loud, coarse "*haar-haair-haair*," chattering "*kek-kek-kek-kek*" and various whining sounds.

PEREGRINE

broad rump

uniformly barred

rump paler than back and tail

blue-grey above

broad black 'moustache'

FEMALE significantly larger than MALE

barred below

JUVENILE similar to adult but browner; **streaked black on buff below**, with pale tail tip.

175

Nightbirds

Introducing nightbirds

Tawny and **Long-eared Owls** are nocturnal hunters but may be discovered at a daytime roost, Tawny Owls often when being mobbed by small birds, Long-eared Owls more often by discovering piles of white droppings and grey pellets beneath their perches. **Short-eared Owls** hunt by day and groups can be watched in winter in areas where voles are numerous. **Barn Owls** are nocturnal except on cold winter days and if feeding young, when they hunt well before dusk. **Little Owls** are visible all day, on open perches, but actually feed at dusk. Tawny and Little Owls are frequently heard. **Nightjars** are best located by the males' songs and appear just before dark on summer evenings. They feed mainly at dusk and dawn, flying erratically over heathland and woodland clearings.

Nightjars (*p. 182*)

Small (thrush-sized) and slender, with long wings and tail, 'flat' head and tiny bill. 'Dead wood' patterning provides remarkable camouflage when at rest by day, usually on the ground or perched along a branch. Flight agile, buoyant. Sexes differ slightly. Summer visitor.

NIGHTJAR

Owls

Stocky (thrush- to crow-sized), with a distinctive large head and large, forward-facing eyes. Flight characteristics differ between species: **Little Owl** flies with bounding undulations; **Tawny Owl** is heavy and direct; **Barn Owl** flies low, diving headlong into long grass; and the **'eared' owls** have a more buoyant, wavering hunting flight. Sexes alike – juveniles are downy for a few weeks and then look like adults.

IDENTIFY BY:
► size
► facial pattern
► eye colour
► wing pattern

LONG-EARED OWL

TAWNY OWL

BARN OWL

Owls compared

Range in size from thrush to crow, but thickset and large-headed, so tend to look large.

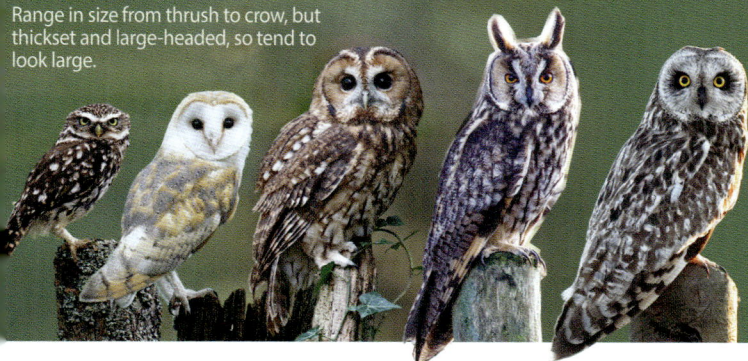

| LITTLE OWL | BARN OWL (p. 178) | TAWNY OWL (p. 179) | LONG-EARED OWL (p. 181) | SHORT-EARED OWL (p. 180) |

(p. 178) (p. 179) (p. 181) (p. 180)

Locally common (introduced)

Often seen on large, bare branch overlooking a field, or on a low stump, stone or hump in the ground; hunts at dusk.

WHERE farmland/parks with old trees, farm buildings/ruins, quarries, rocky islands

EATS small mammals, invertebrates, worms

Little Owl *Athene noctua*

L 23–27·5 cm | WS 50–57 cm

ID Small but stocky; short-legged, short-winged and very short tail. Weak facial disk; **pale 'eyebrows'; yellow eyes** outlined with black. Dark brown, with **white mottling** above and wavy dark streaks beneath. **IN FLIGHT**, quick, **swooping, bounding action**, like a woodpecker; **sweeps up to perch**.

VOICE Loud, clear, nasal whistles – "*kleee-ow*," "*chi-chi-chi*;" song an evenly repeated, rising "*keeeah*."

LITTLE OWL

Distinctive profile and undulating flight, even in silhouette.

Often seen on open perch by day. Typically bolt upright on branch, looking like a broken stump.

pale 'eyebrows'

Juvenile pale, downy at first, but soon looks like adult.

J MAY–JUN

A

Small birds often call and attract attention to a **Little Owl** in daylight.

Barn Owl has rather short wings with a large, heavy head and body seemingly 'suspended' beneath.

Scarce

Usually seen at dusk or after dark in car headlights; hunts by day in cold winter weather and in summer, when feeding young.

WHERE farmland, woodland/moorland edge, rough grassland, marshes

EATS small mammals

Barn Owl *Tyto alba*

L 33–39 cm | WS 80–95 cm

ID Medium–large, 'white owl'; may stand on post, looking narrow-bodied and 'knock-kneed', but head large, broad. Wide, **heart-shaped face** with black eyes and narrow dark 'V' over bill. Sandy or **golden-buff** above, with grey, 'pepper-and-salt' speckling; dark bars on spread wings. **IN FLIGHT**, hunts over open, grassy areas; looks very large-headed, with broad-based wings; clean **white underparts**. Quick, slightly jerky wingbeats, **hovers briefly before headlong dive** into grass after prey.

VOICE A shrill, bubbly shriek; various hissing, squealing notes.

BARN OWL

Large tree holes and nest boxes are often used by Barn Owls, but many still roost and nest in buildings.

white wings

black eyes; pale bill

bright white face and body

Hard to see but silhouette against sky distinctive; this is the owl that hoots.

WHERE woodland, parks, large gardens

EATS small mammals, birds, invertebrates, worms

Tawny Owl *Strix aluco*

L 37–43 cm | WS 81–96 cm

ID Woodpigeon-sized (*p. 156*); sits upright, with big, **round head** and short tail: 'rugby-ball' shape when relaxed. **Rufous** or **grey-brown** with **white 'shoulder' spots** and cross-barred streaks beneath. **Black eyes** face forwards in **flat, rounded face**.

TAWNY OWL

Tawny Owl, the most common large owl in Britain (but not Ireland), is rufous, but in N Britain greyer birds are more frequent. Tawny Owls have permanent territories and leave telltale white droppings under a roost tree, but pellets of undigested material are regurgitated randomly (Barn and Long-eared Owl pellets are found under the roost).

VOICE Calls after sunset, occasionally during day: loud, nasal "*ke-wick!*," "*wik-wik-wik*" and variations; pure or breathy, trembling hoot – "*hooo! hu–hu–huwoooo-o-o.*" Young call is a hissy "*shee-eep*" (see Long-eared Owl (*p. 181*)).

If small birds find a Tawny Owl by day they call noisily and attract others to join a crowd – this can sometimes be a useful way of finding a roosting owl.

rounded when relaxed

black eyes; pale greenish bill

short, broad wings thickly barred

A

J MAR–JUN

Juvenile owls move away from the nest while still in down, but after a few weeks look much like adults.

Short-eared and Long-eared Owls have a similar wing pattern in flight, with a **dark 'wrist' and wingtips** separated by a **contrasting orange-buff patch**; the underwing is white with a small, black, crescent-shaped mark and dark wingtips. Short-eared Owl has more solidly dark wingtips and a white trailing edge to the innerwing, as well as a whiter body.

WHERE moorland and heathland; in winter, also wet pasture, marshes	
EATS small mammals, birds	

Scarce, nomadic/migrant from NW Europe

Look for birds hunting by day over open space. Winter roosts are typically on the ground.

Short-eared Owl
Asio flammeus

L 33–40 cm | WS 95–105 cm

ID Large; often **flies by day**. Yellowish-brown; some very pale, others darker; all have white belly. Facial disk rounded; broad, whitish 'fan' around bill; eyes strikingly **pale yellow**, in 'wedge' of black.
IN FLIGHT, hunts **low over open areas**, with buoyant, harrier-like (*p. 169*) action and frequent glides.

VOICE Emphatic, tuneless, wheezy "*eeyah!*;" song in flight, deep, booming "*bu-bu-bu-bu*" combined with sharp wing-clap.

SHORT-EARED OWL

Short-eared Owls are more marbled than streaked above, blotched buff without the row of white 'shoulder' spots characteristic of Tawny Owl (*p. 179*). Numbers vary, depending on vole populations.

dark tips

pale belly

tail has few black bars

white trailing edge

yellow eyes in dark patches; black bill

WHERE forest, forest edge, shelter belts; in winter also thickets, hedgerows near open areas

EATS small mammals, birds

Scarce, resident/migrant from NW Europe

May be located by spring song after dark, though calls of young easier to detect (APR–AUG). Winter roosts are in trees and bushes.

Long-eared Owl *Asio otus*

L 31–37 cm | WS 86–98 cm

LONG-EARED OWL

ID Large, round-headed, upright. Hunts at night, roosts by day in tree or thicket, marked by droppings and regurgitated grey 'pellets'. Olive or yellowish-brown; wide facial disk surrounds white **'V' above bill**. **'Ear' tufts long**, upright, although often laid flat; eyes **deep orange** in black vertical stripe, inside **buff cheek**. **IN FLIGHT**, like Short-eared Owl, with orange-buff patch on outer part of wing (see *opposite*), but wings marginally broader, more finely barred across rear edge and towards the tip; body darker.

VOICE A short, moaning, cooing hoot, "*oh*" or "*ooh*". Young bird calls loud, distinctive: plaintive "*pee-ee*" or "*pyeee*" (like a 'squeaky-gate'), louder, sharper, less hissy than young Tawny Owl (*p. 179*).

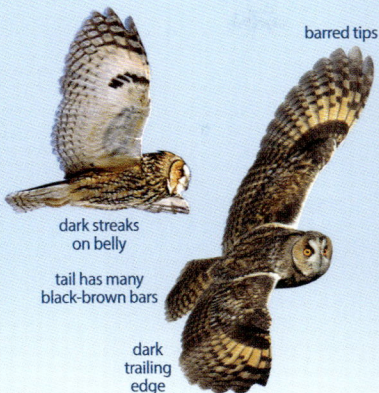

barred tips

dark streaks on belly

tail has many black-brown bars

dark trailing edge

orange eyes; black bill

white 'V' above bill

If alert or alarmed, stretches slender and upright, 'ears' raised and face narrowed

181

Nightjars

A **Nightjar** is usually only seen perched as a distinctive silhouette, churring from a songpost at dusk.

Scarce, locally fairly common APR–SEP; winters in Africa

Requires a special effort at dusk: visit a suitable heath and find a good vantage point. Listen, and watch for a distinctive shape flying low, silently and erratically against the sky. If a bird is singing, wait for the prolonged song to 'run down', as this is a signal that the bird is about to fly: look without binoculars, unless the position has first been pinpointed.

WHERE heathland, moorland/woodland edge/ clearings, bracken-covered slopes, young/ cleared plantations

EATS insects, principally large moths

Nightjar
Caprimulgus europaeus

L 24–28 cm | WS 52–59 cm

ID Small (thrush-sized), long-winged, long-tailed, slender, with tiny bill and legs. Grey, brown and buff in 'dead-branch' pattern. **Active at dusk**, silhouette in flight or perched on branch. **Flat, tapered head**, slim body and **long tail** distinctive. IN FLIGHT, **long, tapered wings**; **tail almost as long**, closed or widely spread and twisted as floats, swoops and glides. MALE has **white spots on wingtip** and tail corners.

VOICE Abrupt, nasal, mechanical *"gooik!"* (beware Tawny Owl's *(p. 179)* *"ke-wick"*). Song a vibrating, **churring trill for minutes on end**, periodically changing pitch, which 'runs down' before whiplash clap of wings.

NIGHTJAR

no white spots on wing or tail

F

fans/twists tail when making sudden turns

M

white spots on wing and tail

cryptic coloration; rarely seen by day

'Near-passerines'

are a loose collection of birds that are seemingly more closely related to perching birds than any other group.

Kingfishers   **Cuckoos**   **Parakeets**   **Woodpeckers**

The **Kingfisher** is diminutive, as demonstrated by this individual sitting on a reedmace spike.

Scarce, locally fairly common

Despite its striking colours, a Kingfisher can be remarkably inconspicuous when perched in thick waterside vegetation – but a sudden splash as one dives for small fish often reveals its presence.

WHERE freshwater areas; lakes, rivers, ponds, marshes; in winter, coasts and saltmarsh

EATS fish, aquatic insects, freshwater shrimp

Kingfisher *Alcedo atthis*

L 17–19 cm | **WS** 25 cm

ID Small (barely as big as a Starling (*p. 200*)), waterside bird with **big head**, **long bill**, tiny, red legs and very short tail. Greenish to deep **blue above** with vivid **electric blue rump**; orange below; blue, orange and white on head. MALE bill black with very little orange. FEMALE bill two-thirds orange on lower edge. JUVENILE duller plumage, darker legs than adult.

IN FLIGHT, fast, straight, low, with whirring wings.

VOICE High whistle "*chi-k-keee*" or "*ki-kee*," and trilled variants.

A typical view may be little more than a flash of turquoise-blue as a bird whizzes past.

KINGFISHER

Sits upright or leans forward on a perch to look for prey beneath; may hover before diving.

white patch on neck

electric blue back and rump

long bill (black on male; some orange on female)

short, red legs

Cuckoos

A **Cuckoo** may resemble a hawk at distance, but the drooped wings and broad tail create a unique shape.

Locally fairly common
APR–SEP; winters in Africa

When calling, often perches on an outside branch or quite low in a tree; as soon as the "cu-coo" stops, watch for a low-flying Cuckoo.

WHERE moors, and heaths, reedbeds, farmland; although decreasing across much of the south, numbers appear to be relatively healthy farther north

EATS invertebrates, particularly caterpillars

Male **Sparrowhawk** and Cuckoo can be confusing on occasion.

broader wingtip

head no raised

barred underwing

pale band on underwing

slender head slightly raised

broad-based, tapered wings

Cuckoo *Cuculus canorus*

L 32–36 cm | WS 54–60 cm

ID Fairly large (size of Collared Dove (*p. 157*)), slim, long-winged, short-legged, with **small head** and **short, downcurved bill**. **Long, broad, white-spotted tail** often swayed sideways. ADULT **pale grey**, underparts white, barred dark grey. JUVENILE greyish or rufous-brown, barred dark and scalloped white above; **whitish patch on nape**. IN FLIGHT, broad wings taper to swept-back tip; **white band** beneath; **pointed head slightly raised**.

VOICE Soft, far-carrying "*cu-coo*" (loud and penetrating at close range); FEMALE has loud, bubbling, chuckling trill. MALE calls low, wheezy "*gek-eh-eh-eh-eh.*"

Males are grey; females can be grey or rufous (rare), grey females typically have buff on neck/breast.

CUCKOO

J MAY–JUN

wingtips drooped beneath broad, spotted tail

Cuckoos lay their eggs in the nests of other birds (in this case a Reed Warbler). Young birds call incessantly to be fed; they fledge in May/June and begin their migration to Africa in August/September, long after the adults have left in June/July.

Parakeets

Ring-necked Parakeets often form flocks and screech noisily as they dash by overhead.

Locally common (introduced)

Easy to see in some areas such as London parks/suburbs, best tracked down by following up calls from birds perched in treetops; large, communal roosts in tall trees in winter, located by fast-flying flocks of screeching birds.

WHERE woodland edge, urban parks, suburban gardens with feeders, orchards

EATS fruit, seeds, nuts

Ring-necked Parakeet *Psittacula krameri*

L 37–43 cm (incl. tail 18–23 cm) | **WS** 42–48 cm

ID Large, long-tailed, round-headed, **green**; long pointed tail and short, thick, curved, **red bill**. **IN FLIGHT**, fast and direct or twisting; blade-like, swept-back wings; **spike-like tail**.

VOICE Loud, frenzied squeals and screeching notes unmistakable, frequently given in flight.

RING-NECKED PARAKEET

Look carefully at parakeets: several other species may be seen flying free, some of which have bred. **Alexandrine Parakeet** *Psittacula eupatria* is perhaps the most frequent and told by its **purplish 'shoulder' patch**.

black-and-yellow underwing

long, spike-like tail

black throat and neck ring well-defined on male

round head

bright green plumage

round, red bill

Woodpeckers are small to medium-sized, heavily built, short-legged and short-tailed. Generally found in trees, where the tail is used as a support when perching upright on a branch. Sexes look similar; juveniles differ slightly from adults.

IDENTIFY BY:
▶ size
▶ overall colour
▶ upperpart pattern
▶ head pattern

EAT All: seeds, nuts, berries, insects (especially those found in/on tree bark)
Green Woodpecker: also ants on the ground

GREEN WOODPECKER

LESSER SPOTTED WOODPECKER

GREAT SPOTTED WOODPECKER

J JUN–OCT

When feeding on the ground, has a head up, tail down, very short-legged profile. Juvenile is greyer and has more spotted underparts than adult.

WHERE woodland edge, lawns, parks, gardens, heaths; often feeds on the ground

Common

Often heard but more difficult to see well. If disturbed from the ground, flies up to tree or stump, sidling round out of sight at the back.

M

red crown

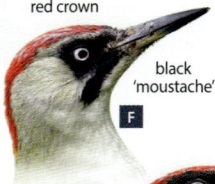

black 'moustache'

F

pale eye in black face

red in 'moustache'

M

Green Woodpecker *Picus viridis*

L 30–36 cm | WS 45–51 cm

ID Large (**size of Jay** (*p. 238*)); when on ground, tail down/head up. Upperparts **green** with **bright yellow rump**; underparts greenish-white. White eye in black patch beneath **red cap**. Black 'moustache', with a red centre on MALE. JUVENILE pale green, finely barred and speckled blackish. **IN FLIGHT, bounding**, showing yellow rump.

VOICE Very distinctive and far-carrying: ringing "*kew kew kew*" and variations.

Best located by their call, but will associate with tits, Treecreepers and finches moving through treetops. Often high in thinner branches, where hard to see.

Lesser Spotted Woodpecker
Dryobates minor

L 14–16·5 cm | WS 24–29 cm

ID **Sparrow-sized**, rather dainty; back and wings **barred** black-and-white; white may be merged on middle of back, but no clear 'shoulder' patch. Underparts buff, no red. MALE has red cap. **IN FLIGHT**, bounding (like Nuthatch (*p. 226*) but tail pointed, not square).

VOICE Call distinctive: a peevish, nasal or squealed "*pee-pee-pee-pee-pee.*" 'Drum' a little longer than Great Spotted Woodpecker's (about 1 second), sometimes half-pausing in the middle.

buff cap

red cap

small bill

F

M

M

white bars on back (may be merged)

Fluttery flight, often in thin upper branches.

no red under tail

Striking visitors to feeders, often in gardens, dominating smaller birds. Listen for the call or follow up the spring 'drum', trying not to disturb the bird.

Great Spotted Woodpecker
Dendrocopos major

L 23–26 cm | WS 38–44 cm

ID **Thrush-sized**, thickset; **black, white and red** with big **white oval patch** on both sides of the back. Yellow-buff beneath, sometimes stained brownish from tree resin, **vivid red** under tail. MALE has red patch on nape; JUVENILE has red on crown (extends further back in male). **IN FLIGHT**, **sweeping undulations**.

VOICE Call distinctive: a loud, abrupt "*tchik,*" sometimes a longer, trilled note. In spring, a loud, echoing 'drum' made by hammering the bill against wood (or metal), a **short** (about half a second), **even**, rapid drumroll.

M

red on nape

stout bill

no red on head

M

F

big white patch on the sides of the back

juvenile has red on crown (extends back behind eye on male)

vivid red under tail

MJ APR–OCT

187

Aerial Feeders

– **swifts**, **swallows** and **martins** – are small and sleek, with a tiny bill, rounded head, pointed wings, forked tail and small legs. All are summer visitors that winter in Africa and feed by catching insects on the wing. Swifts are classified in a different family to the others, which are often referred to collectively as 'hirundines'.

WHERE aerial, over any habitat; especially suburban/rural areas and near or over water

EAT insects caught in flight

IDENTIFY BY:
- ▶ overall colour
- ▶ face pattern
- ▶ rump colour
- ▶ tail/wing shape

SWIFT

Listen out for the distinctive screeching calls in May/June and look high in the sky on warm days; in wet weather flies low, often over water.

Usually seen over water, from early March; generally keeps quite low; often perches on wires, dead branches, *etc.*

Swift *Apus apus*

L 17–18·5 cm | WS 40–44 cm

ID Uniformly **black-brown** with pale chin. Long, **stiff, scythe-shaped wings**; tapered rear body; forked tail. Never perches in the open. **IN FLIGHT**, fast and direct, with flickering wingbeats and glides; often circles slowly.

VOICE High-pitched **screeching**, especially from fast chasing groups in breeding areas.

SWIFT

Sand Martin *Riparia riparia*

L 12–13 cm | WS 26–29 cm

ID **Pale brown and white** with **brown breast-band**; shallow tail fork. **IN FLIGHT**, light and flickery; rather triangular wings slightly swept back.

VOICE Dry chattering calls around the colony and sometimes on migration.

SAND MARTIN

tapered rear body

forked tail

black-brown overall

long, slender, scythe-shaped wings

can look particularly pale in strong sunlight

short, notched tail

brown breast-band

white belly

brown upperparts

all-dark underwing

! Alpine Swift (p. 259)

Nests mostly in older buildings, in **cavities** in *e.g.* a roof space or under eaves (will use nest boxes); a few use cliffs.

Nests near water in **burrows** in soft cliffs, roadside cuttings, quarries, or in artificial 'Sand Martin wall' pipes.

Hirundines, such as these Sand Martins, line up along overhead wires before migration from August.

AT DISTANCE: **Swift** flickery, quick, stiff beats; 'scythe'-shaped wings; all-black. **House Martin** fluttery; flashes white rump. **Sand Martin** fluttery; uniform above. **Swallow** swooping, wings bent back in fluent beats; long profile, often with tail spike; uniform above, dark throat.

Red-rumped Swallow (p.259)

HOUSE MARTIN   SAND MARTIN   SWALLOW

Locally MAR–OCT	Common MAR–NOV
Usually seen flying high over villages, suburbs, modern estates but perches on wires, sunbathes on roofs. Feeds over lakes in cold/wet weather.	Listen for distinctive calls around farms, villages, from high up on hot days. Usually feeds very low, particularly in bad weather. Perches on wires, *etc.*

House Martin
Delichon urbicum

L 13·5–15 cm | WS 26–29 cm

ID **Blue-black** above with browner wings and **broad white rump**; **white below**, from chin to tail. Pinkish legs feathered white.

IN FLIGHT, quick, swooping or jerky, typically above rooftop height.

VOICE Dry, short, churring/chattering notes.

HOUSE MARTIN

Swallow *Hirundo rustica*

L 14–15 cm (ADULT tail streamers 3·0–6·5 cm long) | WS 29–32 cm

ID **Blue-black** above; **red forehead and throat, dark breast-band**; cream to pinkish below. Deeply forked tail shows **white spots** when spread; when closed forms a thin point. MALE has longer tail streamers than FEMALE. JUVENILE buffish throat; broken breast-band.
IN FLIGHT, elegant, swoops low.

VOICE Liquid *"swilip swilip"* calls; song simple, trills and Goldfinch-like (p. 244) rippling notes.

SWALLOW

short, forked tail

brownish wings

white chin/throat and underparts

broad, white rump

all-dark underwing

cream underparts

dark head

blue-black upperparts

white on underwing

band of white spots across deeply forked tail

M

J MAY–NOV

Builds cup-shaped **nests of mud under the eaves** of buildings; will also use artificial nest boxes.

Builds nests of mud and straw **on a support**, under cover in barn, outbuilding, birdwatching hide, *etc.*

Passerines

Passerines are 'perching birds', with three toes forward, one back. They make up more than half the world's birds and are extremely varied, but all are very different from most of the groups covered earlier in this book, although 'near passerines' such as pigeons are less obviously distinct.

Passerines, even in Britain and Ireland, defy a simple definition. They include most of the birds that come to garden feeders, the typical songbirds of woodlands and gardens, and the various small birds that feed in the fields. The vast majority of passerines are smaller than a Blackbird, some much smaller, including the smallest of all our birds – although the largest is the size of a Buzzard. Despite being referred to as 'perching birds' (which is potentially confusing since many 'non-passerines' also perch in trees, bushes and other tall vegetation), some prefer open ground. There are residents, summer visitors, passage migrants and winter visitors. Of the 248 birds covered in the main part of this book, over one-third (85) are passerines, 82 of which are included in this section (the other three – Swallow and martins – are included in the *Aerial Feeders* section on the previous page-spread). These species can conveniently be divided into 20 'types', as illustrated on *pages 192–193*.

Identification

Generally, if you focus on a bird's size, action/behaviour and bill shape you should be able to name the 'type' of bird fairly easily with experience. The plumage features that are particularly important in the identification of passerines are shown in the annotated image here.

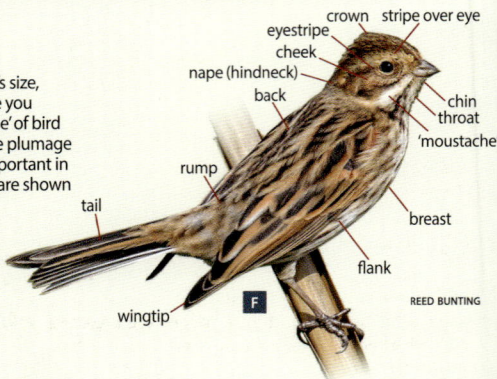

crown · stripe over eye
eyestripe
cheek
nape (hindneck)
back
chin
throat
'moustache
rump
breast
tail
flank
F
wingtip
REED BUNTING

Size

Passerines range from the smallest birds (crests, Wren) to Raven, the size of a Buzzard, with a number of recognizable groupings. Crests/warblers/tits are very small, mostly smaller than a sparrow. A step up are larks and wagtails, most finches and buntings and the sparrows themselves (and some individual species such as Nuthatch) – all easily thought of as 'sparrow-sized'. Bigger than a sparrow but smaller than a dove are the thrushes and Starling; only the crows are substantially larger.

RAVEN

WREN

Bill shape

This is a critical factor that separates 'insect-eaters', generalists and seed-eaters.

Slender – pipits, wagtails, Dunnock, Wren, chats, crests, warblers, Treecreeper.
Rather thick or broad – larks, Waxwing, Dipper, thrushes, chats, flycatchers
Very short and thick – tits.
Heavy or deep – crows.
Conical/triangular – finches, buntings, sparrows.

Action/behaviour

A silhouette, or a shape in a tree, makes detail difficult to see, but the way a bird moves narrows down the possibilities. On the ground, some passerines clearly 'walk', others hop. Some flit boldly from perch to perch, others 'slip' gently through vegetation and a few have sudden, stop-start movements with acrobatic poses. Wing and tail flicks and dips can also be valuable clues.

On ground (how moves)
Walk – larks, pipits, wagtails, Starling, crows.
Shuffle – Dunnock, thrushes, finches, buntings.
Hop – chats, tits, finches, buntings, sparrows.

On perch (how and where)
Grasping trunk – Wren, Nuthatch, Treecreeper, tits.
Upright on branch/twig – Starling, Waxwing, thrushes, chats, flycatchers, crows, finches.
Slipping through foliage – chats, crests, warblers, tits.
Stop-start, acrobatic – Wren, crests, tits.
Up-down tail wag – pipits, wagtails, thrushes, warblers.
Wing and tail flicks – wagtails, Dunnock, Wren, chats, crests, warblers, tits.

Some birds do not form flocks and are generally *solitary* (except when breeding) – e.g. Dipper, Dunnock, Wren, chats, warblers, flycatchers, Nuthatch, Treecreeper.

In flight

The way a bird flies, and whether it forms flocks is often a good key to identification.

Direct – larks, Starling, Waxwing, Dipper, thrushes, crows.
Undulating/swooping – pipits, wagtails, Treecreeper, finches, buntings.
Hovers – crests, Bullfinch.
Out-and-back sallies – wagtails, Waxwing, warblers, flycatchers, House Sparrow.
Flocks (compact) – Starling, Waxwing, thrushes, crows, finches, buntings, sparrows.
Flocks (loose) – larks, pipits, wagtails, thrushes, crows, finches, buntings.

slender

MEADOW PIPIT

thick/ broad

SKYLARK

conical/ triangular

YELLOWHAMMER

Blue Tit in foliage and grasping trunk.

Skylark (*top*) loose flock, **Linnet** (*bottom*) compact flock

Plumages

Some species always look the same, with no very distinct plumages (e.g. Wren, Treecreeper, Carrion Crow); in others male and female look alike but juveniles differ (e.g. Dipper, Robin, Song Thrush); in others, male and female also look different (e.g. Blackbird, Pied Flycatcher, Bullfinch). There may be seasonal differences (e.g. Pied Wagtail, Chaffinch, Reed Bunting). Appearance changes with moult, but in many species also with feather wear/abrasion (see Reed Bunting p. 254). This, for example, results in a drab winter male Chaffinch changing to a bright spring one: buff feather edges obscure brighter colours beneath but wear away to reveal full breeding plumage colours, with no need to replace feathers; only the bill colour changes. Juveniles look dull, spotted or more like females until they moult (usually in late summer/autumn): in many species, wing and tail feathers are retained and may distinguish, for example, year-old thrushes from older birds. However, passerines have few of the obvious intermediate stages so evident in species such as gulls. Age and sex may often be determined with a bird 'in the hand' but can be difficult under normal circumstances.

The types of Passerine

This gallery of images summarizes the key features that identify 20 broad groups of passerines. Features to look for when identifying individual species are shown at the beginning of each group section on the following pages.

Larks (p. 194)

Small; brown, streaked. BILL pointed, stout. TAIL white sides or corners (see *pipits*, *buntings*). LEGS medium-length, hind claw long; walk/run.

SKYLARK

Pipits (p. 196)

Small; brown, streaked. BILL pointed, thin. TAIL white sides (see *larks*, *buntings*). LEGS medium-length, slender; hind claw long or arched; walk/run.

MEADOW PIPIT

Wagtails (p. 198)

Small; black, grey, white, or with yellow and green. TAIL long, white sides. LEGS medium-length, spindly; walk/run.

PIED WAGTAIL

Starling (p. 200)

Medium-small; blackish. BILL sharp, wide-based. TAIL very short. WINGS triangular. Walk/run.

STARLING

Waxwing (p. 201)

Small; crested; pale grey-brown with yellow tail tip. LEGS very short; does not walk.

WAXWING

Dipper (p. 201)

Small; rotund. BILL short, thick, pointed. Wings and TAIL short. LEGS/FEET strong; walks, 'dips'; swims.

DIPPER

Dunnock (p. 202)

Small; dark, streaked, no white. BILL fine, pointed. TAIL slim, horizontal. Hops, shuffles, flicks wings and tail.

DUNNOCK

Wren (p. 202)

Tiny; brown. BILL fine. TAIL short, slim, often cocked. WINGS very short. Bouncy, flitting; does not walk.

WREN

Thrushes (p. 203)

Medium-small; dark or spotted. BILL pointed, quite stout. WINGS rounded or pointed. TAIL square. Run, shuffle, hop, frequently in trees.

SONG THRUSH

Chats (p. 203)

Small; rounded, most multicoloured. BILL medium-slim, pointed. WINGS short. TAIL short. Hop; perch on upright stems, posts; most are infrequent in trees.

STONECHAT

Crests (p. 219)

Tiny; greenish, black-and-white patch on wing. BILL very fine. Acrobatic, in thin twigs, thickets.

GOLDCREST

Warblers (p. 215)

Small; mostly plain colours. BILL thin, pointed. TAIL medium to long, sometimes raised. Perch in trees/bushes/tall vegetation; do not walk.

WILLOW WARBLER

Flycatchers (p. 224)

Small; brownish or pied. BILL slender, pointed, quite broad. WINGS long. TAIL slim. LEGS very short; perch, do not walk or hop.

PIED FLYCATCHER

Nuthatch (p. 226)

Small; flat-backed. BILL wedge-shaped. TAIL short and broad. LEGS short but strong; clings to bark, acrobatic, tail held free; may hop on ground.

NUTHATCH

Treecreeper (p. 226)

Very small; brown-and-white. BILL fine and curved. TAIL quite long, pointed. Creeps on bark, tail used as support; rarely on ground, does not hop or walk.

TREECREEPER

Tits (p. 227)

Very small; multicoloured or brownish. BILL very short, dark, slim triangle. WINGS short. TAIL short, square on most. Acrobatic, darting or flitting, sometimes hop on ground.

GREAT TIT

Crows (p. 232)

Large to very large; black, or mixed black, grey, white, pinkish. BILL strong, thick, arched or pointed, or downcurved. LEGS strong; walk, hop, leap.

CARRION CROW

Finches (p. 241)

Small; multicoloured. BILL triangular, short and thick or rather long and pointed. WINGS short. TAIL notched. LEGS short; perch and hop.

LINNET

Buntings (p. 250)

Small; variably coloured. BILL triangular, thick, or arched. TAIL slim, plain or white at sides (see larks, pipits). LEGS short; perch, hop.

REED BUNTING

Sparrows (p. 255)

Small; brownish or pale, plain beneath. BILL triangular, short, thick. TAIL slim, no white. LEGS short; perch, hop.

HOUSE SPARROW

Larks are rather stocky, ground-feeding birds that walk (do not hop). Two breed and are 'small and streaky brown' birds: pipit-like but heavier, thicker-billed and shorter-tailed and with a small crest that can be raised; in flight they are clearly larger and broader-winged than pipits. One is a winter migrant with distinctive head/breast patterning.

IDENTIFY BY:
▶ head pattern ▶ wing pattern
▶ tail pattern ▶ leg colour

EAT insects, spiders, small seeds picked from the ground

SKYLARK　WOOD LARK　SHORE LARK

Skylark is the only common, widespread lark, typical of wide-open spaces with few trees; winter migrants from Europe form flocks and have higher, more whistling calls than our resident birds. **Woodlark** is very localized, in specialized habitats, but a few may be found on arable fields outside the breeding season. **Shorelark** is a rare winter visitor from Scandinavia, regular only in a few coastal areas.

Locally common resident and winter migrant from N Europe SEP–APR

Flocks can be seen on arable fields OCT–MAR, but in ones and twos in breeding areas MAR–AUG where song is best clue to presence. Call draws attention to birds passing high overhead. Does not perch in trees but sometimes on bush/fence.

WHERE moors, heaths, marshes, downland, pastures; winters in arable fields

Skylark *Alauda arvensis*

L 16–18 cm | WS 30–36 cm

ID Small, brown, streaky. Head and upperparts brown, streaked buff; short, streaked crest; brownish **breast-band** streaked black; white underparts; longish tail; pale legs. **IN FLIGHT**, **whitish trailing edge** to angular wings; **broad white sides** to tail.

VOICE Chirruping "*chrrup*" when flushed and in flight; winter flocks give high, thin whistles. Song **unbroken** fast trills in **rising hover**, often very high up, or shorter phrases from low perch. Deeper notes lost at distance, leaving thin, silvery thread of sound.

prolonged hovering song-flight

white sides to longish tail

white trailing edge

relatively narrow wingtip

crest can be lowered

short, streaked crest

closely streaked breast-band

white underwing

M

WHERE coastal fields and marshes, sandy beaches, muddy tidelines

Rare and local OCT–APR from N Europe

On low-lying coasts, search muddy inlets and shallow creeks edging up into sand dunes or saltmarsh, where creeps or shuffles when feeding on flat ground; sometimes in small flocks.

Shorelark *Eremophila alpestris*

L 16–19 cm | WS 30–34 cm

ID Small, slim, low-slung. Rather plain brown above with **black-and-yellow** head; **unstreaked** whitish underparts; **black legs**. BREEDING MALE well-defined **black 'mask'**, **black cap** with distinct **'horns'** and **black breast-band**. NON-BREEDING MALE/FEMALE duller but retain head and breast pattern. **IN FLIGHT**, white underwing

VOICE Short, simple, squeaky "*eeh*," "*tseep*" or "*ee-du*."

'horns'

black-and-yellow head

B

N/F

WHERE heathland, woodland edge and clearings on sandy soils; winters on downs, farmland

Scarce and local; some dispersal SEP–FEB

Search heathland edge, clear-felled plantations, and listen for distinctive, far-carrying song given in flight or when perched in tree FEB–JUN; creeps and crouches for long periods and looks pale, so hard to see against grass, easier on dark heather.

Woodlark *Lullula arborea*

L 13·5–15 cm | WS 27–30 cm

ID Small, brown, streaky. Rufous cheek; **white stripes over eyes** meet on nape; short, striped crest; black streaks on breast, white underparts; **black-and-white patch** on edge of wing; **very short tail**; pale legs. **IN FLIGHT**, rather rounded wings with no white trailing edge but white band below; **white 'corners'** to tail.

VOICE Quiet or loud, clear "*t'loo-ee*" (emphasis on second syllable). Song slow, **repetitive** series of pure notes: "*leeu leeu leeu, toodl-oodl-oodl, tlui tlui tlui tlui...*" from perch or very high, circling song flight.

no white trailing edge

rounded wingtip

white corners to short tail

pale band under wing

short, striped crest above long white line

finely streaked breast (more like pipit (p. 196) than Skylark)

black-and-white patch on wing

Pipits can look sleek, rounded or slim, not so long-tailed as wagtails but more so than larks. All walk on the ground on thin legs, and have a pointed bill, narrow head, long wingtip and white/grey-edged tail. Three are usually solitary or in pairs, while **Meadow Pipits** may gather in large numbers from September to March, but remain dispersed, flying up separately rather than together as a flock, as would finches.

IDENTIFY BY:
▶ habitat/time of year ▶ flank pattern
▶ leg colour ▶ hind claw shape
▶ call

Pipit calls at-a-glance

Meadow Pipit	thin, quick "seep" or "seep-sip-sip"
Tree Pipit	buzzy, abrupt "teess" or "spiz"
Rock Pipit	thick, slurred "feest" or "sfeep"
Water Pipit	"tsweep" or "feest" midway between Meadow Pipit and Rock Pipit

TREE PIPIT

WHERE farmland, moors, heaths, marshes

WHERE woodland/heaths/plantation edge, bushy slopes

Common resident, passage migrant MAR–MAY, JUL–OCT, and visitor from N Europe SEP–APR

Scarce APR–OCT; winters in Africa

Look on any heath or moor or along freshwater edges. Often in **loose** groups/flocks; **present all year**. Often crouched, creeping along ground.

Visit likely sites from APR and listen for birds singing from a high perch. Does not form flocks; **absent in winter**. Unlike other pipits, habitually walks along tree branches.

Meadow Pipit
Anthus pratensis

L 14–15.5 cm | WS 22–25 cm

ID Small; olive- or yellowish-brown above, streaked blackish; breast buff-white with sharp black streaks; **thick black streaks on flank**. Legs **orange-pink**; hind claw **very long**. Flight hesitant, jerky, fluttering; rises in **short, springy bounds**. Tail sides white.

VOICE Thin, quick "seeip-sip-sip," stronger "sip sip." Song simple, **rapidly repeated** thin notes and quick trills, from ground or in song flight: rises steeply, 'parachute' descent with tail and wings raised in 'shuttlecock' shape.

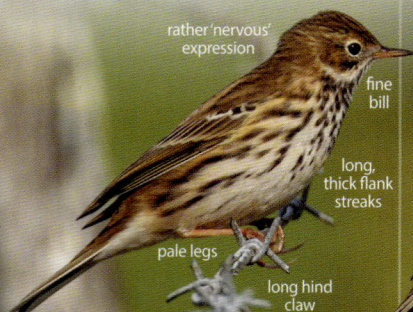

Tree Pipit *Anthus trivialis*

L 14–16 cm | WS 22–25 cm

ID Small; pale olive-brown above, streaked blackish; breast yellow-cream, streaked black; **thin black streaks on flank**. Legs **pink**; hind claw relatively **short**. Flight strong. Tail sides white.

VOICE Call buzzy, abrupt "teeess"or"spiz." Song flight a steep rise then slow descent with outspread wings and tail ('shuttlecock'), usually **starts and finishes on tree or sapling**; also **sings from tree**. Song simple, musical trills before distinctive long final notes "seeya, see-a, seeee-a."

rather 'nervous' expression
fine bill
long, thick flank streaks
pale legs
long hind claw

! Richard's Pipit (p.261)

relatively 'bold' expression
strong bill
fine flank streaks
pale legs
short hind claw

! Olive-backed Pipit (p.261)

Meadow Pipit: breeding birds leave uplands and disperse into lowlands AUG–APR, when joined by N European visitors. **Tree Pipit**: summer migrant only. **Rock Pipit**: resident, dispersing around coasts SEP–APR, when joined by migrants from Scandinavia; few inland. **Water Pipit**: visitor from central European Alps.

EAT very small insects, spiders, small seeds of grasses, sedges and heather

MEADOW PIPIT | TREE PIPIT | ROCK PIPIT | WATER PIPIT

WHERE grassy clifftops, rocks, wave-washed beaches, tidelines, nearby footpaths and buildings. In winter, saltmarshes

WHERE beside lakes, marshy pools and cressbeds inland; also on saltmarshes

Locally common resident/winter visitor from Scandinavia SEP–APR

Quite easy to see along the coast: look for a small, dark bird flitting ahead of you, calling.

Scarce visitor from central Europe OCT–APR

Although a winter visitor, migrants in autumn and spring appear beside inland waters: can be elusive and likely to fly far away if disturbed.

Rock Pipit *Anthus petrosus*

L 15·5–17 cm | WS 23–28 cm

ID Thickset, rather upright, with long, stout bill and **dark** legs. **Dusky grey-olive** with soft streaks above, yellower or whitish below with blurred grey-brown streaks; buff under cheek and on throat. Tail sides pale grey, not quite pure white.

VOICE Call 'thick', slurred, usually single "*feest*" or "*sfeep*." Rising song flight with 'parachute' and simple series of thin trills.

Water Pipit *Anthus spinoletta*

L 15·5–17 cm | WS 23–28 cm

ID Deep-bodied; alert, upright with long, stout bill and **dark** legs. Browner above, **whiter below** than Rock Pipit, with **dull white wingbars** and **whitish stripe over eye**; dark streaks outline **white throat** or bib. In spring, throat and breast **pale pink**. Tail sides **white**.

VOICE Call loud "*tsweeep*" or slightly vibrant "*feest*," midway between thin Meadow Pipit and slurred Rock Pipit.

stout bill (often with yellow at base)

buff under cheek, buff throat

dusky grey-olive overall

tail side grey

underparts yellow-buff with grey-brown streaks

dark legs

white over eye

stout bill

white under cheek, white throat/bib

dull white wingbars

underparts white with grey streaks

dark legs

Wagtails are small, slender and long-tailed, and walk and feed on the ground; as the name suggests, they have the distinctive habit of wagging their tail up and down.

IDENTIFY BY:
▶ head pattern ▶ back colour
▶ colour under tail ▶ leg colour ▶ call

EAT insects, spiders, other intervertebrates, small seeds

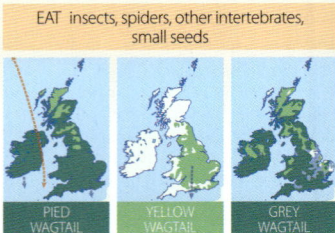

PIED WAGTAIL   YELLOW WAGTAIL   GREY WAGTAIL

Pied Wagtail, the most common wagtail, is found almost anywhere all year, gathering in groups SEP–MAR; birds of the mainland continental European form, **White Wagtail**, appear in MAR–APR and (less easily identified) SEP–NOV. **Grey Wagtail** breeds in more specialized waterside habitats but disperses, joined by continental migrants, SEP–MAR, when it can be seen more widely. **Yellow Wagtail** is a summer migrant only, sometimes seen in flocks APR–MAY and AUG–SEP.

WHERE suburbs, pavements, car parks, open grassland, riversides, fields

Common resident and passage/winter migrant from NW Europe SEP–MAY

Characteristic urban/suburban bird, easy to see around lakesides, near grazing livestock and in muddy farmyards, but just as likely on a house roof or car park; sometimes confiding. Forms large roosts in town centre trees NOV–FEB.

Pied Wagtail *Motacilla alba*

L 16·5–19 cm | WS 28 cm

ID **Black/grey and white** with **white face** and **black bib** or **breast-band**; **wide white wingbars**; white below with grey flank; long tail; spindly black legs. Sexes and ages often difficult to separate. BREEDING MALE **black back, black bib**. NON-BREEDING/IMMATURE MALE/FEMALE **dark grey back**, **black breast-band** JUVENILE paler, duller with yellowish face, dark smudges on breast. **IN FLIGHT**, deeply bounding.

VOICE **Distinctive** cheery "*tsuwee*" or "*churee-wee*," 'brightest' notes similar to Yellow Wagtail, and a sharper "*tissik.*"

White Wagtails in spring with their **pale grey back** are easy to pick out, but in autumn much more difficult and best told by their grey rump (Pied Wagtail has a black or dark grey rump), but this is hard to see.

J JUN–SEP

yellowish face

MB MAR–SEP

black back

black on breast in all plumages

grey back

prominent white wingbars

F

Yellow Wagtail *Motacilla flava*

L 15–16 cm | WS 25 cm

ID Pale **green** or olive above, brown wing with pale edges to feathers and two narrow white wingbars; bright or pale **yellow** below, palest under tail (opposite of Grey Wagtail); **long**, spindly **black legs**. BREEDING MALE unstreaked **bright yellow** below. FEMALE olive-brown above, **plain yellowish-buff** below. JUVENILE yellow-buff below; dark marks on head and throat until about SEP. **IN FLIGHT**, swooping; black tail with white sides.

WHERE arable land, pastures with livestock, grassy areas beside lakes, estuaries, coastal grazing marshes

Scarce, locally common APR–OCT; winters in Africa

Scan grassy places close to water in APR–MAY for migrants and look for small groups among cattle on pasture near the coast in AUG–SEP.

VOICE A loud, sweet "*tsee*" or "*schlee*," or "*sureee*." Song is a weak repetition of short, slurred notes.

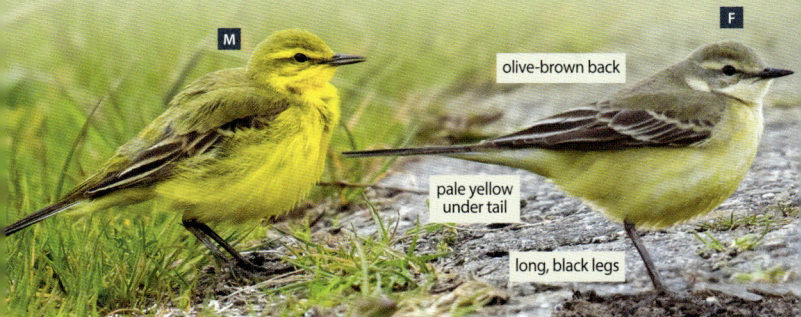

olive-brown back

pale yellow under tail

long, black legs

Grey Wagtail *Motacilla cinerea*

L 17–20 cm | WS 25–27 cm

ID Wagtail with **longest tail**, bright **yellow rear-end** and **short, pale legs**. Slate-grey above with **yellow-green** rump; vivid **yellow** under tail. BREEDING MALE has **black throat**. Flight is deeply undulating; settles with exaggerated up–down tail movement.

VOICE An explosive, metallic "*zi-zi*" or "*tsivit!,*" song rapid, sharp "*tiss-iss- iss*" and "*si-si-si*," penetrating the noise of rushing water.

WHERE flowing, clean freshwater streams, mill races, open or tree-lined; in winter beside lakes, saltmarsh edge, garden ponds, town rooftops

Locally common resident/ migrant from N Europe SEP–MAR

Listen for the distinctive sharp call and look along the edges of rivers and shorelines; usually in ones and twos (not large groups).

grey back

white 'moustache' and black throat

J MAY–MAR

bright yellow under tail

grey flank

short, pale legs

199

Starling, Waxwing & Dipper

STARLING

Starling murmurations can be spectacular: huge flocks swirling and diving in coordinated manoeuvres.

Starling *Sturnus vulgaris*

L 19–22 cm | WS 35–40 cm

ID Small, dark, with short tail; waddling walk or run. BREEDING black with **purple/ green gloss**, buff feather edges on wings and around tail; bill yellow. NON-BREEDING covered in **white spots** that give paler, greyer look with dark 'mask' but wear away by MAR; bill black. JUVENILE dark brown with **blackish bill and 'mask'**; gradually develops white spots on blacker body, head fades to buff. **IN FLIGHT, pointed head**, **square tail**, **triangular wings**.

VOICE Strident whistles, buzzing "*cheer.*" Alarm sharp, clicking "*plik.*" Song (with puffed-out throat, waving wings) rattling, whistling, warbling, mimicry; long, rambling subsong.

WHERE anywhere with scattered trees, towns, villages, moorland edge, reedbeds

EATS insects from ground and also caught high in the air, spiders and other small invertebrates, seeds, berries

Common resident and abundant migrant from Europe SEP–APR

Easy to see despite recent declines; look for winter flocks around cattle or sheep, summer flocks on moorlands, and bigger flocks flying to roost. Often sings from a gutter or TV aerial.

J MAY–AUG

I JUL–SEP

N

Drab JUVENILES quickly grow dark feathers with white spots on body, leaving faded hood.

N SEP–MAR

black bill

yellow bill with blue base (MALE); pink base (FEMALE)

B MAR–SEP

! Rose-coloured Starling (p.259)

Scarce, irregular NOV–MAR, from Scandinavia

Look for flocks in likely good feeding spots with abundant berries, such as shopping centre car parks, particularly in occasional 'invasion' years. Acrobatic when feeding; drinks from puddles

WAXWING

Waxwing *Bombycilla garrulus*

L 18–21 cm | WS 32–35 cm

ID Small, stocky; short legs. Unmistakable: **pale pinkish-grey and brown** (looks greyish in dull light) with distinctive wide **crest**; **black bib** and eyestripe; **grey rump**; **yellow tail-tip**; **rufous under tail**. ADULT MALE long yellow stripe along wingtip, with broad white tip to each feather (forming 'V' shapes); broad yellow tip to tail; sharp edge to black bib. ADULT FEMALE short yellow stripe along wingtip; each feather with a narrow white tip; narrow yellow tail tip; soft edge to black bib. IMMATURE no pale 'V's on wingtip.

VOICE A far-carrying, silvery trill, "*sirrrr*." Greenfinch (*p. 245*) and Blue Tit (*p. 229*) make similar sounds in spring.

M

Dipper *Cinclus cinclus*

L 17–20 cm | WS 25–30 cm

ID Small, rather bulky and **rotund waterside bird**. **Dark brown** with **white breast**. **Swims, dives** or walks into fast-running water to pick food from the bottom. Perches on rock or branch, with taut, vertical **bobbing** as though 'on springs'. JUVENILE grey, mottled white; dark mottling on breast. **IN FLIGHT**, fast and low, following stream on **whirring** wings.

VOICE Call distinctive, a hard, deep, rasping "*dzit*." Song penetrates sound of running water: bright, prolonged, disjointed warble with whistles and trills.

Scarce and local; very rare migrant (with black belly) from N Europe OCT–MAR

Look from bridges or vantage points that give a good view along a river. Check rocks in the middle of the river, particularly those with telltale white droppings.

DIPPER

201

Dunnock & Wren

Sings in upright stance from open perch.

EAT insects, spiders, seeds

Loud, energetic songster, with cocked tail and raised head.

WHERE bushy and wooded areas: including heath, moors, clifftops, gardens, parks

WHERE coastal cliffs to upland tops, islands, moors, heaths, woodland, gardens, parks

Common resident and migrant from N Europe
SEP—MAR

Look along the sides of footpaths or along the edge of a lawn for small, dark shapes lurking in the shadows, sometimes 3–4 waving their wings in display. Usually sings at a mid-height, a little above the ground but not high in the canopy.

Common, locally abundant; slightly different forms on N & W Scottish islands

Heard far more often than seen, but wait quietly and one may pop up from a bramble patch, or behind some garden bric-a-brac, call irritably, bob a couple of times, and dive back down out of sight.

Dunnock *Prunella modularis*

L 13–14.5 cm | WS 19–21 cm

ID Small, dark, deep-chested; horizontal or crouched posture, **creeping and shuffling**, legs flexed, wings flirted, tail flicked. Rich brown above, **streaked black; greyer face and underparts**, smudgy dark brown **streaks** on grey flank. **Thin bill** and bright orange-brown legs.

DUNNOCK

VOICE Bright, even whistle, *"peeeh"* and thin, vibrant *"si-i-i-i-i-i-i."* Song is a fast, thin, high, but slightly 'flat' warble, of even speed and pitch.

Wren *Troglodytes troglodytes*

L 9–10.5 cm | WS 13–17 cm

ID **Tiny, rotund**; quick, jerky movements. Warm brown, **barred crosswise** on wing and flank; **pale stripe over eye**. Tail **short** and narrow, often (but not always!) **pointing upwards**. Thin bill; pinkish legs.

WREN

VOICE Calls short *"chek,"* a longer, rolling/rasping *"cherrrr,"* and an irregular scolding rattle. Song loud, vibrant, powerful: a fast, ringing warble with a low, quick trill at or near the end.

greyish head

plain wing; streaked flank

grey breast

short tail (often cocked)

white stripe over eye

barred wing and flank

brown breast

Thrushes and Chats

Thrushes (p. 204)

Six species, three resident (but also winter migrants), one summer migrant, two winter visitors (very few breed). Small–medium-sized; long but stout body and relatively small head with thick bill; wingtip falls short of rather long tail; legs strong. Perch and sometimes feed in trees, but mostly feed on ground.

IDENTIFY BY:
► overall colour
► underpart colour/pattern
► underwing colour

REDWING

Chats (p. 208)

Seven species, two resident, four summer migrants, one migrant but also rare breeder. Small (larger than most warblers but smaller than thrushes); strong-billed and short-tailed.

IDENTIFY BY:
► upperpart colour
► head pattern
► tail and rump colour

ROBIN

Plumages

Sexes differ in 7 species, alike in 6; no marked seasonal changes in thrushes but marked in 5 chats. Juveniles generally spotted but look like females until October–January. Thrushes often 'sunbathe', helping rid plumage of parasites.

BLACKBIRD (JUVENILE)

In flight

Thrushes direct, fast even in enclosed woodland; often loose groups. Mistle Thrush in longer lines, Fieldfare and Redwing in larger flocks. **Chats** more flitting, rarely in long flights, often fly from perch to ground or from bush to bush.

FIELDFARE

Behaviour

Thrushes eat berries but mostly feed on ground with run-pause action, looking/listening with cocked head. **Chats** are woodland or open-ground birds perching on low bushes; all tend to drop down for food, hopping on the ground.

SONG THRUSH (smashing snail)

STARLING
FIELDFARE
REDWING
FIELDFARE
FIELDFARE
REDWING

Thrushes

Blackbird and Song Thrush songs

Blackbird gives relaxed, flowing warbles and trills at different tempos, phrases often petering out before a pause: notes may be repeated but each phrase is succeeded by a different one.

Song Thrush has a different rhythm, with stronger, strikingly varied musical, strident or whistled phrases, each repeated two to six times.

Common resident and migrant from N Europe
OCT–MAR

A very familiar garden bird, often on lawns; song often dominates the woodland dawn chorus.

WHERE forests, woodland clearings, heaths, gardens, parks, farmland with trees, hedges

EATS worms, insects, other invertebrates, fruit, berries, seeds, sometimes lizards and newts

Blackbird *Turdus merula*

L 23·5–29 cm | WS 40–45 cm

ID Large, dark, round-headed, long-tailed; often **raises tail** and lowers it slowly. MALE **black** with **yellow bill** and eyering. IMMATURE MALE has dark bill until DEC/JAN, browner wings (may have blackish body, pale hood). FEMALE **dark brown**; throat brown or whitish; underparts brown mottled darker, not spotted black. JUVENILE more **rufous**, mottled dark brown and red-brown below, some have ill-defined pale breast-band.

VOICE Vibrant, "*shrreee;*" soft "*chook;*" loud "*chak;*" repeated loud "*pink pwink pwink,*" especially at dusk. Repeated rhythmic sequence in alarm; full alarm a **clattering, screechy rattle**. Song long, **musical, throaty and flute-like**, separate phrases often peter out.

JUVENILE Blackbirds calling to be fed give low, churring or rippling notes.

uniformly brown

diffusely mottled breast

yellow eyering

M

F

M

BLACKBIRD

204

Thrushes in flight

Look at underwing colour and underparts pattern.

REDWING (p. 207)

FIELDFARE (p. 207)

M
white gorget

red

white

streaked

white belly

RING OUZEL

M
plain or 'scaled'

SONG THRUSH (p. 206)

buff

M

BLACKBIRD

spotted

plain or mottled

F

white

pale wingtips

MISTLE THRUSH (p. 206)

spotted belly

Scarce MAR–NOV; winters in S Europe/N Africa

Listen for distinctive song in breeding areas and follow up with care, as usually wild and unapproachable, flying off over skyline. Watch for migrants at regular sites in MAR–APR and OCT–NOV, feeding on the ground or in bushes.

WHERE upland crags, moors and fields, eroded peat bogs; migrants on isolated hills, heaths, coastal sites with berry-bearing bushes

EATS worms, insects, other invertebrates, lizards, berries, seeds

Ring Ouzel *Turdus torquatus*

L 24–27 cm | WS 41–45 cm

ID Large, dark, slender, long-winged with sleek, flat-backed shape; does not raise tail like Blackbird. MALE sooty-black with clear **white breast-band** and **silvery-grey panel on wing**; from AUG, pale lacy pattern beneath and breast-band duller. FEMALE/JUVENILE dark brown, **pale feather edges below**; dull breast-band.

VOICE Scolding, hard "*tuc tuc tuc*," rolling "*churr.*" Song wild, loud, recalls Mistle Thrush (p. 206), based around a few clear whistles, phrases distinctly separated: "*tulee tuleee tulee; tiu-lee tiu-lee tiu-lee.*"

FI

Very restricted breast-band for the first few months, but scaly feather edges; pale upperwing distinctive.

F

M

pale panel on wing

pale breast-band partially obscured

pale feather edges

white breast-band

RING OUZEL

EAT **All**: worms, insects, other invertebrates, fruit, berries, seeds. **Song Thrush**: also snails

Common resident and migrant from NW Europe OCT–MAR

Distinctive loud song draws attention to bird singing from exposed perch. Unobtrusive feeder, rustles leaves; flies low into cover if disturbed.

Song Thrush *Turdus philomelos*

L 20–22 cm | WS 33–36 cm

ID Small, short-tailed, rather solitary. Pale **brown** above, creamy-buff below with **'V'-shaped black spots**. JUVENILE buff feather edges. **IN FLIGHT**, pale orange-buff underwing. **VOICE** Thin, sharp "*tik*" or "*sip*;" alarm like weak Blackbird (*p. 204*) rattle. **Song** strident, with rich, fluty whistles, shouted notes, in **short phrases**, **each repeated** at an even tempo.

WHERE mixed and deciduous woods, parks, gardens, farmland with trees, hedges

warm brown

closely scattered 'V'-shaped black spots

SONG THRUSH

Common resident/migrant from NW Europe

Loud song from FEB, usually from a high treetop. Feeds on open ground, wary, flies into treetops if disturbed. Feeds on Rowan and Holly NOV–JAN.

Mistle Thrush *Turdus viscivorus*

L 26–29 cm | WS 43–45 cm

ID Large; small-headed; **upright**; **strong, springy hops**. Pale **greyish-brown** above, creamy-buff below with **round black spots**. **Dark 'shoulder' spots** and **pale feather edges** on wing; tail has whitish sides. JUVENILE pale with dark-edged, cream spots on back. **IN FLIGHT**, pointed head; long, squared tail; long wings show **white below**.

VOICE Call dry, rattling "*tchrrr-tchrrr-tchrrr*." Song fluting, melodic, slow repetition but little variation, often from high treetop.

WHERE woodland of all kinds, heath, moorland edge, villages, farmland with old trees

white tip to tail

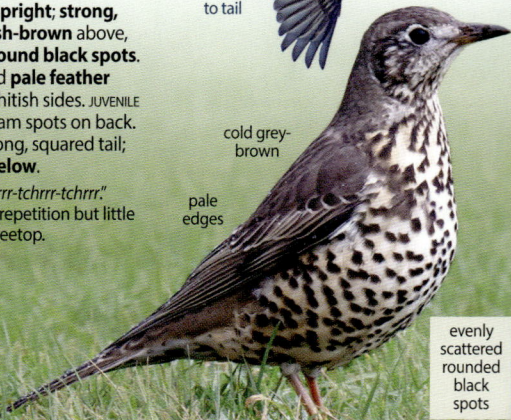

cold grey-brown

pale edges

evenly scattered rounded black spots

MISTLE THRUSH

Common SEP–APR from N/E Europe, Iceland; very rare breeder in N Scotland

Look on open pastures and check areas with berried bushes or fallen fruit. Listen at night for high-pitched call from birds overhead. In severe weather flocks may be seen moving west by day.

Redwing *Turdus iliacus*

L 19–23 cm | WS 30–34 cm

ID Small, short-tailed, social. **Dark brown** above, **cream stripe over eye**, dark cheek and 'moustache'; white below, **streaked** black; flank **brick-red**. IN FLIGHT, in loose flocks; pointed head, swept-back wings, short, square tail; **red underwing**.

VOICE High, thin "*seeeeh*;" rattling notes. Song short fluty phrases. Spring flocks produce a rambling chorus.

pale stripe over eye

red flank

streaked underparts

REDWING

Locally common OCT–APR from N/E Europe; very rare breeder in N England/Scotland

WHERE woodland, farmland with hedgerows and trees, heaths, orchards

Mixes with Redwing, on fields or in hedgerows: sometimes scores/hundreds in loosely coordinated flocks that fly into nearby treetops if disturbed; listen for the distinctive calls.

Fieldfare *Turdus pilaris*

L 22–27 cm | WS 40–42 cm

ID Large, social. **Grey head and rump**, brown back and **black tail**. Black 'mask'; yellow bill. **Orange** breast, white below, flank heavily spotted black. IN FLIGHT, usually in loose flocks; **white underwing**.

VOICE Low, chuckling chatter "*chak-chak-ak*" or softer "*chuk-uk-uk-uk*;" nasal "*swee-eep*." Occasional 'subsong' from spring flocks.

grey rump

grey head with blackish 'mask'

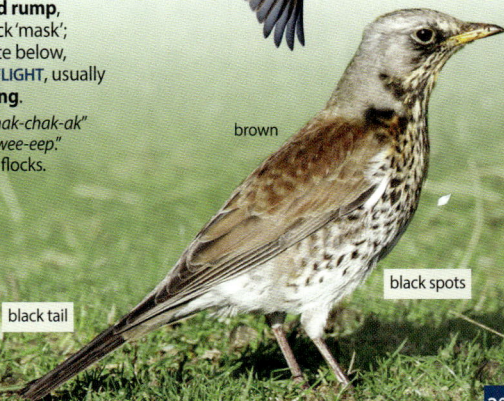

brown

black spots

black tail

FIELDFARE

207

Chats

Male **Robins** sing for most of the year, and often do so at night in well-lit streets, car parks, *etc.*

Very common resident and migrant from
N Europe SEP–MAR

Familiar bird of mid-level canopy, flitting down to
ground to feed and back up again; moves with
bouncy hops on ground, and habitually flicks
wings and tail. Often visits feeders.

Robin *Erithacus rubecula*

L 12·5–14 cm | WS 22–25 cm

ID Rounded or slim,
depending on conditions
(more rounded in cold
weather). Sexes alike: warm
brown above; **orange-red
breast**; beady dark eye; pale
legs. JUVENILE brown with pale spots above,
buff with dark crescents below; patchy red
from JUN–OCT, depending on hatching date.

VOICE Typical call is a sharp "*tik*;" a thin, high
"*see*" can be frustratingly hard to pinpoint.
Song a **long**, fluent, melody, more or less
melancholy, with **frequent changes in speed**
and characteristic long-drawn notes.

Sexes alike; no seasonal change but dull, pale
and faded by late summer, bright again after
early autumn moult.

ROBIN

WHERE forest, scrub, gardens, parks, suburbs;
rocky coasts with bushes to high ground

EATS insects, other invertebrates, seeds, berries

J APR–OCT

JUVENILE has typical Robin character but lacks red;
only likely to be confused with juvenile Redstart
(*p. 210*) but has pale legs and a brown tail.

Male **Nightingales** sing by day as well as at night but are usually very well hidden.

Typically heard singing deep inside a thicket, but with patience and a careful, quiet approach may be glimpsed on the ground or a song post.

WHERE dense, often damp, deciduous thickets, woods, woodland/heathland edge and around flooded gravel pits

EATS insects, spiders, other invertebrates

Nightingale
Luscinia megarhynchos

L 15–16·5 cm | WS 26–28 cm

ID Rather large chat; unstreaked pale rufous-brown above; plain head with pale ring around large, dark eye; **brighter rufous tail**, often raised. Grey-buff below with long, whitish feathers under tail.

VOICE Call a low, grating "*kerrrr*" or clear, whistled "*wheep*." Song dramatic, easy to hear: long, rambling, varied pace, pitch and quality, many deep, full-throated notes; long pauses. Long, thin "*seeee seeee*" suddenly changes to deep, fast 'gobbling' notes.

NIGHTINGALE

On the ground, a Nightingale dips and bobs its head and tail, Robin-like, but is hard to see in low thickets; migrants appear in unlikely places.

Nightingale looks like a large Robin with no red: the tail is more rufous, and often raised.

bold black eye in plain face

long, rufous tail

long wingtip

Male **Redstarts** often sing high in the canopy, frequently dropping down to feed on the ground.

Locally fairly common APR–OCT (but rare in Ireland); winters Africa

Easiest to see in western oakwoods when singing in spring, but can be elusive in the canopy. Unlike other chats, habitually quivers tail.

WHERE mixed/deciduous forest, heath/woodland/moorland edge

EATS insects, other invertebrates, seeds, berries

Redstart
Phoenicurus phoenicurus

L 13–14·5 cm | WS 25 cm

ID Robin-like (*p. 208*); **orange-red rump and tail**; plain wing (rarely with weak pale panel); black legs. MALE grey back; **white forehead**; **black face** (looks greyish from AUG); orange breast. FEMALE grey-brown above, **orange-buff** below. JUVENILE as female but pale spots (resembles juvenile Robin but has red tail and black legs).

REDSTART

Migrants are usually found in thickets or trees, but on exposed coasts can sometimes be seen perched in the open, even on wire fences.

VOICE Call sweet "*hu-eep*" or "*hweep*," like Chaffinch (*p. 242*) or Willow Warbler (*p. 223*), "*wheet-tiktik*;" ticking alarm. Song low, vibrant "*srree srree srree*" before short musical warble.

! Bluethroat (*p. 261*)

M

black face;
orange breast

plain wing

orange rump
and tail sides

F

orange-buff
breast

Black Redstarts often use stone walls and concrete structures as substitutes for natural crags.

Rare and local summer migrant MAR– SEP and winter visitor from N/C Europe SEP–MAR

Wintering birds on coast easiest to see – look on roofs, groynes; breeds in some railway stations (*e.g.* in London) and best located when singing.

WHERE breeds inaccessible urban/industrial sites (*e.g.* power stations, factories); winters sheltered rocky coasts. Does not perch in trees

EATS insects, other invertebrates, seeds, berries

Black Redstart
Phoenicurus ochruros

13–14·5 cm | WS 25 cm

ID Robin-like (*p. 208*); grey, with **rusty-red tail**; pale panel in wing; black legs. MALE **smoky-grey, blacker on face and breast**; prominent **white panel** in wing. ONE-YEAR-OLD MALE (often breed) greyer. FEMALE/JUVENILE/NON-BREEDING MALE brownish-grey, with plain grey head.

VOICE Call a sharp "*weet*" or "*weet-t'k t'k.*" Song fairly quiet but far-carrying, a trill followed by a dry crackle and musical flourish.

BLACK REDSTART

Migrants and wintering birds favour areas of rubble or stony places, or weed-strewn shorelines on low coasts.

Flash of orange tail catches the eye in short, low flights.

white panel in wing

black face and breast

pale panel in wing

grey breast

rusty-red tail sides

EAT insects, spiders, other invertebrates, worms

STONECHAT | WHINCHAT

Male **Stonechats** are very conspicuous, even at a distance.

Locally common resident and migrant from W Europe SEP–MAR

Listen for the distinctive call and look for a small, upright, round shape on an exposed perch.

Stonechat *Saxicola torquatus*

L 11·5–13 cm | WS 21–23 cm

ID Rounded; plain head (no white stripe over eye); short, **plain**, blackish tail. MALE blackish above; often white patch in wing; **black hood, white neck patch** (suffused brown from AUG); rufous breast, white belly. FEMALE brown, streaked black above; **dark brownish hood**; **throat streaked buff-brown**, often with pale crescent below; rusty-buff breast. IMMATURE pale stripe over eye (shorter and thinner than on Whinchat); whitish chin; throat streaked brown.

VOICE Call a distinctive sharp whistle "*whee*" or "*whee-tak*." Song fast, chattering, squeaky warble, sometimes in flight.

WHERE heathland, moorland, rough grassland, on bushes, walls, wires; often near coast, particularly in autumn/winter

MB

Broad, black tail often raised in wind and in short flight from perch down to ground.

MN SEP–MAR

black head

white neck patch

at most faint pale stripe over eye

black throat and rufous breast

MB MAR–SEP

dark tail

F

Whinchats call nervously when breeding but are generally less obvious than Stonechat.

Scarce APR–OCT; winters in Africa

Upright on exposed perches in suitable open habitat in the N and W, particularly MAY–JUL; migrants can often be seen perched up on bushes/tall stalks in grassy places near the coast AUG–SEP.

Whinchat *Saxicola rubetra*

L 12–14 cm | WS 22–24 cm

ID Rather slim; **long, pale stripe over eye**; short, brown tail with **white on side**. BREEDING MALE pale buff-brown above, streaked black; often shows white in wing; **black 'mask'**, white stripe over eye; bright apricot throat and breast. NON-BREEDING MALE/FEMALE/IMMATURE brown-and-buff; buff stripe over eye; unstreaked throat.

VOICE Call a sweet "*siu*" and "*siu-tektek.*" Song rattles and clicks, dry ticking before fast, musical flourish.

WHERE rough grassy heaths, moorland edge, bracken-covered slopes, young plantations

F/I

White tail sides but dark rump (far more white on Wheatear (*p.214*)): Stonechat has all-black tail.

pale stripe over eye

apricot throat/ breast

MB APR–AUG

white tail sides

F/I

Wheatears are often seen on open grassy areas or fences during migration, sometimes in loose groups.

Locally common MAR–OCT; winters in Africa

Upright and usually on the ground or stones/walls in open areas. Look for migrants especially MAR–APR and AUG–SEP; if disturbed flits ahead a little way showing prominent white rump.

EATS insects, other invertebrates, seeds, berries

WHERE breeds upland pastures, stony slopes, heaths; migrants on coastal grassland, shingle beaches, footpaths, or inland arable fields, cropped grass, often near water

Wheatear
Oenanthe oenanthe

L 14–16·5 cm | WS 27–28 cm

ID Rather large, fairly slim chat; extensive **white patch on rump** and tail, with **black centre and tip creating bold 'T' shape**. BREEDING MALE blue-grey above with blackish wings; **black 'mask'**; whitish below. NON-BREEDING MALE pale buff-brown with bright buff feather edges on wings; dark 'mask'. FEMALE/IMMATURE grey-brown above, buff below; cheek and wings brown.

VOICE Whistled *"wheet"* and hard *"chak"* calls. Song in short song flight or from low perch, quick chattering and ticking phrase with musical chirps.

WHEATEAR

IN FLIGHT, low, quick, direct on broad wings; bold flash of white on rump and tail,

MB

MN AUG–NOV

pale stripe over eye
and dark 'mask'

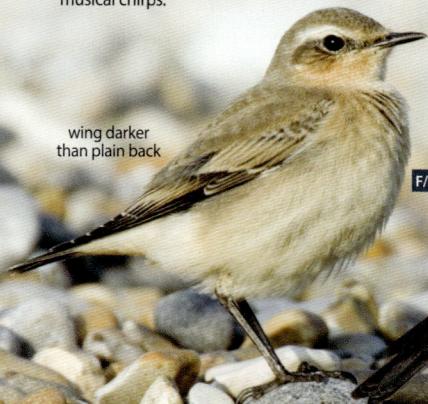

wing darker
than plain back

blackish tail reveals
white sides when
spread

F/I

MB MAR–AUG

Crests and Warblers

comprise 14 small birds: four resident, others summer migrants but two regular in smaller numbers in winter. They are slim-billed and creep, ho and/or flit through foliage and upright stems. Crests are acrobatic but warblers far less so. The two crests are similar but distinctive; warblers form three broad groups.

Crests (p. 219)

Tiny, with distinctive yellow/orange crown stripe and black-and-white wing patch.

GOLDCREST

Phylloscopus Warblers (p. 222)

Three 'green' species, living in foliage, with fine bill, pale stripe over eye, slender legs. Easily distinguished by songs; call-notes "*sweet*".

CHIFFCHAFF

Plumages

Sexes alike in most species but differ in some *Sylvia Warblers*; seasonal change minor; juveniles distinct in some species.

In flight

Quick, flitting, not so strong as chats, nor as dashing as tits; **Wetland Warblers** fly low and fast, Dartford Warbler whirrs low; *Sylvia Warblers* 'heavier' than lightweight *Phylloscopus*.

Behaviour

Crests often hang upside down and hover. **Warblers** more horizontal, but **Wetland Warblers** cling sideways to upright stems. Two species sing in hurried, flappy display flight. Migrants often in unexpected places.

Wetland Warblers (p. 220)

Four 'brown' warblers, two plain, two streaked, with slim bill, round tail; all associated with dense wetland vegetation. Easily distinguished by songs; call-notes churring or clicking.

SEDGE WARBLER

Sylvia Warblers (p. 216)

Five small or slightly bulky warblers, greyish or brownish, some with white tail sides; rather thick bill. Easily distinguished by songs; call-notes hard or tacking.

WHITETHROAT

SEDGE WARBLER

GOLDCREST

REED WARBLER

DARTFORD WARBLER

Sylvia Warblers are quite stout, short-billed and strong-legged, clumsier than Phylloscopus warblers, less acrobatic than tits; calls are characteristically hard, harsh or grating but some have rich, warbling songs. Sexes look alike or differ slightly.

IDENTIFY BY:
▶ head pattern   ▶ wing/underparts colour
▶ eyering colour   ▶ song

EAT small insects, other invertebrates, berries

WHITETHROAT   DARTFORD WARBLER   LESSER WHITETHROAT

Male **Whitethroats** give a hurried, scratchy song from a low perch or wire.

Locally common APR–OCT; winters in C Africa

Listen for distinctive song from dense scrub particularly in APR–JUN and look for bird perched up (sometimes on overhead wire), with throat puffed out, tail raised and swinging, sometimes making a display flight, before diving into cover.

WHERE hedgerows, nettle beds and bramble patches, low thickets; berried bushes in AUG–SEP

Autumn birds look pale sandy-buff with dark streaks on rufous wings.

Whitethroat *Sylvia communis*

L 13–15 cm | WS 18–22 cm

ID Small; bright rusty-brown above with **ginger-rufous feather edges** on wing; **white throat**; pinkish-buff below. Long, slim, brown tail with white sides. Broken narrow white eyering; **pale yellow-orange** legs. MALE head grey. FEMALE/JUVENILE head brownish; wing pale brown, with bright with rufous panel and blackish feather centres.

VOICE Varied calls include nasal, slightly buzzy *"aid-aid-aid;"* longer, buzzing *"churrr;"* rhythmic *"wichety-wichety."* Song (in **bouncy, wing-waving song flight**, from exposed perch, or from cover) fast, churring, scratchy warble with fast rise-fall rhythm.

no contrast between cap and cheek

rufous on wing

brownish head

slim tail often tilted or angled sideways

M

pale legs

F

Dartford Warbler

Sylvia undata

L 13–14 cm | WS 16–18 cm

ID Very small; long tail, often raised, exaggerates size. **Dark grey above, reddish below; red eyering; tail long and thin.** MALE dark grey head; throat and **breast brownish-red.** FEMALE/JUVENILE paler browner; paler throat.

VOICE Call a low, **buzzing**, nasal "*chairrrr*." Song a bright, fast sequence of whistles and buzzy notes in jumbled warble.

Scarce and very localized; mostly on lowland heathland sites in S England

Listen for a short, buzzing churr in areas of thick gorse and heather and watch for a long-tailed warbler appearing briefly on top of a bush or making a low, dipping dash to a new patch.

WHERE low, dense heathland, gorse, often with small pines

red eyering

M

F/J

rufous/orange-brown breast

Lesser Whitethroat

Sylvia curruca

L 11·5–13·5 cm | WS 17–22 cm

ID Small, sleek; grey-brown above (no rufous); grey head with faint, broken, whitish line over dark eye and white crescent below; darker **grey cheek** contrasts with white throat and side of neck; pale grey-buff below. Dark tail with white sides. **Blue-grey** legs.

VOICE Clicking, hard or sharp "*tet*" or "*tuk*" call; high "*see*." Song a low warble before loud, **wooden rattle**: "*tuk-atuk-atuk-atuk-atuk-atuk-atuk*" (warble/rattle often reversed or one element absent).

Scarce APR–OCT; winters in Africa

The distinctive song is given from within thick cover during APR–JUN; approach slowly, as they are rather skulking and often disappear through the back of bush. Expect a glimpse of a grey-brown 'whitethroat' with blue-grey legs.

WHERE dense thickets, old hedgerows

grey cap, darker cheek

grey-brown above

blue-grey legs

! Barred Warbler (*p.260*)

217

Garden Warbler and **Blackcap** are often in the same wood: many songs are distinctive, others difficult to be certain unless the bird is seen.

EAT **All**: small insects, other invertebrates, berries
Blackcap: also seeds (winter)

Blackcap	**VOICE** Hard "*tek*" or "*tak*" calls, repeated in alarm. Song an accelerating **fluty warble, vigorous and musical**, becoming more strident; **more forceful** than Garden Warbler (which it mimics).
Garden Warbler	**VOICE** Call "*chek*" or "*tsak*;" alarm softer, 'chuffing' "*cha cha cha*." Song like Blackcap's but generally longer, simpler, more even with **fast, flowing/bubbling tempo**, less forceful finish.

BLACKCAP

GARDEN WARBLER

WHERE woodland, bushy clearings, thickets (not frequent in gardens)

Garden Warbler *Sylvia borin*

L 13–14·5 cm | WS 20–22 cm
ID Rather stocky; plain, pale brownish above, buff beneath, with **no marked pattern**. Head round, **plain**, with thin, whitish eyering, faint pale stripe over eye and diffuse grey neck patch; blue-grey bill slightly **thick and stubby**. Sexes/ages alike.

Locally common APR–SEP; winters in Africa

Look for a slow-moving, skulking warbler, singing in foliage or thick undergrowth; may fly to a new perch up to 100 m away and sing again.

plain head

dull brown upperparts and plain wings

WHERE woodland with dense shrub layer, thickets, large gardens; feeders in winter

Blackcap *Sylvia atricapilla*

L 13·5–15 cm | WS 20–23 cm
ID Rather stocky; plain, apart from **darker cap**. MALE **grey-brown**, paler below and on wide grey collar; **round, black** cap falls **short** of bill. FEMALE/JUVENILE pale grey-brown with **rufous cap**.

Common migrant MAR–NOV, winters S Europe / N Africa; scarce OCT–MAR from N Europe

MAR–JUN listen for loud song, often from tree-top, sometimes low down; AUG–OCT check patches of brambles, Elder, *etc.* with berries. A few winter in gardens and visit feeders NOV–MAR.

Beware superficially similar Marsh and Willow Tits (*p.230*), which are stockier, with a black bib.

black cap

pale chin

M

rufous cap

F/J

Crests

Crests are tiny, acrobatic birds of woodland and scrub: greenish, with a black-and-white wing patch and yellow/orange crown stripe, and high, thin, penetrating songs/calls. Sexes differ slightly; juveniles lack crown pattern of adults.

IDENTIFY BY:
▶ head pattern   ▶ song

Goldcrest	**VOICE** Song high-pitched, rhythmic, with **slight terminal flourish**: "*si-sissi si-sissi si-sissi sissi-siswee-it*". Call 3–4 notes: "*ssee-ssee-ssee*" or "*zree-zree-zree*" (less shrill than Long-tailed Tit (*p. 228*)) or sharp "*sit*."
Firecrest	**VOICE** Song variable, accelerating trill without repetitive rhythm or terminal flourish of Goldcrest: "*zi-zi-zi-zizizizizizi*". Call sometimes single, often 2–3 notes, first longer: "*zee-zi-zi*," often indistinguishable from Goldcrest.

GOLDCREST   FIRECREST

Listen for high-pitched song and calls (although beyond hearing range for many people) and look high in trees for a tiny bird feeding acrobatically from twigs, occasionally hovering; both species also feed low down and can often be almost oblivious to humans and easy to see.

Common resident and migrant from N Europe SEP–MAR	Scarce and local resident (but increasing) and migrant from W/C Europe SEP–MAR

Goldcrest *Regulus regulus*

L 8·5–9·5 cm | WS 14–15 cm

ID Tiny, dumpy; olive-green, paler below; prominent white wingbars. **Thin black crown** with **yellow central streak** (orange on MALE when spread). Pale face; dark 'moustache' but no white over eye and no black eyestripe.

Firecrest *Regulus ignicapilla*

L 9–10 cm | WS 14–15 cm

ID Tiny, rounded; bright green above with yellowish 'shoulder'; prominent white wingbars. **Broad black crown** with orange-yellow stripe (vivid orange on MALE when spread). Face **striped: white band over black eyestripe**.

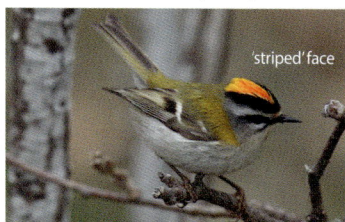

plain face

'striped' face

narrow black crown, yellow centre

broad black crown, orange centre; white stripe over eye

219

Wetland Warblers are small, with a rather long, pointed bill and long feathers under the tail; they are quite easy to identify given good views. Sexes look alike.

EAT small insects and other invertebrates

IDENTIFY BY:
- ► head pattern ► back pattern
- ► tail shape ► song

WHERE reedbeds, mixed fen, waterside willows; scrub/trees on migration

WHERE mixed marsh and riverside vegetation, bramble patches, thickets

Locally common APR–OCT; winters in Africa

May rustle reed stems before short, low flight across open space, or sidle up a stem to sing. Sometimes seen feeding in adjacent trees.

Locally common APR–OCT; winters in Africa

The song (or song flight) is usually the first giveaway sign; often in bushier places than Reed Warbler, although the two can be found together.

Reed Warbler
Acrocephalus scirpaceus

L 12·5–14 cm | WS 18–20 cm

ID Slender; low forehead slopes into quite long, pointed bill. **Plain brown**, buff below. ADULT has pale **rufous-brown rump and tail**, white throat (puffed out when singing). JUVENILE slightly more rufous overall.

VOICE Low, slurred "*tcharr*," softer "*kresh*," grating "*krrrr*." Song **rhythmic, repetitive**, each phrase repeated 2–4 times, lower, more even than Sedge Warbler, without high trills: "*chara-chara-krrik-krrik-krrik charee charee charee….*"

Sedge Warbler
Acrocephalus schoenobaenus

L 11·5–13 cm | WS 18–20 cm

ID Small; pale sandy-brown with **white stripe** over eye. Back and wings **softly streaked** above **pale sandy-brown rump**; throat silvery-white and flank bright buff.

VOICE Hard "*tuk*" and short, flat "*trrrr*" calls. Song **energetic, varied, scratchy** or more musical without rhythmic repetition. Begins with **sweet, musical** "*tsweee*" notes. Sings upright on exposed or hidden perch, or in whirry **song flight**.

J JUN–OCT

When feeding, often adopt a horizontal posture.

Sedge Warbler is the only wetland warbler with a display flight.

sloping forehead

plain back

white throat

buff underparts

rufous-brown rump and tail

slim tail

A

Marsh Warbler, Savi's Warbler (p.260)

white over eye

streaked back

white throat

buff flank

sandy-brown rump paler than brown tail

slim tail

GRASSHOPPER WARBLER

REED
WARBLER

SEDGE
WARBLER

GRASSHOPPER
WARBLER

CETTI'S
WARBLER

WHERE marshes and drier areas with long grass and bushy growth

WHERE marshes, riverside thickets, overgrown ditches, brambles

Scarce or rare APR–OCT; winters in Africa

Best located by distinctive 'reeling' song at dusk or in warm, sultry weather. Secretive, creeps mouse-like in low, dense vegetation; usually seen only with quiet, slow approach; if flushed, flits low, twists down with **rounded tail** fanned.

Local, uncommon (declines in hard winters)

Easy to hear but skulks deep in dank undergrowth. Often sings once, then, frustratingly, sings again somewhere else. When seen, movements jerky, low, leaps between clumps of vegetation (very like Wren (p.202)).

Grasshopper Warbler
Locustella naevia

L 12·5–13·5 cm | WS 16–18 cm

ID Slender; slim bill; small, flattish head; short, **curved** wing; long pale feathers extending beneath rounded tail give distinctive, tapered-at-both-ends shape. Pale olive to yellowish, **softly streaked grey-brown**; **dark streaks under tail**.

VOICE Sharp "*tik*" or "*psit*" calls. Song a **prolonged**, high, **reeling trill**, often for minutes on end, with **mechanical**, loud ticking quality, but thinner, whirring trill on one note at distance (volume changes occasionally).

Cetti's Warbler
Cettia cetti

L 13–14 cm | WS 18–20 cm

ID Small, dark, dumpy; uniform **rufous-brown above**, with **grey cheek**, **pale line over eye**; grey below (**darker** overall than Reed Warbler). Tail quite long, **square, dark rufous** (sometimes cocked).

VOICE Short, hard, sharp "*quilp!*" or "*plit*" calls, loud and distinct or quiet. Song a **sudden loud outburst**: short notes, momentary pause, then **fast** series of ringing notes – "*chwee; chwee: chuwee-wee-wee-wee-wee chwit-it!*"

softly streaked back

streaked underside

short, curved wing

broad, rounded tail

rather long, dark square tail

plain rufous-brown upperparts

thin pale line over eye

pale throat

greyish flank

Phylloscopus **Warblers** are small with a fine bill; greenish (paler below) with a dark line through the eye and a paler stripe above it. Their movements are light and active but they rarely hang beneath perches. Calls are variations on a sweet, rising "*hweet;*" songs **distinctive**. Sexes look alike.

IDENTIFY BY:
▶ calls & song ▶ head pattern ▶ leg colour

EAT small insects, other invertebrates, berries

CHIFFCHAFF | WILLOW WARBLER | WOOD WARBLER

CHIFFCHAFF

Phylloscopus **Warblers** are extremely vocal when they arrive in spring and the species have very different songs.

Common summmer and passage migrant MAR–OCT, most winter S Europe/N Africa but some remain, mainly in the south

Listen for the onomatopoeic song, from treetops, from MAR onwards; a few overwinter in damp woodland and scrub close to water, where the call is usually the best clue to their presence.

Chiffchaff *Phylloscopus collybita*

L 10–12 cm | WS 15–21 cm

ID Rounded; rather short-tailed; slightly rounded head and short wings. Distinctive frequent **downward 'tail dip'**. **Dusky olive** with paler fringes to dark wing and tail; pale stripe over eye, **white crescent** below; very pale greenish-cream or yellowish underparts. Bill dark; **legs thin, brown-black**. JUVENILE (MAY–OCT) greener above, yellower below.

VOICE Simple "*hweet*" call, **less disyllabic** than Willow Warbler, less forceful than similar note of Chaffinch (*p.242*). In summer/autumn, slurred "*shrilip*" or "*shlip*." Short "*hoot*" in autumn. **Song distinctive:** even-paced notes in random sequence, "*chip-chap-chi-chap-chap-chi-chee,*" interspersed with low "*grrt-grrt;*" frequent in autumn.

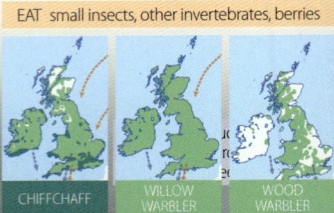

Phylloscopus warbler Identification

Chiffchaff and **Willow Warbler** are both small and active, greenish warblers that present real difficulties unless they are singing. Chiffchaff has rounder head, shorter wing and tail than Willow Warbler, more monosyllabic call, and often dips tail. **Wood Warbler** is distinctly green/white, with long wing and short tail.

Chiffchaff	CALL: "*hweet*","*shrilip*" or "*hoot*" SONG: even-paced "*chip-chap…*"
Willow Warbler	CALL: disyllabic "*hoo-eet*" SONG: descending cadence
Wood Warbler	CALL: "*piuw*" SONG: fast silvery trill

! Dusky Warbler (*p.260*)

rather diffuse pale stripe over eye

rounded head

thin, dark bill

short wingtip

dark legs

Scarce and local (rare in Ireland) APR–SEP;
winters in Africa

Best located by song, high in canopy in breeding
areas APR–JUN

Wood Warbler *Phylloscopus sibilatrix*

L 11–12·5 cm | WS 16–22 cm

ID Long-wings **often drooped** beside **short,
broad tail**. Distinctly green above, **clear white
below** with pale lemon-yellow lower face/
upper breast (yellow often only on throat);
long, yellow stripe over eye; broad, dark
eyestripe. Wing feathers edged yellow-green.

VOICE Call "*piuw*." **Song** mixes sweet,
sad "*siuuw-siuuw-siuuw*" with more
frequent metallic **ticking** that
runs into **fast silvery trill**
"*ti-ti-ti-ti-tikikitrrrrrrrrrrrrr*."

broad yellow stripe
over dark eyestripe

greenish
above

wing feathers
edged
yellow-green

short
tail

long
wingtip

white
underparts

Common APR–OCT; winters in Africa

Easily detected by sweet, musical song in spring –
a repeated phrase from high trees to low bushes.
Migrants best located and identified by call.

Willow Warbler *Phylloscopus trochilus*

L 11–12·5 cm | WS 15–21 cm

ID Rather sloping forehead and **long wings**.
Flicks but **does not 'tail dip'** like Chiffchaff.
Pale grey-green or olive above, bright or
'clean', paler yellow-cream below, with whiter
belly. Fairly strong **yellowish stripe over eye**;
weak eyering, paler cheek. Bill pale at base;
legs pale orange-brown (some dark with
pale feet). JUVENILE **yellower** below with yellow
stripe over eye.

VOICE Call "*hoo-eet*", clearly **more disyllabic**
than Chiffchaff and very similar calls of Redstart
(*p.210*) and Chaffinch (*p.242*). Song musical,
sweet, fluent, descending phrase with flourish
at end.

WHERE woodland, moorland and lowland
heathland with scattered trees, thickets

J JUL–OCT

In autumn, dusky green above with dark wings
and tail; pale yellow below, no bright white.

yellowish
stripe
over eye

sloping
forehead

thin bill,
pale at
base

long
wingtip

pale legs

whitish belly

Yellow-browed Warbler, Greenish Warbler,
Icterine Warbler (*p.260*)

223

Flycatchers are small, upright and very short-legged, with a slightly thicker, broader bill than warblers (*p. 215*); although round-bodied, the slim tail and long wings give a characteristic shape, and the large, dark eyes add a distinctive, alert expression. They snatch flying insects in the bill in short 'sallies' from a perch. Both are summer visitors, and appear as migrants outside their breeding areas.

IDENTIFY BY:
► head pattern
► wing pattern

EAT insects and other small invertebrates

PIED FLYCATCHER

SPOTTED FLYCATCHER

WHERE woodland and edges of clearings, moorland fringe, parks, gardens

Scarce, declining mid-MAY–SEP; winters in Africa

Look for small bird sitting on an open perch under the canopy or along woodland edge, flicking wings and dipping tail, and flying out to catch flying insects, **returning to same position** or close by.

Spotted Flycatcher *Muscicapa striata*

L 13·5–15 cm | WS 23–25·5 cm

ID Upright, long-winged, short-legged; pale **grey-brown** with **streaked crown**; silvery-buff feather edges on wing; underparts pale grey-buff or whitish with subtle **grey-brown streaks**. Sexes look alike. JUVENILE spotted buff above.

VOICE Calls, from perch or in flight: thin, scratchy, slightly vibrant "*sirrr*" or "*tseeet*." Song variable, a weak repetition of calls, or longer, more musical, thin, squeaky phrases.

Although now scarce in much of southern Britain, may still occupy open-fronted nest boxes or even nest in hanging baskets in gardens.

! Red-breasted Flycatcher (*p. 260*)

streaked crown

pale fringes to wing feathers

subtle dark streaks on breast/ flank

slender, brown tail

Male **Pied Flycatchers** sing repeatedly from quite low perches, but also high in the canopy.

Pied Flycatcher *Ficedula hypoleuca*

L 12–13·5 cm | WS 21·5–24 cm

ID Rounded; quite like a small chat with a longer tail and long wings, often **drooped**; **white in wing** (female Chaffinch (*p. 242*) has two white wingbars and a thicker bill). BREEDING MALE **black-and-white** with one or two white spots on forehead, **white patch on wing**. NON-BREEDING MALE/FEMALE/JUVENILE **brown-and-white**, blacker on wing with short white bar and narrow lengthwise white streak.

VOICE Sharp "*pwit*," sweet "*huit*" or "*huit-tik*" calls. Song staccato or stop-start, whistled phrase, some mimicry; several variants in irregular sequence.

> **Pied Flycatcher**, **Redstart** (*p. 210*) and **Wood Warbler** (*p. 223*) comprise a trio of typical western oakwood species in Britain, often occurring together.

WHERE mainly deciduous woodland, particularly western oak woodland; migrants in trees, bushes near coast

Locally fairly common APR–AUG; winters Africa

Visit breeding areas MAY–JUN and look around nestboxes; watch for birds descending to **pick insects from the ground**, as well as flycatching and landing on **new perch**.

Nest box schemes restore bird populations where old trees with holes are scarce. Pied Flycatchers are quick to take advantage in oakwoods.

! Red-breasted Flycatcher (*p.260*)

MB APR–JUL

unstreaked crown

white wing patch

broad, white-sided tail

F/J

unstreaked breast

Nuthatch & Treecreeper both require trees but Nuthatch will also feed on the ground/ around walls; Treecreeper clings to bark, but also feeds in low, dense thickets.

EATS nuts, seeds, insects and other small invertebrates	WHERE all woodland types, well-wooded parks and gardens

Locally common (absent from Ireland)

Listen for repetitive, piping whistles and loud tapping sounds, particularly from large Beech, oak or chestnut trees. Often visits feeders.

Nuthatch *Sitta europaea*

L 12–14·5 cm | WS 22·5–27 cm

ID Alert, agile, short-tailed, flat-backed and 'neckless', with 'wedge'-shaped head and bill; **bold black stripe through and behind eye**. Silky **blue-grey** above, buff below, with rusty flank. **Tail short and square** with black-and-white corners. **IN FLIGHT**, straight, flitting with no agility, heavy body and **very short, square tail**.

VOICE Distinctive loud, clear, **shouted whistles**, often fast series – "ch'wit;" "hwit hwit hwit;" tit-like (p. 228) "sit" calls. Song a clear "wheee wheee wheee".

Searches methodically, often hanging upside down, **climbing up and down trees and walls**.

NUTHATCH

EATS insects and other small invertebrates; some small seeds	WHERE mixed and deciduous woodland, parks, gardens

Common; rare migrant from N Europe OCT–MAR

Thin, high calls often suggest a tit, but look on upright trunks or beneath lower sloping branches for small bird creeping along.

Treecreeper *Certhia familiaris*

L 12·5–14 cm | WS 17·5–21 cm

ID Brown above, white below; long, spiky tail; short legs but long toes and claws. Upperparts warm brown with pale spots and streaks: a side view reveals white underparts. Bill **fine and downcurved**. **IN FLIGHT**, round wings show a broad, pale central band; thin tail.

VOICE Thin, slightly vibrant or sibilant "sreee;" song frequent, a little like Willow Warbler (p. 223) in pattern but thinner, flowing phrases with flourish at the end.

Inconspicuous, **creeps in a spiral up** a tree trunk or moves along a branch (sometimes underneath) using its tail for support, before flitting down to the base of another tree and repeating the process.

TREECREEPER

blue-grey back

rufous below

straight bill

curved bil

brown back, mottled white

white below

Tits share a name but comprise three different families. **Bearded Tit** lives in reedbeds, is bright tawny-orange and has a small, pointed, orange bill and a long, slender tail; **Long-tailed Tit** occurs in woods and bushy areas, is black, white and pinkish and has a tiny bill and a very long tail; **'True' tits**, generally found in woodland habitats, are blue/green/yellow or black/brown/buff, and have a short, thick bill, short but strong legs and toes and a relatively short tail.

Bearded Tit

Bearded Tit breeds in reedbeds, but sometimes uses reedmace and other tall wetland vegetation.

Scarce resident and eruptive migrant from W Europe SEP–MAR

Secretive and hard to see feeding on ground beneath reeds; listen for 'pinging' calls and rustling reeds. The best chance is to visit a regular reedbed breeding site. In AUG–OCT, may disperse and appear unexpectedly elsewhere.

WHERE reedbeds; in winter, other wet fen vegetation

EATS insects and other small invertebrates, seeds, shoots

Bearded Tits 'burst out' of reeds in short, whirring flight

Bearded Tit *Panurus biarmicus*

L 14–15·5 cm | WS 16–18 cm

ID Small, **long-tailed**; **Bright tawny-orange**, wings streaked black and cream; triangular **golden-orange bill**. MALE **blue-grey head, drooped black 'moustache'**. FEMALE buff head, with dark stripe beside crown. JUVENILE blackish on back and tail.

VOICE Call distinctive: quite loud, metallic, pinging "*ching*" or "*p-chink*"; scolding alarm. Song a little-heard, soft "*tchin-tchick-tchray*".

BEARDED TIT

grey head

black 'moustache'

black line beside crown

tawny-orange

long, slim tail

227

Long-tailed Tit

Common

Easy to find almost everywhere following recent increase: listen for the high-pitched call from dense scrub or high canopy and watch for flocks of 10–20 flying single-file across open spaces. Often visits feeders, usually in small groups.

Long-tailed Tit *Aegithalos caudatus*

L 13–15 cm | WS 16–19 cm

ID Tiny, acrobatic, with erratic movements. **Long, slim tail.** ADULT black and dull white, with **black stripe** below white crown and **pink 'shoulder'**.

VOICE High, thin, unemphatic "*see-see-see*" or "*si-si-si*" (shriller, less emphatic than Goldcrest (*p.219*)); distinctive short, abrupt, low "*brr-p*" mixed with dry, trilled "*ts-rreet*" and metallic "*pit*."

The only other long-tailed bird in a tree might be a larger Pied Wagtail (*p.198*) in a winter roost.

LONG-TAILED TIT

WHERE woodlands, bushy places, hedgerows, gardens; will visit garden feeders

EATS insects and other small invertebrates, especially their eggs/larvae; a few small seeds

J MAY–AUG

JUVENILE is dull with dark cheeks, but moults to adult plumage when a few weeks old.

white crown

pink 'shoulder'

long, slim tail

A

'True' Tits

'True' Tits are small, lively woodland birds with striking head patterns. Two of the six species are blue/green/yellow and four are black/brown/buff; vocalizations include thin, high notes, rhythmic calls and buzzing sounds. Form mixed flocks, roaming through woodland from July to March, and many visit gardens and other habitats at times.

IDENTIFY BY:
▶ overall colour ▶ head pattern
▶ wing pattern ▶ voice

EAT insects, spiders, other small invertebrates, berries, fruit, seed

CRESTED TIT

Strong feet allow tits to perch at any angle.

LONG-TAILED TITS

BLUE TIT

Blue Tit *Cyanistes caeruleus*

L 10·5–12 cm | WS 17–18 cm

ID Barrel-shaped, acrobatic feeder; leaps and **hangs from twigs**, with frequent **wing flicks**. Pale green above, yellow below with **thin** dark central streak. **Blue cap** edged white; pale blue nape; **white cheek edged dark blue**, black chin. Blue on wing and tail most vivid on spring MALE.

VOICE High, sharp "*si-si-si*," frequent rhythmic "*sisi-du*" and "*tzisi-di-di*" calls. Song a slurred, trilled "*see-see-si-surrrrr*."

BLUE TIT

WHERE woodlands, bushy places, hedgerows, gardens, reedbeds

Common resident/winter visitor from NW Europe

Use feeders to get close views, but also check woodland almost everywhere; listen for more rhythmic notes amongst general high-pitched calls from mixed flocks JUL–MAR.

blue cap edged white

blue tail

Both sexes have a narrow dark streak down centre of breast.

A

J late MAY–JUL

JUVENILE is like adult but greener overall, with yellow cheek (no clear blue and white on head).

Great Tit *Parus major*

13·5–15 cm | WS 18–20 cm

ID Largest tit, acrobatic, but has rather deliberate movements. ADULT green above, yellow below with **broad black stripe** down breast. **Blue-black head** with **white cheek**.

VOICE Varied, many strident, off-key call notes: "*pink*" or "*chink*" (like Chaffinch (p. 242)); "*pink-a-tchee tchee*;" "*tsweet*;" "*tsi-uti-uti*." Song loud, see-sawing two- or three-note, whistle: "*tsee-tsoo tsee-tsoo tsee-tsoo*" or "*tchee-tchu*" or "*tchi-too-tcha*." Loud bill-tapping on bark.

GREAT TIT

WHERE woodlands, parks, hedgerows, gardens

Common resident/winter visitor from NW Europe

Listen for strident two-note calls in woodland/gardens, and check feeders. Unfamiliar call notes and loud tapping sounds often lead to this bird!

blue-black head with white cheek

white sides to tail

M

Broad black breast stripe (widens between legs on MALE)

J late MAY–JUL

JUVENILE is like adult but has greenish yellow-cheeks until the autumn moult.

229

Marsh Tit and **Willow Tit** are both broadly brown-and-buff with white cheeks, a black cap and black bib. Most features overlap so care is needed to tell them apart, but the "*pit-chew!*" call is only given by Marsh Tit.

Marsh Tit *Poecile palustris*

L 11·5–13 cm | WS 18–19·5 cm

ID Sleek; back greyish, wing usually **plain** (weak pale panel at most). Bill may show **pale patch at base**. Flank **dull buff**. On most the black cap is glossy and the black bib rather small and square.

VOICE Cheerful, whistled "*pit-chew!*" rules out Willow Tit. Thin "*si-si*," quick, easy, lightweight "*tsi-tsi-chair chair chair*" ("*chair*" is **scarcely stressed**). Song simple, flat rattle: "*chi-ip-ip-ip-ip*" or more ringing "*witawitawitawitawita.*"

MARSH TIT

WHERE woodland, parks, often damp areas

Scarce, increasingly rare; absent from Ireland

Increasingly hard to find: try damp woodland/willow thickets and listen for characteristic buzzing call; may visit feeders.

wing typically plain

Male **Blackcap** can look similar but has a short cap and an all-grey chin.

Willow Tit *Poecile montanus*

L 12–13 cm | WS 17–20 cm

ID Stocky and rather thick-necked; back brown, pale fringes on wing feathers often create lengthwise **pale panel**. Bill **all-dark**. Flank tinged **rusty-buff**; black cap dull and black chin relatively wide, inverted 'V'-shape.

VOICE **Absence** of Marsh Tit's "*pit-chew*" note helpful; frequent high "*tsi-tsi*" before deep "*chair chair chair*;" ("*chair*" is long, **deeply nasal buzz**). Song "*tsew-tsew-tsew*" (like Wood Warbler (*p.223*)) or rare brief, melodic, warble.

WILLOW TIT

WHERE woodland, thickets, old hedges, often damp areas with flooded willows

Rare; absent from Ireland

In likely areas, listen for the call: the deep, nasal buzz is the best feature (as is the "*pit-chew*" for Marsh Tit): look low down in damp thickets. Very occasionally visits feeders.

Once common but now reduced to a tiny fraction of its previous numbers and range for reasons unknown.

pale panel in wing

glossy cap
pale bill base
MARSH TIT
'square' bib

dull cap
WILLOW TIT
'V' bib

Coal Tit *Periparus ater*

L 10–11·5 cm | WS 17–21 cm

ID Tiny, with **no yellow, blue or green**. Quick, staccato movements, acrobatic. Visits feeders but briefly, taking food away to eat or hide nearby. Large black head, **white cheek; clear-cut white patch on back of head**; extensive black chin, **buff underparts** without central dark streak. **Two white bars** across wing.

VOICE Sharp "*tsooo*" or "*tsee*" and melancholy variations, especially in autumn; short, sharp, hard, 'spitting'"*split*". Song emphatic two-note rhythm, simple "*see-too, see-too*".

WHERE mixed and coniferous woodland, thickets, gardens

Common resident/winter visitor from N Europe

Generally in woodland canopy, often near conifers if present, but also feeds on the ground and comes to feeders. Often joins mixed tit flocks.

COAL TIT

white patch

two white wingbars

White patch on back of head is unique to Coal Tit.

Crested Tit *Lophophanes cristatus*

L 10·5–12 cm | WS 17–20 cm

ID Buff-brown with no bright colours but striking **pointed crest** (barred black and white); black eyestripe extending around cheek, and black throat continuing as collar.

VOICE Thin, rolling or purring note with distinct rhythm – "*p'trrr-up*" or "*burrur-ur-eet*." Also, high, thin "*seeet*" notes. Song shrill notes followed by lower trill, "*si-si-see see tr-rr-rruh*."

WHERE pine woods in northern Scotland

Scarce and local

Typical of old 'Caledonian' Scots Pine forest and pine plantations; call is best clue to its presence. Regularly visits feeders, where easy to see.

CRESTED TIT

The Crested Tit's spiky crest is not always immediately obvious seen from below.

231

Crows are a small group of largely opportunistic, widespread birds that persist despite long-standing 'control' and persecution. Medium- to Buzzard-sized, with a robust, arched bill, broad wings that are more or less 'fingered' at the tip, and strong legs and feet. Most are predominantly black or black-and-grey; **Jay** and **Magpie** are brightly and distinctively patterned. All are frequently seen in flight: size, shape and actions become recognizable with experience. Sexes look alike.

IDENTIFY BY:
► head and tail features   ► voice

CARRION CROW

Crows in flight

JACKDAW
(p. 237)

CARRION CROW
(p. 235)

RAVEN
(p. 236)

CHOUGH

ROOK
(p. 234)

HOODED CROW
(p. 235)

MAGPIE
(p. 239)

JAY
(p. 238)

ROOKS

'Black' crows compared

CHOUGH

ROOK
(*p. 234*)

HOODED CROW
(*p. 235*)

CARRION CROW
(*p. 235*)

JACKDAW
(*p. 237*)

RAVEN
(*p. 236*)

Chough *Pyrrhocorax pyrrhocorax*

L 37–41 cm | WS 75–90 cm

ID Jackdaw-sized; **glossy black**, with small head, and unique long, **downcurved red bill** and **red legs**. Moves with bouncy hops, **long wings** dipped and flicked.

IN FLIGHT, **square, 'fingered' wings**; pairs or groups soar around cliffs, dive with half-closed wings, frequently followed by a steep, bounding rise.

VOICE Jackdaw-like but longer, more **ringing, piercing**: shouted "*chee-aah*," "*chaaa*," "*chrri*."

WHERE Coastal and (rarely) inland cliffs/quarries, adjacent grassy areas, heaths, beaches

EATS beetles, ants, spiders and worms

Scarce and local

Look on pastures with anthills and cattle near clifftops in SW Cornwall, SW Wales, Anglesey, the Isle of Man, Islay and in Ireland; listen for the characteristic call from birds in flight.

square, 'fingered' wings, often swept back

red bill

red legs

CHOUGH

233

'Black' Crows are heavily built, but sleek; usually perch with body sloping, tail down; walk freely on quite long, strong legs.

IDENTIFY BY:
▶ **bill shape and colour**   ▶ **wing shape in flight**
▶ **tail shape in flight**   ▶ **calls**

ROOK | CARRION CROW | HOODED CROW

Rook *Corvus frugilegus*

L 41–49 cm | WS 80–90 cm

ID Social, nesting in **treetop colonies** (Jackdaws (*p. 237*) often nest alongside but not Carrion Crows). **Peaked crown; pointed bill**, wide at base; **heavily feathered** over thighs. ADULT **bare, grey-buff** face. JUVENILE black face; basal bristles form distinct 'bump' (smaller patch in line with top of shorter, blunter bill on Carrion Crow); bill pale at base. **IN FLIGHT**, long head and bill; long **round or wedge-shaped tail**; tapered wingtips often curved well back, wings frequently raised in 'V'. Acrobatic in wind, **often soars** high up.

VOICE Deep caws and croaks, typically "*craa-craa-craa;*" loud, far-carrying, high "*crroo-crroo-crroo;*" choked trumpeting notes with musical squeaks and squeals; deep, mechanical, wooden rattle in flight.

WHERE farmland, moorland edge, woodland, copses, coastal cliffs with grassy tops, suburbs

EATS worms, insects, larvae, seeds and grain

Common

Frequently by *e.g.* roadsides and car parks looking for dead insects and scraps. Noisy flocks swirl over colony at any time of year.

WINGTIP tapered | WINGTIP broad
HEAD long, slim | HEAD short, broad
TAIL long, round/wedge-shaped | TAIL rather short, square
ROOK | CARRION CROW

basal bristles form raised 'bump'

pale base to bill

J ALL YEAR

peaked crown (steep forehead)

pale face

long, pointed bill

A

heavily feathered thighs

WHERE farmland, moorland, woodland edge, beaches, cliffs, suburbs, rubbish tips	EATS almost anything: worms, insects, small birds and mammals, dead animals, seeds

Common resident; Hooded Crow also scarce migrant from N Europe OCT–MAR outside normal breeding range

Usually ones/twos but often numerous in areas with abundant food (especially beaches, rubbish tips and fields spread with slurry); sometimes feeds with Rooks, but does not associate with them at rookery. Generally shy but can be approachable in urban areas.

Carrion/Hooded Crow *Corvus corone/[cornix]*

L 44–51 cm | WS 85–90 cm

ID Two distinct forms: all-black **Carrion Crow**; grey-and-black **Hooded Crow**. Broad, rounded head; all-black face; **heavy, slightly arched, black bill**; basal bristles form a small patch in line with the top of the bill; flank/belly smoothly feathered. JUVENILE dull black.

IN FLIGHT, short, broad head; short, **square tail**; broad-tipped, oblong wings. Rarely soars.

VOICE Calls hard, rough, explosive "*kraang-kraang-kraang*" or "*kraaa*," and harder, faster "*dairr dairr*" or soft "*krr-krr-krr*."

grey-and-black

HOODED CROW

The two forms are sometimes treated as separate species.

Hybrids have a 'ghost' Hooded Crow pattern, grey areas darker or streaked black; may persist for generations.

basal bristles form small patch

broad, rounded head

heavy, arched, black bill

all-black

smoothly feathered flank

CARRION CROW

235

A **Raven** looks massive close-up but size can be deceptive at long range.

Locally common
Distinctive deep calls draw attention to approaching birds long before they appear. May be flocks of 100 or more: always check soaring 'crows' (but beware Rook, which also soars).

WHERE cliffs from coast to high peaks, moorland, heathland, forested areas, pastureland with sheep or pig fields

EATS dead animals, associated insects and larvae; small mammals and birds; all kinds of edible waste

Raven *Corvus corax*

L 54–67 cm | WS 125–135 cm

ID Very large (close to Buzzard (p. 164) in size). **All-black**, with **long, deeply arched bill**. Head rounded, peaked or flat; throat sometimes shows loose 'beard', bulbous in flight.

IN FLIGHT, soars expertly, long wingtips often flexed back or angled down. **Tail long and wedge-shaped**, spread in 'diamond' or rounder (like Rook (p. 234)) when closed.

VOICE Carries far: loud, echoing, abrupt, hollow *"prruk-prruk-prruk;"* higher, more ringing *"tonk!;"* many other notes include loud *"quak quak"* in synchrony from pairs; subdued whistles, rattles, clicks at close range.

Uniquely, when flying, often **rolls upside down** and back again with wings angled; often flies fast in pairs, one 'on the shoulder' of the other.

RAVEN

long wings, often curved back or angled down

long, wedge-shaped tail

massive, arched bill

'bearded' throat

all-black

The **Jackdaw** is the most pigeon-like (*p. 154*) crow in shape and actions; often seen on roofs and chimneys.

Common

Easy to see, but may be overlooked amongst Rooks: check for smaller, faster-flying 'crows' in flocks. The rather sharp, high-pitched calls are distinctive and often given in flight.

WHERE arable and pasture land, woodland, parks, coastal cliffs, quarries, suburban areas

EATS insects, other small invertebrates, seed and grain, small birds, eggs and small mammals

Jackdaw *Corvus monedula*

L 30–34 cm | WS 70–75 cm

ID Small; grey-black, with **black face and cap**, **pale grey 'shawl'** and **whitish eye**.

IN FLIGHT, wings rather rounded, often slightly curled back; flies with quick, **flickery beats**. Flocks often soar, swirl out from trees, cliffs or tall buildings, turning in synchrony.

JACKDAW

VOICE Metallic "*jak*," "*chak*" or "*kya*," but very varied: even a single bird can produce a prolonged, rapid, bouncy cacophony of sharp, barked, shouted or squeaky notes. Noisy, staccato chorus from flock going to roost.

rather rounded wings

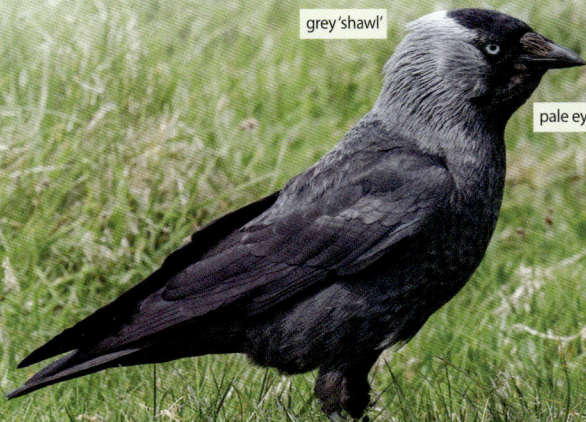

black cap

grey 'shawl'

pale eye

▶ CROWS IN FLIGHT *p. 232*

Jay & Magpie have the typical thick, arched bill, short legs and broad wings of crows, but look very different from the 'black' crows and from each other. Both are boldly patterned: Jay brightly coloured and with a white rump; Magpie essentially black-and-white with a long tail.

IDENTIFY BY:
▶ overall colour ▶ tail shape ▶ calls

Jays are conspicuous when flying high between woodland patches and during autumn movements.

Common resident and migrant from NW Europe OCT–MAR

Listen for harsh calls in woodland, and approach cautiously, as shy and easily disturbed. Often feeds on the ground, with bouncy movements, searching for acorns buried the previous autumn.

WHERE woodlands, thickets, parks and large gardens

EATS insects and other invertebrates, birds' eggs and chicks, acorns, seeds, grain and shoots

Jay *Garrulus glandarius*

32–35 cm | WS 50 cm

ID Unmistakable: medium-sized, thickset; pinkish, with **black 'moustache'**; patch of **electric blue** near bend of wing; black-and-white wingtip; **white rump** and black tail.
IN FLIGHT, broad wingtips spread and pressed well forward in springy, elastic beats.

VOICE Subdued or loud 'mewing'; more frequently, harsh screech of alarm or irritation – a hoarse, tearing "*shraairk!*"

JAY

white rump

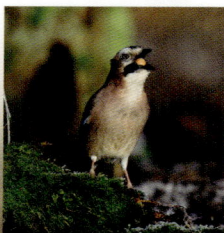

Jays are closely associated with oaks: they carry acorns in their throat.

Magpies often gather in treetops, occasionally in large numbers.

Conspicuous, and a frequent sight in a range of habitats with trees.

Magpie *Pica pica*

40–51 cm (incl. tail 20–30 cm) | WS 56–61 cm

ID Unmistakable: large, **long-tailed, black-and-white**. Tail glossed green, blue and purple. **White 'shoulder'-patch, belly and wingtip** contrast with black plumage. JUVENILE has shorter tail. **IN FLIGHT**, steady, quick beats (frequent faster 'shudder') with steep, closed-winged dive to ground or perch.

VOICE Loud, chattering, staccato "cha-cha-cha" calls, and variations.

WHERE farmland, woodland edge, heathland, villages, gardens, parks, suburbs

EATS insects, other small invertebrates, birds' eggs, chicks, grain and berries

MAGPIE

Magpies often take ticks from large wild or domestic animals.

239

Finches, Buntings and Sparrows are small, short-billed, round-headed birds, slim to rotund, with a square or notched tail and short legs. All hop or shuffle on the ground.

Finches (pp. 242–249)

Essentially triangular bill adapted primarily for shelling seeds, with mandibles the same size, although shape varies greatly between species, and colours may change between seasons. Underparts plain or streaked. Wings and tail may be plain, or have streaks or patches of white or brighter colours.

Buntings (pp. 250–254)

Conical bill adapted for feeding on seeds, particularly grasses, with the upper mandible narrow and lower one broad and deep. Underparts streaked or plain. Wings have thin bars or large white patches. Tail is plain, or dark with white sides (like pipits (see *p. 196*), which are much thinner-billed).

Sparrows (p. 255)

Thick bill adapted primarily for eating seeds, with the upper mandible deeper than the lower one. Underparts are unstreaked, ruling out many finches and most buntings. Wings have pale bars and the tail is plain.

CHAFFINCH

YELLOWHAMMER

TREE SPARROW

UPPER MANDIBLE
same size as lower

LINNET

GAPE forward point

UPPER MANDIBLE smaller than lower, usually 'lid'-like

YELLOWHAMMER

GAPE backward point

UPPER MANDIBLE
deeper than lower

HOUSE SPARROW

GAPE square corner

GOLDFINCHES

'FRINGILLA FINCHES' (pp. 242–243)	'YELLOW-WINGED' (pp. 244–245)	'BROWN' (pp. 246–247)	'SPECIALIST' (pp. 243 & 248–249)
BRAMBLING	SISKIN	REDPOLL	CROSSBILL

Finches compared: '*Fringilla* **finches**' – peaked head, broad wingbars, pale underside; '**yellow-winged**' – broad yellow wing bars or streaks but are otherwise quite different from one another; '**brown**' – more or less streaky brown with pale wing bar or white streaks; '**specialist**' – individual, with bills adapted to different foods.

Plumages

In some species, male and female differ in breeding plumage but are more alike in non-breeding colours. Fresh feathers have broad, pale fringes obscuring brighter colours beneath. In late February–April the fringes crumble away, and stronger patterning beneath is revealed; bill colour may also change.

MI [JAN] MN [NOV] MB [MAR]

J [AUG] FN [OCT] FB [MAR]

Behaviour

Most **finches** are more acrobatic feeders than buntings; some are fine songsters and a few, unlike any bunting or sparrow, sing in 'song flights'. **Buntings** often feed on the ground, where they have a crouched posture; songs are simple, with monotonous phrases given from a perch. **Sparrows** generally feed on the ground but sometimes take insects, even in flight; songs hurried jumbles of loud, forceful, chirping notes. Some species visit feeders.

GREENFINCHES

In flight

Finches and **buntings** fly up to reveal flashes of colour on wings, rump and tail; harder to see in trees, where **Redpolls** and **Siskins** fly in tight groups, easier on **Chaffinch**, **Brambling** or **Bullfinch** that have more relaxed flight lower down. **Finches** on open ground fly up in large (100+) bouncy flocks (*e.g.* **Linnet**); **buntings** split up in flight (except **Snow Bunting** flocks); **House Sparrows** move noisily from thicket to thicket; flocks in cereals dash to nearest hedge in whirring mass, then back down again.

LINNETS

BRAMBLING

CHAFFINCH

EAT All: seeds (winter), insects (summer)
Brambling: Beech mast; **Bullfinch**: buds

CHAFFINCH   BULLFINCH   BRAMBLING

AT DISTANCE, **Chaffinch** and **Brambling** look similar and frequently associate in winter. Look for **Brambling**'s orange breast contrasting with whitish belly (plus flank spots); **Chaffinch**'s breast is pink or grey-buff with little or no contrast with belly, wings black-and-white.

IN FLIGHT, listen for Brambling's distinctive **nasal call** and look for the telltale **white rump** and nearly all-black tail; Chaffinch call a **smooth "chup"** and has a **grey/green rump** and black tail with white sides.

BRAMBLING

CHAFFINCH

Common resident and winter visitor from N Europe OCT–APR

Can be seen and heard almost everywhere; comes to feeders, often tame where used to people (cafe gardens, *etc.*).

WHERE woods, thickets, parks, villages, gardens, farmland with hedgerows

Chaffinch *Fringilla coelebs*

L 14–16 cm | **WS** 25–26 cm
ID Long-bodied, thick-billed; **plain** back; unmarked underparts with little contrast. **White wingbar** and tail sides; grey-green rump; blue-grey/pinkish bill. MALE orange-pink cheek and breast, bluish cap (buff edges SEP–MAR). FEMALE/JUVENILE olive-grey above, olive-buff below. **IN FLIGHT**, white wingbars and white sides to tail; **grey/green rump**.

Chaffinches in winter typically form small flocks (but can be in the hundreds) on stubble, often with other finches. At this time resident birds are joined by visitors from Europe and Scandinavia.

VOICE Call a high, ringing "*pink*;" **IN FLIGHT**, "*chup*." Spring/summer, a repeated, monotonous "*huit*." Song a bright, rattling "*chip-chip-chip cherry-erry-erry*," accelerating into final flourish.

MB

MALES often sing stridently from an exposed perch, with white wing patches exposed.

MB MAR–AUG

bill never yellow

white 'shoulder' patch can be hidden

white bar across middle of wing

F

Bullfinch *Pyrrhula pyrrhula*

L 15·5–17 cm | WS 22–29 cm

ID Thick-necked, heavy-bodied with **black cap and chin**; **white rump**; blue-black wings with broad, **pale grey wingbar**. MALE **red-pink breast**. FEMALE grey-buff beneath. JUVENILE like female, but with a brown head. **IN FLIGHT**, pot-bellied, flitting; bold white rump and extensive white under tail.

VOICE Call a low, hollow whistle "*peooo*" or "*heeew*," penetrating in spring. Song quiet, vibrant, creaky sounds.

Common resident/migrant from NW Europe OCT–APR

Unobtrusive; a distinctive piping "*peooo*" from within a dense bush is usually the first clue to the presence of a pair or small group.

WHERE deciduous woodland, mature orchards, parks, large gardens with shrubberies, farmland hedgerows; also frequent in dense thickets on grassy downland

blue-black wings and tail

M

black cap and chin

white rump

F

Brambling
Fringilla montifringilla

L 14–16 cm | WS 25–26 cm

ID Form as Chaffinch; **patterned back; orange-buff breast**, white belly; **dark flank spots. Orange-buff wingbar**; white rump. MALE WINTER black-and-buff head; yellow bill (head and bill black in summer). FEMALE/IMMATURE **dark bands** beside **paler crown and nape; pale grey collar. IN FLIGHT**, narrow **white rump**.

Scarce, erratic winter visitor from N Europe OCT–APR

Look in woods (especially beneath Beech with a good mast crop); carefully check Chaffinch and other finch flocks in arable fields; will visit feeders (usually on spilled seed beneath); also heathland birch woods in spring.

WHERE woods, parks, farmland

MB MAR–SEP

By late March, MALES are nearly in their full, black-headed breeding plumage.

VOICE Call a twangy, coarse, nasal "*tswairk*" or "*tsweep*," harder "*chup*" than Chaffinch.

orange 'shoulder'

yellow bill

MN SEP–MAR

dark flank spots

white belly

F

'Yellow-winged' finches in flight:
look for flight and flock 'style', and plumage details.

In spring, male Greenfinches perform a distinctive bat-like, stretched-winged song flight.

	GOLDFINCH	GREENFINCH	SISKIN
FLIGHT	light, erratic, bouncy	strong, long undulations	rapid, short undulations
FLOCK	small, tight, coordinated	quite tightly bunched	coordinated, swirling, bounding
PLUMAGE	**broad yellow band across wing; white rump; black tail with white spots**	**yellow streaks on outerwing only; green rump;** broad yellow patches on tail	**thin yellow band across wing; yellow rump;** broad yellow patches on tail

GOLDFINCH

Common resident and winter visitor from C Europe OCT–APR

Look for in tall, leafy trees in summer; rest of the year anywhere where its preferred food is readily available; the tinkling calls are often the first indication of a flying flock.

WHERE weedy waste ground and field margins, bushy thickets, downland and grassland where tall, seed-rich plants are abundant, gardens

EATS soft, small seeds, particularly of tall composites (*e.g.* thistles, teasels and ragworts); also Alder and pine; some insects in summer

Goldfinch *Carduelis carduelis*

L 12–13·5 cm | WS 20–25 cm

ID Unmistakable, small, dainty. **Red, white and black head; yellow pattern on black wing;** white rump; **black tail with white spots**.

VOICE Slurred, sweet, musical "*swilp*," "*swilip*," "*sililip*;" also harsh, churring rasp. Song (given from trees) fast, tinkling trills and chattery notes.

Garden niger seed feeders can be an irresistible draw.

JUVENILE as adult, but with a plain head.

GOLDFINCH

red/white/black head unique

yellow band on wing

dark patch on side of breast

A

no yellow on tail

Common resident/winter visitor from N Europe

Favours thicker, unkempt bushes; in winter in small flocks in weedy fields. Regular at garden feeders, where it prefers larger seeds.

Greenfinch *Chloris chloris*

L 14–16 cm | WS 24–27 cm

ID Large, thickset with large, **pale bill**; **yellow edge to grey/brown wing**; **yellow sides to tail base**. MALE **apple green**. FEMALE brownish-green, softly streaked above. JUV as female but paler and streaked below.

GREENFINCH

VOICE Call a short "*jup*;" loud, erratic trill "*jup-jup-up-up*." JUVENILE has loud "*chup*," like Crossbill (*p. 248*). Song includes loud, nasal "*dweeez*;" and a range of **ringing, musical trills**.

Common resident/winter visitor from N Europe

Inconspicuous when high in trees; readily comes to feeders with niger seed (especially JAN–MAR).

Siskin *Spinus spinus*

L 11–12.5 cm | WS 18–22 cm

ID Small, slender, acrobatic feeder. Green back with soft dark streaks; **white belly**, **streaked flank**; **dark wing with broad yellow bands**; **yellow sides to noticeably forked tail**. MALE has **black cap and chin**. FEMALE/JUV as male but duller, no black chin.

SISKIN

VOICE Call **distinctive, ringing, squeaky** "*tluee*," "*tilu*" or "*tzsy-ee*." Also, hard, harsh rattle or churr; fast medley from treetop flocks. Song (from perch or in fluttery flight) fast, twittery, squeaky with trills and light, buzzy, wheezy notes.

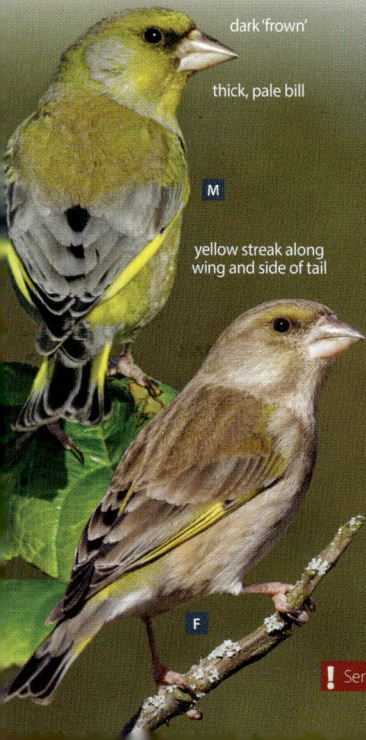

dark 'frown'

thick, pale bill

M

yellow streak along wing and side of tail

F

acrobatic when feeding

dark cap and chin

M

thin, pale bill

yellow-green bar across wing

F

dark streaks on flank

! Serin (*p. 261*)

245

'Brown' finches in flight: focus on wing/tail pattern and calls.

EAT small and medium-sized seeds; small invertebrates and their larvae

	LINNET	REDPOLL	TWITE
WING	streaky white patch	pale buff bar	streaky white patch
TAIL	white streaks on sides	all-dark	white streaks on sides
FLIGHT CALL	twittering *"chet-et-et"*	metallic *"chuch-uch-uch"*	dry chatter and twangy *"twaa–it"*

LINNET	REDPOLL	TWITE

LINNET

Linnet *Linaria cannabina*

L 12·5–14 cm | WS 20–24 cm

ID Brownish with **white streaks on outerwing and tail**; grey bill. In winter, in dull light, looks dark, greyish, with **whitish cheek marks** and pale eyering. MALE **grey head**, red forehead; **red-brown back** and **red breast**. FEMALE/JUVENILE no red; back ginger-brown, faint dark streaks.

VOICE Call a flat, twittering, dry *"chet-et-et,"* softer than Redpoll. Twangy *"tsooee,"* less forceful than Greenfinch (*p. 245*). Song a musical, sweet warbling.

WHERE reeds, bushy heath, moorland, scrub; migrants/in winter on fields, edges of estuaries and 'waste' ground with low, weedy vegetation

Locally common resident and winter visitor from N Europe SEP–MAR

Listen for twittering calls from 'bouncy' flocks in flight; look for birds feeding on/from the ground or coming to puddles to drink.

MN AUG–MAR

pink forehead

red forehead and grey bill

MB MAR–JUL

red-brown back

white streaks on wing and tail

white chin and red breast

pale marks above/below eye

grey head and bill

white mark on cheek

! Common Rosefinch (*p. 261*)

F/J

Redpoll *Acanthis flammea*

L 11·5–14 cm | WS 18–26 cm

ID Slim, lightweight.
Streaky brown, whiter on belly, with **buff wingbar**, **red forehead**, small **black chin** and **blackish streaks on flank**; yellow bill. BREEDING MALE **pink-red over breast** and pink on rump; less pink in autumn/early winter.

VOICE Hard chattering calls: fast, metallic "*chuch-uch-uch-uch-uch*;" twangy "*tsooeee*." Song, in long, bouncy song flight, mixes calls with jingly trill "*trrrreeeee*."

Locally common

Listen for distinctive calls from flocks flying over and look for birds feeding acrobatically in canopy (also feeds on ground).

WHERE breeds birch/mixed woodland, heath, moorland edge; winters in areas with birches, Alder, poplars, willows and Larch; will visit feeders

The widespread form is 'Lesser' Redpoll; in OCT–APR, larger, paler 'Common' (or 'Mealy') Redpoll occurs as a scarce migrant from N Europe.

red forehead and yellow bill

black chin

buff wingbar

F/J

flank streaked black

MB FEB–JUN

From FEB–JUL, MALES have bright pink cheeks, rump and breast.

Twite *Linaria flavirostris*

L 12·5–14 cm | WS 22–24 cm

ID **Buff-brown** with **buff wingbar** (like Redpoll) and **white wing and tail streaks** (like Linnet). **Tawny-buff throat**. MALE has deep pink rump FEB–JUN. In winter, both sexes have **yellow bill** (pale greyish in summer).

VOICE Call **twangy, nasal, buzzing** "*twaa-it*": flight note quick chatter, harder than Linnet, closer to Redpoll. Song fast, twittering, mixing twangy call and rattling trills.

Scarce, local resident/migrant from N Europe OCT–APR

Scan saltmarshes in winter for circling flocks and listen for distinctive calls. From APR–AUG, look around crofts near the coast in Scotland and Ireland.

WHERE breeds on moorland fringes in uplands and coastal areas with rough grazing; winters on low-lying coasts around estuaries, saltmarsh

brown head and yellow bill

buff throat

buff wingbar

white streaks on wing and tail

N JUL–FEB

MB FEB–JUN

Deep pink rump on MALE is often hard to see.

Crossbills, as a group, are identifiable as such by their heavy, large-headed, upright shape and thick, **arched bill that is crossed at the tip**. There are three closely related species that cannot always be positively identified.

Crossbills are inconspicuous when feeding, but often perch in the open, calling, before flying off.

Scarce resident; irruptive migrant from N Europe

Feed quietly in conifers: listen for falling cones. Often on treetops; drink from puddles.

Crossbill *Loxia curvirostra*

L 15–17 cm | WS 27–30 cm

ID MALE dull red, **brighter on rump**. FEMALE greenish, **rump yellower**, wings plain. JUVENILE greenish, streaked dark; males gradually gain orange, becoming more intensely red with age.

VOICE Purring notes build to ringing "*jip-jip-jip*" as birds fly off; forceful "*djeep-djeep-djeep*." Often an excited chorus from groups. Song buzzing, trilling, whistled sounds.

All crossbills eat dry seeds and must drink frequently.

IN FLIGHT, heavy, long-winged, with quick, bounding action; no obvious markings.

EAT conifer seeds, shoots, berries, occasionally fruits, insects

COMMON CROSSBILL

SCOTTISH and PARROT CROSSBILLS

uniform wings

hooked bill tip

JUVENILE greenish-brown, cold buff below with dark streaks; bill rather small at first.

Crossbills compared

Crossbill is the most widespread species but may occur in some Scottish forests on Speyside and Deeside with the scarce, very local endemic **Scottish Crossbill** and the very rare **Parrot Crossbill**. Separating the three depends on subtle differences in form and call – best identified from sound recordings

CROSSBILL

'fat-cheeked'

SCOTTISH

'bull-necked'

deepest bill

PARROT

Crossbill

VOICE Calls "*jip-jip-jip*" or "*djeep-djeep-djeep*."

Scottish Crossbill
Loxia scotica

L 16–18 cm | WS 27–30 cm
Deeper, heavier bill than Crossbill; rather 'fat-cheeked'.
VOICE Very slightly deeper than Crossbill.

Parrot Crossbill
Loxia pytopsittacus

L 16–18 cm | WS 28–32 cm
Deepest, heaviest bill of all crossbills, barely crossed at tip; rather 'bull-necked'.
VOICE Like Crossbill but deeper, harder quality: "*tup*" rather than "*jip*."

| WHERE | deciduous woods, well-wooded parkland |
| EATS | seeds, nuts, mast, cherry kernels, some small invertebrates |

Rare, localized; occasional influx from N Europe

Shy and hard to find; faithful to traditional sites but now lost from many areas. Sharp call may draw attention to birds perched on treetops: look for a large, thick-necked, short-tailed finch (much like Crossbill). Also feeds on the ground, often under Hornbeams, but easily disturbed so scan likely areas from a distance.

Hawfinch *Coccothraustes coccothraustes*

L 16·5–18 cm | WS 29–33 cm

ID Large, big-headed, upright. Mostly tawny-brown; orange-buff on head; black 'mask' and chin; grey collar; dark brown back. **Large bill** (blue-and-black MAR–AUG, yellowish SEP–MAR). MALE blue-black panel below **brown-and-white wing band**; FEMALE pale grey wing panel. JUVENILE head and underparts grey-buff, barred black. **IN FLIGHT**, fast, **long-winged** but **short-tailed**, with **large patches of white** on wing and **white tail tip**.

VOICE Call hard, dry, clicking or ticking "*tik!*;" sharp, quietly explosive "*tsip*" or "*chip*" (very like Robin (*p. 208*)) or "*tik-ik-ik*". Quiet, variable song, repeats ticking calls.

HAWFINCH

JUVENILE underparts yellowish, barred black; chin pale.

prominent white wing patches

short tail

pale grey wing panel

blue-back wing panel

F

large bill

M

white-tipped tail

Buntings are rather finch-like, with a triangular, quite sharp bill. Except for Corn Bunting, sexes look different; juveniles resemble females; plumage changes through the year.

IDENTIFY BY: ▶ head, wing and tail pattern ▶ rump colour

EAT seeds, especially small grass seeds, invertebrates

CORN BUNTING

SNOW BUNTING

CORN BUNTINGS   YELLOWHAMMERS

CORN BUNTINGS

Corn Buntings often perch on roadside wires and fences; in winter they join mixed finch/bunting flocks.

Corn Bunting
Emberiza calandra

L 16–19 cm | WS 26–32 cm

ID Largest bunting, stocky; keeps low and **hops** on ground (unlike larks (*p. 194*)). Pale brown, streaked darker; buff beneath with black streaks. **Plain tail** with no white. **IN FLIGHT**, **thick, arched, pale bill**, **plain brown tail** and **plain wings** in flight rule out larks.

VOICE Call loud, full "*quik*" or "*plip*." Song short, monotonous, 'crunching glass' or 'shaking keys' quality – **short** notes followed by rising, straining trill "*tuc-tuc-tuc-tss-rr- rreeeee*."

WHERE arable land, grassy downland

Scarce, locally fairly common

Best located by distinctive song in expansive farmland with low, gappy hedges and fences, or grassy downland with scattered bushes. Often on a fence, mound of earth, or singing from overhead wire or bush top.

plain wings

plain tail

stocky

Sings from a low, open perch where it looks large, heavy, with tail tilted down and head often tipped back.

thick, pale bill

boldly streaked

plain tail

Pale, dull rump and plain brown tail, unlike other buntings and larks.

Snow Buntings often form flocks in winter, flying low and showing flickering white wing patches.

Snow Bunting
Plectrophenax nivalis

L 15·5–18 cm | WS 32–38 cm

ID Long-bodied, short-legged. BREEDING MALE **black-and-white**. In winter, all birds rich buff-brown, streaked black; **tawny-brown on crown**, cheek and breast side. **Unstreaked below**. Bill yellow, legs black. IN FLIGHT, MALE has **white wings** with black tips; FEMALE/IMMATURE have less white (on innerwing).

VOICE Rippling, rhythmic "*til-lil-il-it!*"; bright, whistled "*pseu*," often combined. Song short, disjointed phrases mix full, vibrant or strident whistles and thin, wistful notes.

WHERE shingle beaches, weedy areas near coast; high mountain peaks/plateaux in summer

Scarce winter visitor SEP–APR from Iceland/Scandinavia; very rare breeder

Most easily seen in winter, particularly on east coast; a few also winter on Scottish moorland and can be seen around ski resorts. About 60 pairs breed in Scottish mountains. Can be confiding.

MI

MB MAR–AUG

tawny-brown crown and cheek

BREEDING MALES are strikingly pied with no hint of brown.

MN AUG–MAR

yellow bill

white wing panel

rufous breast side

F/I

unstreaked underparts

251

Male **Yellowhammers** give a 'little bit of bread and no cheese' song.

YELLOWHAMMER   CIRL BUNTING

WHERE downland with scrub, bushy heaths/moors, pastures with hedgerows, arable land

Locally common resident and migrant from N Europe SEP–MAR

Listen for the distinctive song, which can be heard into AUG or SEP, and look for a male perched upright on a bush. Feeds on the ground.

IN FLIGHT, quick, bounding; rusty rump, and long, blackish tail edged white.

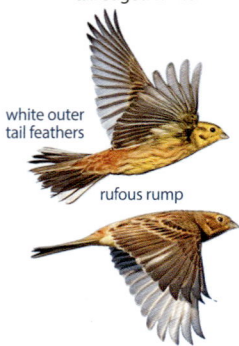

white outer tail feathers

M

rufous rump

F

Yellowhammer *Emberiza citrinella*

L 16–17 cm | WS 23–29 cm

ID Long, slim; **rump rufous-orange**; long tail blackish with white sides. BREEDING MALE **yellow head** with blackish lines; orange-brown breast/flank. NON-BREEDING MALE/FEMALE/IMMATURE pale rufous, streaked black, above; head/underparts pale yellow-buff to yellow (strongest on MALE), streaked black-brown.

VOICE Calls clicking "*tswik*," "*tik*" and rasping "*tzu*". Song high, even-pitched metallic notes, one or two high/low at end – "*sip-ip-ip-ip-ip-ip- seee-u*" or finishing with longer "*-seeee*".

yellow head, blackish lines

brown, streaked black

yellow throat

MB MAR–SEP

FEMALES and IMMATURES may be dull, buffish (see *opposite*) or brighter yellowish: often difficult to tell age/sex.

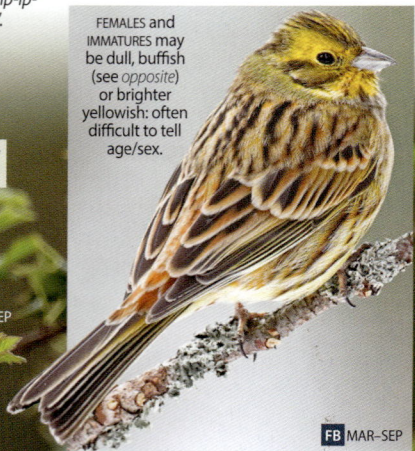

FB MAR–SEP

rufous-orange rump

FEMALE rufous-brown above; **rufous-orange rump**; yellowish head and underside

Cirl Buntings are usually inconspicuous unless singing, but can be heard from quite some distance.

WHERE old pastures, arable fields with dense hedgerows and scattered trees, bushy slopes

Rare and very local resident

Subject of a successful conservation project in south-west England. Visit the coastal strip around south Devon and listen for the song. Can be seen at sites where seed is supplied, feeding on the ground with a crouched posture.

Cirl Bunting *Emberiza cirlus*

L 16–16·5 cm | WS 22–25 cm

ID Long, slim; **rump dull olive**, long tail blackish with white sides. BREEDING MALE **black-and-yellow 'face'**, black throat (greyish SEP–MAR); greenish breast-band. FEMALE/IMMATURE **buff-brown**, streaked black; chestnut 'shoulder'; whitish spot on cheek.

VOICE Call elusive high, thin, quiet "*si*" or "*zit*." Song a short trill on one note; fast, thin, metallic "*ts-r-r- r-r-r-r-r-r*"; or slightly slower, more distinct "*tsi-tsi-tsi-tsi-tsi- tsi-tsi-tsi*".

'Yellow' bunting variation

NON-BREEDING FEMALE/IMMATURE Yellowhammer/ Cirl Bunting are difficult to identify; Cirl Bunting is greyer, less rufous/yellowish overall, and usually has a more prominent pale spot on rear of cheek.

F/I

YELLOWHAMMER

F/I

whitish spot usually more prominent

CIRL BUNTING

MB MAR–SEP

black-and-yellow face

chestnut, streaked black

black throat

dull olive rump

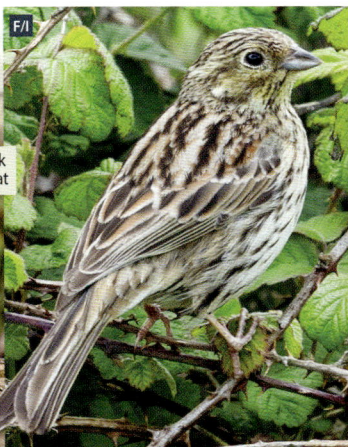

F/I

FEMALE grey-brown, rufous mostly on shoulder; **dull olive rump**; dull head and underside

253

Reed Bunting is the only bunting that breeds in reedbeds and males are conspicuous in spring.

Locally common resident and migrant from N Europe SEP–MAR

Listen for the distinctive song and look for a male perched up on a bush, reed or other exposed perch (but not in trees), usually around wetlands; occasionally visits seed feeders in winter.

WHERE wet moorland, boggy heathland, marshes, riversides

EATS seeds, especially small grass seeds, invertebrates; feed chicks on caterpillars'

Reed Bunting *Emberiza schoeniclus*

L 14–16 cm | WS 21–28 cm

ID Long, slim; streaked red-brown, buff and black; long **tail blackish** with **white sides**. BREEDING MALE **black head**, **white collar and 'moustache'** (suffused brown AUG–FEB). FEMALE/IMMATURE buff, streaked blackish; often two cream stripes along back. Head dark brown with **paler stripe over eye**, **blackish surround** to cheek and pale cream 'moustache' edged black.

VOICE Call a simple "*tseup*" and high, thin "*tseee*." Song, monotonously repeated from a low perch, a disjointed, short phrase: "*sup-jip-chilee-up*."

REED BUNTING

Plumage variation
Reed Bunting shows a wide range of head patterns at different ages and times of the year.

MN AUG–FEB

Brown feather edges on head from AUG; wear away in FEB–APR to reveal black-and-white.

MI AUG–FEB

IMMATURE MALE intermediate between JUVENILE and ADULT MALE until FEB when adult plumage becomes evident.

FB FEB–AUG

BREEDING FEMALE dark brown with pale stripe over eye, blackish edge to dark cheek, pale cream 'moustache'.

blackish tail with white sides

black head

MB FEB–JUL

white collar

white 'moustache'

black lower cheek and pale 'moustache'

pale stripe over eye

cream stripes

white sides to tail

F/I ALL YEAR

! Lapland Bunting, Little Bunting *(p.261)*

Sparrows are small and finch-like, short-legged with triangular bill, but unstreaked beneath. Sexes look different in **House Sparrow**, alike in **Tree Sparrow**; juveniles resembles females. Small seasonal differences in males.

IDENTIFY BY:
▶ head pattern

! Common Rosefinch (p.261)

EAT seeds, scraps, invertebrates

HOUSE SPARROW   TREE SPARROW

WHERE farms, villages, parks, arable land, coasts

Common

Although declining, still a familiar sight in many areas, especially smaller villages, family groups/loose flocks squabbling in hedges and thickets; often visits feeders.

House Sparrow *Passer domesticus*

L 14–16 cm | WS 18–25 cm

ID Pale, brown; **thick bill**; unstreaked below; plain brown tail. MALE **grey crown**, **edged red-brown**; pale grey cheeks; **black throat and bib**. In winter, pattern obscured by pale feather tips. FEMALE/JUVENILE **pale brown** with **broad, buff stripe** over cheek; **unstreaked** grey-buff below.

VOICE Loud chirrups and cheeps, "*cheep*," "*chwilp*," "*shreep*;" song includes calls in prolonged, rich, loud, emphatic but unmusical performance.

paler and duller in winter

pale buff stripe over cheek

grey crown and red-brown nape

grey cheek

black bib

MN AUG–MAR

F

MB MAR–SEP

Tree Sparrow
Passer montanus

L 12–14 cm | WS 18–22 cm

ID Sexes alike: brown-and-buff; rather small bill; streaked black and brown above, unstreaked buff below; **all-brown cap** and white cheek with **black spot**; plain tail often raised when on ground.

VOICE Hard "*tek*" or "*tet-et-et*" calls in flight, and cheerful "*tsuwit*." Song higher, more chattering, less dynamic than House Sparrow's.

WHERE farmland, parkland with old trees, wet thickets and waterside places

Rather scarce and local

Very much a 'countryside' sparrow, not closely associated with buildings, but regularly visits seed feeders, where easy to see.

black spot on white cheek   chestnut cap

small black bib

A

Rare migrants and regular vagrants

Very rare species to reach the shores of Britain and Ireland include (from left to right) the **Black-browed Albatross** from the Southern Ocean; the exotic **Collared Pratincole** from southern Europe and the **Black-and-white Warbler** – one of more than 50 species of American landbird that have been observed.

Birds are amazing, not least for how they find their way around the world, year after year. A Willow Warbler singing in a wood in spring will very likely be the same individual as last year, occupying the same territory, having flown all the way from Africa where it spent our winter in the very same site that it has used before. Birds do, though, sometimes go astray and Britain and Ireland are ideally placed to pick up 'vagrants' from far and wide. In fact, almost 400 species – around 60% of those ever recorded in these islands – have occurred as rare migrants or vagrants. These range from the seabirds from the tropics and Southern Ocean to diminutive American warblers, that somehow manage to survive crossing the Atlantic, blown along by fast-moving weather systems in Autumn!

Despite the large number of rare species, the 247 that may be considered as 'frequent' in Great Britain or Ireland (those that breed annually or for which over 1,000 individuals are recorded most years) – and which are covered in detail on the preceding pages – represent more than 99% of the total individual birds that are likely to be seen. However, a few of the 'rarities' breed in tiny numbers most years, and others occur as 'regular' migrants or vagrants (i.e. an average of 25 or more individuals per year). In addition, there are a few others that often have long-staying individuals that are fairly easy to see with a little effort. The 45 species that fall into any of these categories are included in this section. Although none are easy to find, if you put in the time and effort you may make your own discoveries of rare and unexpected birds – and doing so certainly adds to the excitement of watching birds.

KEY | **Individuals per year:** ● >50 ; ● 30–50; ● <30 | * = **Has bred** | Origin in status box

Vagrant | N America | most AUG–MAR (some long-stayers); freshwater/estuaries	Vagrant | Arctic | all year (some long-stayers); coasts/estuaries (usually with Eider)
American Wigeon *Mareca americana* ●	**King Eider** *Somateria spectabilis* ●
L 48–56 cm | WS 76–89 cm	L 55–63 cm | WS 87–100 cm

Female almost identical to female Wigeon (p. 53).

Female very like female Eider (p. 61).

White-billed Diver *Gavia adamsii* 🔴

L 77–90 cm | WS 135–150 cm

Like Great Northern Diver (p. 67) but **bill all-white** (no dark on upper edge).

American Golden Plover *Pluvialis dominica* 🔴

L 24–27 cm | WS 55–60 cm

Like a greyish Golden Plover (p. 119) with **dusky underwings**.

Black-winged Stilt 🔴* *Himantopus himantopus*

L 33–36 cm | WS 60 cm

Unmistakable.

Long-billed Dowitcher 🔴 *Limnodromus scolopaceus*

L 27–30 cm | WS 48–50 cm

Like a cross between a Knot (p. 127) and a Snipe (p. 120).

Pectoral Sandpiper 🟢 *Calidris melanotos*

L 19–23 cm | WS 43–47 cm

Like Dunlin (p. 124) with **sharp breast-band** and **pale legs**.

Temminck's Stint 🟢* *Calidris temminckii*

L 13·5–15 cm | WS 30–35 cm

Like Little Stint (p. 125) with **yellow legs, no 'V' on back**.

Buff-breasted Sandpiper 🟠 *Calidris subruficollis*

L 18–20 cm | WS 43–47 cm

Like a diminutive Ruff (p. 129).

Lesser Yellowlegs 🔴 *Tringa flavipes*

L 23–25 cm | WS 65–67 cm

Like Redshank (p. 133) with **yellow legs, plain wings**.

Ring-billed Gull *Larus delawarensis* 🔴

Vagrant | N America | most OCT–MAR (some long-stayers); coasts/lakes

L 41–49 cm | WS 112–124 cm

2Y **1Y**

Like pale Common Gull *(p. 94)* with **black band on thicker bill**, **pale eye**; FIRST YEAR has streaked tail.

Caspian Gull *Larus cachinnans* 🟢

Migrant | E Europe | all year, most AUG–MAR; beaches/lakes/tips

L 55–60 cm | WS 138–147 cm

A

Like Herring/Yellow-legged Gulls *(pp. 96/97)* MALE with **longer bill**; JUVENILES with **U-shaped** pale

Glossy Ibis 🟢
Plegadis falcinellus

Migrant | S/E Europe | all year; wetlands/marshes

L 55–65 cm | WS 88–105 cm

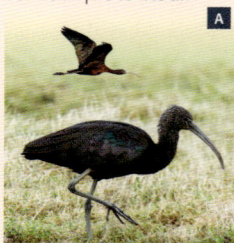

A

Unmistakable.

Purple Heron 🔴
Ardea purpurea

Migrant | S/W Europe | most APR–SEP; reedbeds

L 70–90 cm | WS 120–138 cm

A

Like slender Grey Heron *(p. 141)* with **striped rufous neck**.

Migrant | S/C Europe (some escapes) | most APR–OCT; meadows/marshes

tertial tips.

L 95–110 cm | WS 180–218 cm

A

Unmistakable.

Spotted Crake 🔴*
Porzana porzana

Rare breeder/migrant | N/E Europe | most MAY–JUN/AUG–OCT; wetlands

L 19–22·5 cm | WS 37–42 cm

A

Like Water Rail *(p. 146)* with **short bill** and **spots**.

Rough-legged Buzzard 🟢
Buteo lagopus

Visitor | Scandinavia | most E England and Scotland, OCT–MAR; coasts/moors/farmland

L 49–59 cm | WS 120–150 cm

A

Like Buzzard *(p. 164)* with a dark belly and **white rump**.

Snowy Owl 🔴*
Bubo scandiacus

Vagrant | N Europe | most N/W Isles (regular long-stayers); moorland (has bred)

L 53–65 cm | WS 120–150 cm

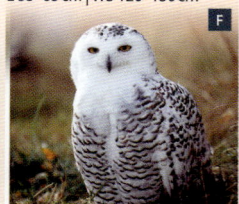

F

Unmistakable; FEMALE barred black; MALE all white.

Bee-eater ●*
Merops apiaster

L 25–29 cm | WS 36–40 cm

A

Unmistakable.

Alpine Swift ●
Tachymarptis melba

L 20–23 cm | WS 57 cm

A

Like large Swift (p. 188) with **white belly and throat.**

Red-rumped Swallow ●
Cecropis daurica

L 14–19 cm | WS 27–32 cm

A

Like Swallow (p. 189) with a **reddish rump.**

Hoopoe ●*
Upupa epops

L 25–29 cm | WS 44–48 cm

A

Unmistakable.

Rose-coloured Starling ●
Pastor roseus

L 19–22 cm | WS 37–42 cm

A

J

ADULT **unmistakable**; JUVENILE like juv. Starling (p. 200) with **pale bill.**

Golden Oriole ●*
Oriolus oriolus

L 19–22 cm | WS 44–47 cm

M

F

Unmistakable.

Great Grey Shrike ●
Lanius excubitor

L 21–26 cm | WS 30–34 cm

A

Unmistakable.

Red-backed Shrike ●*
Lanius collurio

L 16–18 cm | WS 24–27 cm

F/J

M

MALE **unmistakable**; FEMALE/JUVENILE rufous with dark bars.

Woodchat Shrike ●
Lanius senator

L 17–19 cm | WS 25–27 cm

J

A

ADULT **unmistakable**; JUVENILE cold greyish; **whitish 'shoulder'.**

Migrant | N Europe | most E coast, most AUG–OCT; woodland edge/scrub

Red-breasted Flycatcher
Ficedula parva
L 11–12 cm | WS 18·5–21 cm

Small flycatcher with **white patches on black tail.**

Migrant | W Europe | most N Isles/E coast, most MAY–JUN/AUG–SEP; woodland/scrub

Icterine Warbler
Hippolais icterina
L 12–13·5 cm | WS 22 cm

Large warbler (*p.215*) with **plain face** and **pale wing patch.**

Migrant | C/NE Europe | most N Isles and S/E coasts, most SEP–OCT; woodland/scrub

Barred Warbler
Sylvia nisoria
L 15·5–17 cm | WS 22–25 cm

Like large Lesser Whitethroat (*p.217*) with **paler head and bill.**

Vagrant | Siberia | most SEP–NOV; woodland/scrub

Greenish Warbler
Phylloscopus trochiloides
L 9·5–10·5 cm | WS 16–18 cm

Like Willow Warbler (*p.223*) with a **single wing bar.**

Migrant | Asia | most OCT–NOV; woodland/scrub

Yellow-browed Warbler
Phylloscopus inornatus
L 9–10·5 cm | WS 15–16 cm

Like Willow Warbler (*p.223*) with a **double wing bar.**

Migrant | Asia | most OCT–NOV; woodland/scrub

Pallas's Warbler
Phylloscopus proregulus
L 9–9·5 cm | WS 14–16 cm

Like Yellow-browed Warbler with **yellow rump.**

Vagrant | Asia | most OCT–NOV; woodland/scrub

Dusky Warbler
Phylloscopus fuscatus
L 10·5–12 cm | WS 16–19 cm

Like brown Chiffchaff (*p.222*) with bolder eyestripe; **sharp "tek"** call.

Migrant | W Europe | most JUN–SEP; marshes/scrub

Marsh Warbler
Acrocephalus palustris
L 13–15 cm | WS 18–20 cm

Like Reed Warbler (*p.220*) with **more musical, mimetic song.**

Rare breeder/migrant | C Europe, | most near E/S coast, APR–AUG; large reedbeds

Savi's Warbler
Locustella luscinioides
L 13·5–15 cm | WS 16–18 cm

Like Reed Warbler (*p.220*) with **low, purring trill** song.

Wryneck ●*
Jynx torquilla

L 16–18 cm | WS 25–27 cm

A/J

Unmistakable.

Richard's Pipit ●
Anthus richardi

L 17–20 cm | WS 26–30 cm

I

Large, long-legged pipit (*p. 196*);
sparrow-like (*p. 255*) "***speew***" call.

Olive-backed Pipit ●
Anthus hodgsoni

L 14–15·5 cm | WS 24–27 cm

I

Like olive-green Tree Pipit (*p. 196*)
with **pale ear spot.**

Migrant | C/N Europe | most N
Isles/E coast, most MAY/AUG–
SEP; wetlands/reedbeds

Migrant | C/N Europe | most
N Isles/E coast, most MAY–JUN/
AUG–OCT; woodland/scrub

Bluethroat ●*
Cyanecula svecica

L 13–14 cm | WS 23–25 cm

N

Similar to Redstart (*p. 210*) with
blue throat and **rusty gorget.**

Serin ●*
Serinus serinus

L 11–12 cm | WS 18–22 cm

A

Tiny finch; like Siskin (*p. 245*) with
yellow rump.

Common Rosefinch ●*
Carpodacus erythrinus

L 13·5–15 cm | WS 24–25 cm

N/I

Sparrow- (*p. 255*) or Linnet-like
(*p. 246*) with **two pale wingbars.**

Visitor | NW Europe | most N
Isles/E coast, most SEP–MAR;
stubble/low-lying coasts

Little Bunting ●
Emberiza pusilla

L 12–13·5 cm | WS 18–20 cm

N/I

Like Reed Bunting (*p. 254*) with
rusty cheeks; "***tik***" call

Ortolan Bunting ●
Emberiza hortulana

L 15–16·5 cm | WS 21–27 cm

N/I

Pink bill and pale eyering.

Lapland Bunting ●*
Calcarius lapponicus

L 15–16 cm | WS 24–27 cm

B

N/I

Like Reed Bunting (*p. 254*) but dark
cheek **corner, rufous** wing panel.

Further reading

This book has been designed to help people identify the birds they see with maximum confidence and minimum fuss. Naming birds is the first step towards caring about them and their future. An unknown bird flying across the road, or feeding in the garden, can easily be ignored: but it is not so easy to ignore something once its identity is known. Taking notice helps people become more aware of the natural world around them, and of the problems it faces.

This book is a pocket guide, pure and simple. It need not look in greater detail at the processes behind the various plumage changes that help make some birds such a problem to identify, on the one hand, but so interesting on the other. It is, in a way, a primer. Watching birds is a learning process, which never stops. Experience makes things easier but fortunately comes from enjoyment: looking, finding, seeing and appreciating birds. It is not always easy, but never a chore.

If readers want to take their interest in Britain's birds further, perhaps stepping up to a more exhaustive identification book that has room to deal more fully with trickier identification challenges, the best-selling companion advanced guide, *Britain's Birds: An identification guide to the birds of Britain and Ireland* by the same team, takes the same reader-friendly style, clear design and stunning photography to a higher level. It covers many more species (over 640) in greater depth, with much more of the detail that the present book deliberately omits.

If you are encouraged to look further and take your hobby forwards, you will also enjoy David Lindo's *How to Be an Urban Birder* – in it, David looks at ways to expand your interest in birds without travelling too far from home.

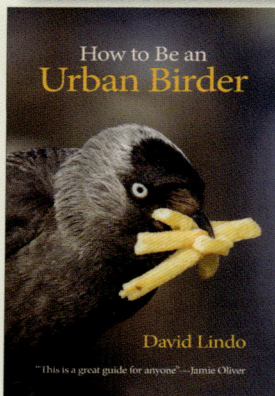

BirdLife International

BirdLife International brings together 115 Partner organizations worldwide, striving to conserve birds, their habitats and global biodiversity. BirdLife is widely recognized as the world leader in bird conservation, combining rigorous science with feedback from projects on the ground to implement successful conservation programmes. BirdLife's online Data Zone contains a wealth of information on birds and conservation, including up-to-date global species distribution maps (upon which the maps featured in this book are based). For more information, visit: **http://datazone.birdlife.org/species/search**.

Acknowledgements and photographic credits

This book has been produced as a follow-up to the highly popular *Britain's Birds: An identification guide to the birds of Britain and Ireland* first published in 2016. Feedback from readers indicated that a 'pocketable' version of the book focusing on the birds most likely to be seen would be invaluable – and here you have it. Many of the people who generously contributed to *Britain's Birds* have also been involved in the production of this *Pocket Guide* and our sincere thanks go to everyone who has influenced the final product.

A special mention goes to Rachel and Anya Still for their invaluable contributions behind the scenes. We also extend our grateful thanks to Brian Clews for his continuing commitment and dedication in helping to source images, and comments on the final proof of the book. Thanks, too, go to Ian Burfield and Jim Lawrence at BirdLife International for their support, Mark Balman and Hannah Wheatley, also at BirdLife International, for their help in providing the distribution maps, and to Chris Batty for his invaluable comments on the captioning of the photos. We also thank Robert Kirk, Publisher, Field Guides & Natural History, at Princeton University Press, for his encouragement and help throughout this project, Gill Swash for proof-reading the final text, Bob Self for helpful comments and The Urban Birder, David Lindo, for kindly writing the foreword.

The production of this book would not have been possible without the generous support of the many photographers who kindly supplied images. Although the majority of the 1,690 images featured were taken by the authors, 96 other photographers contributed one or more images and our thanks go to them all. Some 44 of these photographers are represented by the Agami photo agency in the Netherlands (agami.nl) and we would like to express our gratitude to Marc Guyt and Roy de Haas, who manage this agency, for their invaluable help.

A number of photographers generously provided access to their entire portfolio of images and their images are featured extensively throughout the book. They all spend many hours behind the camera, using their technical expertise, extensive local knowledge and understanding of wild birds in pursuit of the perfect picture. We would particularly like to thank Martin Bennett, Mark Darlaston, Dave Kjaer, Mike Lane and Markus Varesvuo.

The contribution of every photographer is gratefully acknowledged and each image is listed in this section, together with the photographer's initials, as follows (images sourced via Agami are indicated with an ^ after the photographer's initials):

Dave Appleton [DA]; **Aurélien Audevard**/Agami [AA^]; **Glenn Bartley**/Agami [GB^]; **Roy & Marie Battell** (moorhen.me.uk) [RMB]; **Martin Bennett** [MB]; **Alex Berryman** [AB]; **Han Bouwmeester**/Agami [HB^]; **Dermot Breen** (dermotbreen.blogspot.co.uk) [DB]; **Graham Catley** [GC]; **Keith Chapman** [KC]; **Roger & Liz Charlwood** (WorldWildlifeImages.com) [RLC]; **Trevor Codlin** [TC]; **Stephen Daly** (andalucianguides.com) [SD]; **Mike Danzenbaker**/Agami [MDan^]; **Mark Darlaston** [MD]; **Ian Davies**/Agami [ID^]; **Roy de Haas**/Agami [RdH^]; **Raymond De Smet** (pbase.com/raydes) [RDS]; **Greg & Yvonne Dean** (WorldWildlifeImages.com) [GYD]; **Oscar Diez**/Agami [OD^]; **Dean Eades** (Birdmad.com) [DE]; **Dick Forsman**/Agami [DF^]; **Steve Gantlett** (sgbirdandwildlifephotos.co.uk) [SGan]; **Saverio Gatto**/Agami [SG^]; **Hans Gebuis**/Agami [HG^]; **Alain Ghignone**/Agami [AGh^]; **Antonio Gutierrez** [AGu]; **Marc Guyt**/Agami [MG^]; **Hugh Harrop** (hughharropwildlifephotography.blogspot.com) [HH]; **Ron Hindhaugh** (flickr.com/photos/16309940@N05) [RHi]; **Rob Hume** [RHu]; **Tom Johnson** [TJ]; **Martin Jones** [MJ]; **Arto Juvonen**/Agami [AJ^]; **David Kjaer** (davidkjaer.com)

[DK]; **Jainy Kuriakose** [JK]; **Mike Lane** (nature-photography.name) [ML]; **Vincent Legrand/
Agami** [VL^]; **Wil Leurs/Agami** [WL^]; **Ralph Martin/Agami** [RM^]; **David Massie** [DMa];
Bence Mate/Agami [BM^]; **Karel Mauer/Agami** [KM^]; **Michael McKee** (michaelmckee.
co.uk) [MM]; **Arnold Meijer/Agami** [AM^]; **Tim Melling** (flickr.com/photos/timmelling)
[TMe]; **David Monticelli/Agami** [DMon^]; **Denzil Morgan** (facebook.com/Denzil-Morgan-
Photography-786259851389520) [DMor]; **Pete Morris/Agami** [PM^]; **Tomi Muukkonen/
Agami** [TMu^]; **Jerry O'Brien** [JOB]; **Daniele Occhiato/Agami** [DO^]; **Rob Oliver/Agami** [RO^];
Arie Ouwerkerk/Agami [AO^]; **Jari Peltomäki/Agami** [JPel^]; **Joe Pender** [JPen]; **Rene Pop/
Agami** [RP^]; **Markku Rantala/Agami** [MR^]; **Rob Riemer/Agami** [RR^]; **Chris van Rijswijk/
Agami** [CvR^]; **Ran Schols/Agami** [RSc^]; **Reint Jakob Schut/Agami** [RJS^]; **Glyn Sellors** [GS];
Charles J. Sharp (flickr.com/photos/93882360@N07) [CJS]; **Tom Shevlin** [TS]; **Brian E. Small/
Agami** [BES^]; **Walter Soestbergen/Agami** [WS^]; **Helge Sorensen/Agami** [HS^]; **Laurens
Steijn/Agami** [LS^]; **Rachel Still** [RaS]; **Robert Still** [RSt]; **Brian Sullivan/Agami** [BS^]; **Andy
& Gill Swash** (WorldWildlifeImages.com) [AGS]; **Tim Taylor** (wildimaging.co.uk) [TT]; **Roger
Tidman** [RTi]; **David Tipling** (birdphoto.co.uk) [DT]; **Ralph Todd** [RTo]; **Jacques van der Neut/
Agami** [JvdN^]; **Harvey van Diek/Agami** [HvD^]; **Menno van Duijn/Agami** [MvD^]; **Nils van
Duivendijk/Agami** [NvD^]; **Markus Varesvuo** (facebook.com/markus.varesvuo) [MV]; **Fred
Visscher/Agami** [FV^]; **Mike Watson** [MW]; **Steve Wilce** (breconbeaconsbirder.com) [SW];
Wim Wilmers/Agami [MM^]; **Edwin Winkel/Agami** [EW^]; **Phil Winter** (flickr.com/photos/
philwinter) [PW] and **Steve Young** (birdsonfilm.smugmug.com) [SY].

Five images are reproduced under the terms of the Creative Commons Attribution-
ShareAlike 2.0 or 2.5 Generic licenses and the photographers' names are given in full
followed by "(CC + relevant licence)" in the list. Other images sourced via the photographic
agencies Shutterstock (shutterstock.com) are also credited in full. Two of the images are in
the Public Domain but the photographers' names are not known; these are indicated as
"[(PD)]".

> The following codes are used: 1Y = 1st year; 2Y = 2nd year; 3Y =3rd year; A = adult; B = breeding;
> C = chick; F = female; f = female; I = immature; J = juvenile; M = male; N = non-breeding. Where necessary, 'action'
> codes are added: f = flying (when necessary qualified with (a) = from above; (b) = from below; (f) = from
> front; (s) = from side); p = perched or standing; s = swimming. Other codes: (btm) = bottom; (h) = head.

Cover: Goldfinch [ML].

Title page: Oystercatcher [HH].

INTRODUCTION p6: Avocets and **Black-headed Gulls** [DT]. **p7: Goldfinch** bathing [AGh^]; **Hoopoe** [HH].
p9: Blue Tit [DT]; **Sanderling** both [HH]; **Fieldfare** f (a) [MG^], f (b) & p [MV]. **p10: Gannet** both [AGS]; **egrets**
[MG^]; **Curlew** both [HH]. **p11: Willow Warbler** [DT]; **Curlew Sandpiper** [DT]; **Buzzard** p (tree) [MV], p (ground)
[KM^], p (post) [MvD^]. **p12: Meadow Pipit** [AGS]; **Starling** flock [DT]. **p13: Black-headed Gull** p [RHu], others
(2) [DT]; **birds** in tree [RSt]. **p15: cormorant**, **auk (larger)** (top), **Moorhen** (h) & **swan** [AGS]; **auk**, **duck (diving)**,
Fulmar, **phalarope** & **gull (larger)** (btm) [HH]; **grebe (smaller)** [MB]; **Gannet** & **skua** [MD]; **goose** [SG^]; others
(8) [DT]. **p17: sandpiper**, **plover (smaller)**, **plover (larger)**, **goose** & **Crane** [HH]; **Moorhen** [DO^]; **Buzzard** [KM^]
tern [AO^]; **duck** & **heron** [AGS]; others (9) [DT]. **p19: auk** [HB^]; **pigeon** [WL^]; **cormorant**, **crow** & **eagle** [AGS]
buzzard [SG^]; **falcon** [TMu^]; **hawk** [WS^]; others (4) [DT]. **p21: chat**, **pipit**, **sparrow** & **thrush** [AGS]; **bunting**
[Andreas Trepte (photo-natur.net) (CC 2.5)]; **finch** (right) [DO^]; **Starling** & **Waxwing** [HH]; **flycatcher**, **lark** &
wetland warbler [RM^]; **Dunnock** [SG^]; **crest** [WS^]; others (12) [DT]. **p23: cormorant**, **Fulmar**, **goose**, **heron**,
wader (large) [AGS]; **gull (smaller)** & **wader (small)** [DO^]; **duck**, **Spoonbill** & **tern** [DT]; **Kingfisher** [EW^]; **grebe**
[KM^]; **shearwater** & **storm petrel** [MD]; **swan** [MV]; **plover** larger [MvD^]; others (7) [HH]. **p25: buzzard**, **crow**,
eagle, **'gamebird'**, **kite**, **lark** & **swallow** [AGS]; **harrier** [HH]; **parakeet** [KC]; **finch**, **pipit** & **wagtail** [MG^]; **thrush**
[MV]; **Starling** [PM^]; **falcon** [RM^]; **woodpecker** [RMB]; **pigeon** [RSc^]; others (7) [DT]. **p26: garden** [RaS];
Peregrine [RSc^]. **p27: birds** all (7) [DT]. **p28: woodland and birds** all (5) [DT]. **p29: woodland and birds** all (4)
[DT]; **heathland** [RHu]; **Stonechat** [DT]. **p30: farmland** [RHu]; **birds** all (3) [DT]. **p31: open ground** [ML]; **birds**
all (3) [DT]. **p32: lake** [ML]; **birds** all (4) [DT]. **p33: reedbed and birds** all (6) [DT]. **p34: coastal wetlands** [RHu]
birds all (5) [DT], except **Black-headed Gull** [HH]. **p35: coastal cliffs** [RHu]; **Turnstone** [HH]; **birds** others (6) [D

WILDFOWL p36: Whooper Swan, **Egyptian** & **Pink-footed Geese** & **Wigeon** [DT]; **Brent Goose**, **Shelduck**,
Scaup & **Eider** [HH]. **p37: Pink-footed Goose** both, **Bewick's Swan**, **Mallard**, **Shoveler**, **Teal** & **Goldeneye** [DT]; **Mallard**
MB & upend [AGS]; **MN** & **F** [AGS]; **Gadwall** [BES^]. **p38: Mute Swan** f & A [DT], M (h) [HH], J & I [AGS]; **Whooper
Swan** & **Bewick's Swan** f [DT]. **p39: Bewick's Swan** flock [HH], others (3) [AGS]; **Whooper Swan** A (h) [DT], J (h)
[AGS], A s [HH]. **p40: Greylag Goose** main both [HH], (inset) [(PD)]. **p41: Bean Goose** all (3) [HH]; **Pink-footed
Goose** all (3) [DT]; **White-fronted Goose** f [DT], Greenland [GC], I (h) & A [HH].

p42: Canada Goose A [AGS], (h) [HH], f [DT]; **Barnacle** & **Brent Geese** A (h) [DT]. **p43: Brent Goose** flock & f [DT], pale [HH], dark [AGS]; **Barnacle Goose** f [DT], A [HH]. **p44: Mute** & **Bewick's Swans** [DT]; **Whooper Swan** [AGS]; **Brent Goose** both [AGS]; **White-fronted Goose** (a) [HH], (b) [DT]; **Barnacle Goose** both [DT]; **Pink-footed Goose** both [DT]; **Bean Goose** a [MV], (b) [HH]; **Canada Goose** [BES^]; **Greylag Goose** (a) [DT], (b) [HH]. **p45: Shelduck** (top) & f [DT], J [DO^], M (h) [HH], f [DT]; **Egyptian Goose** f [DT], A [CJS].
p46: Mallard, Teal, Pintail, Shoveler, Merganser, Pochard, Wigeon, Tufted Duck, Red-crested Pochard, Smew, Scaup & **Gadwall** [DT]; **Garganey, Goosander, Shelduck, Long-tailed Duck, Goldeneye, Common** & **Velvet Scoters** & **Eider** [HH]. **p47: Wigeon** & **Pintail** [AGS]; **Teal** & **Mallard** [DT]; **Garganey** & **Gadwall** (h) [HH]; **Shoveler** [RM^]. **p48: Mallard** M [RM^], F (a) [AO^], F (b) [Ana Gram (Shutterstock)]; **Shoveler** M [BES^], F (a) [AGS], F (b) [MV]; **Pintail** M & F (a) [DT], F (b) [Imran Shah (CC2.0)]; **Pochard** M [JPel^], F (a) [TMu^]; **Gadwall** M [AB], F (a) [RTi], F (b) [MV]; **Wigeon** M [DT], F (a) [AGS], F (b) [MV]; **Teal** M [DO^], F (a) [MV], F (b) [RM^]; **Garganey** M & F (a) [DO^], F (b) [DT]. **p49: Goldeneye** both [MV]; **Smew** both [MV]; **Shelduck** [DT]; **Red-breasted Merganser** M [HH], F [MV]; **Goosander** M [DT], F [MV]; **Eider** M & F [HH], MI [MvD^]; **Long-tailed Duck** both [MV]; **Scaup** both [MV]; **Common Scoter** both [MV]; **Velvet Scoter** both [MV]; **Tufted Duck** both [MG^]. **p50: Mallard** M (eclipse) [DT], f f [DO^], others (3) [HH]. **p51: Gadwall** M & f [AGS], f f [RM^], f [HH]; **Shoveler** M f [DT], others (3) [HH]. **p52: Teal** f f [RM^], others (4) [DT]; **Garganey** M f [DO^], others (3) [DT]. **p53: Wigeon** f f (a) [RTi], f f (b) [MV], others (3) [AGS]; **Pintail** M & M f [DT], f f [Imran Shah (CC2.0)]. **p54: Mixed flock** [MV]; **Tufted Duck** M f [HH], f f [MV], M & F [DT]; **Pochard** F f [TMu^], F s [AGS], others (2) [DT]; **Scaup** M f & F f [MV], M & F [DT]. **p56: Red-breasted Merganser** all (4) [DT]; **Goosander** M [HH], others (3) [HH]. **p57: Goldeneye** M f & F f [MV], M & F [HH]; **Smew** M f & F f [MV], M & F [HH]. **p58: Black Swan** [AGS]; **Snow Goose** [(PD)]; **Bar-headed Goose** [HH]; **Muscovy Duck** [Underworld (Shutterstock)]; **Mallard** [AGS]. **p59: Red-crested Pochard** M f & F f [MV], M & F [DT]; **Mandarin Duck** M (inset) [DT], F & F [AGS].
p60: Long-tailed Duck all (7) [HH]. **p61: Eider** flock [DT], others (6) [HH]. **p62: Scoters and Long-tailed Duck** flock [MV]; **Common Scoter** M & (inset) [HH], F [MV]; **Velvet Scoter** M & (inset) [HH], F [MW].

WATERBIRDS p63: Cormorant [AGS]; **Great Crested Grebe** J [Maciej Olszewski (Shutterstock)], N [MB]; others (6) [DT]. **p64: Cormorant** B & B (h) [MvD^], N (h) [DO^], others (4) [DT]. **p65: Shag** (top) [HH]; **Cormorant** dive [RM^]; **Shag** B (h) [DT], others (6) [HH]. **p66: Red-throated Diver** f (b) & f (b) [DO^], N/J [HH], others (3) [DT]. **p67: Black-throated Diver** f [TMu^], N [DO^], B (b) [HH]; **Great Northern Diver** f [BS^], N [HH], B [SG^]. **p68: Great Crested Grebe** f [KM^], N [HH], B [DT]; **Red-necked Grebe** N [DO^], B [HH].
p69: Little Grebe both [DT]; **Black-necked Grebe** N [RM^], B [MvD^]; **Slavonian Grebe** N [AA^], B [VL^].

SEABIRDS p70: Guillemot, Fulmar & **Gannet colony** [HH]; **Manx Shearwater** & **Storm Petrel** [MD]; **Gannet** [AGS]. **p71: Gannet, Guillemot** & **Puffin** [DT]; **Sooty Shearwater** (right) [HH], others (4) [MD]; **Gannets** feeding [DT]. **p72: Razorbill** [AGS]; **Guillemot** both [DT]. **p73: Guillemot** colony [DT]; **Black Guillemot** B [HH]; **Puffin** B [DT]. **p74: Razorbill** f [MV]; **Guillemot** f [MV]; **Puffin** f (b) [HH], f (a) [MV]; **Black Guillemot** f (a) & B, **Guillemot** B, **Razorbill** B, **Puffin** B & N [HH]. **p75: Razorbill** f [EW^]; **Guillemot** f [HH]; **Little Auk** f [TMu^]; **Black Guillemot** f [TS]; auks s all (5) [HH]. **p76: Storm Petrel** f (flock) & f (a) [MD]; **Leach's Petrel** both [PM^]. **p77: Fulmar** on cliffs, (h) & f (a) [DT], f (b), s & pair [HH]. **p78: Manx Shearwater** s [DT], others (3) [MD]; **Balearic Shearwater** all (3) [MD]; **Sooty** & **Cory's Shearwaters** [HH]; **Great Shearwater** [DO^]. **p79: Sooty Shearwater** f (b) [DMor], f (a) [MD]; **Great Shearwater** f (b) [DMor], f (a) [DT]; **Cory's Shearwater** f [HH]. **p80: Gannet** J [MD], others (5) [HH]. **p81: Gannet** colony [AGS], 1Y [AGS], others (5) [HH].

GULLS, SKUAS & **TERNS p82: Arctic Skua** p [HH]; others (5) [DT]. **p83: birds** both [DT]. **p84: Herring Gull** 1Y, 2Y [MG], others (4) [MD]; **Pomarine Skua** J [DB], 1Y & A [LS^], 2Y [JPen]; **Black-headed Gull** N (h) [AGS], B (h) [MV]. **p85: Herring Gull** 2Y, 3Y Mar & A [AGS], 3Y Sep [HH]; **Arctic Skua** all (3) [HH]; **Iceland and other Gulls** & **Mediterranean Gull** [MD]; **Pomarine Skuas** [MD]. **p86: Kittiwake** all (5) [HH]; **Little Gull** 1Y [HH], N [NvD^], B [MV]; **Black-headed Gull** 1Y & N [AGS], B [MV]; **Mediterranean Gull** 1Y [HH], N [JPel^], B [SGan]; **Common Gull** N [DT], others (3) [HH]. **p87: Sabine's Gull** [MD]; **Kittiwake** J [HH], A [RM^]; **Little Gull** 1Y [AO^], N [HH], B [MV]; **Black-headed Gull** 1Y [AGS], N [DO^], B [MvD^]; **Mediterranean Gull** 1Y [TC], 2Y [MG^], B [MV]; **Common Gull** J & B [DT], 1Y [RM^]. **p88: Great Black-backed Gull** both [HH]; **Lesser Black-backed Gull** 1Y [AGS], 2Y [RM^]; **Yellow-legged Gull** 1Y [SG^], 2Y [DO^]; **Herring Gull** 1Y [AGS], 2Y [HH]; **Iceland Gull** both [HH]. **p89: Great Black-backed Gull** 3Y [DT], A [HH]; **Lesser Black-backed Gull** 3Y [RM^], A [AGS]; **Yellow-legged Gull** 3Y [AGu], A [AGS]; **Herring Gull** 3Y [HH], A [RM^]; **Iceland Gull** 3Y [CvR^], A [HH]. **p90: Great Black-backed Gull** 1Y [MD], 2Y [AGS]; **Lesser Black-backed Gull** 1Y [MvD^], 2Y [KM^]; **Yellow-legged Gull** 1Y [SG^], 2Y [DO^]; **Herring Gull** 1Y [HH], 2Y [MG^]; **Glaucous Gull** both [HH]. **p91: Great Black-backed Gull** both [HH]; **Lesser Black-backed Gull** 3Y [MG^], A [RM^]; **Yellow-legged Gull** 3Y [DO^], A [RM^]; **Herring Gull** 3Y [HH], A [AGS]; **Glaucous Gull** 3Y [MV], A [HH]. **p92: Black-headed Gull** 1Y & N [SG^], 1Y f [RM^], N f [MV], B f [MG^], B (h) [RHu]. **p93: Little Gull** 1Y & 1Y f [HH], N f [TMu^], B f [RM^], B (h) [MV]; **Mediterranean Gull** 1Y f [TMu^], 2Y f [MG^], & f [HH], B [SGan]. **p94: Common Gull** 1Y f [MV], f [TMu^], 2Y (h) & N (h) [HH], 1Y & B [AGS]. **p95: Kittiwake** (top) [AO^], J f [AGS], B f [RM^], B [GB^], others (3) [HH]; **Sabine's Gull** B (h) [BES^], I/N [MD]. **p96: Herring Gull** A f & 1Y f [HH], A [AGS]. **p97: Herring Gull** both [AGS]; **Lesser Black-backed Gull** (tertial) [AGS]; **Great Black-backed Gull** (tertial) [HH]; **Yellow-legged Gull** (tertial) & 1Y [CvR^], A f & 1Y f [DO^], A [RM^]. **p98: Lesser Black-backed Gull** A f & 1Y f [MvD^], 1Y [AO^], B [AGS]. **p99: Great Black-backed Gull** A f & 1Y [HH], 1Y f [DB], B [AGS]. **p100: Glaucous Gull** all (3) [HH]; **Iceland Gull** all (3) [HH]. **p101: Arctic Skua** f [RM^], Int [PM^], pale & dark [HH]; **Long-tailed Skua** [HH]; **Pomarine Skua** [CvR^]; **Great Skua** [HH]. **p102: Great** & **Arctic Skuas** all (4) [HH]. **p103: Arctic Skua** [RM^]; **Pomarine Skua** J f [Leg^], f (b) [LS^], 1Y [JPen], 1Y f [JPen], f (b) & f (a) [HH]; **Long-tailed Skua** s & J f [RM^], 1Y [HH]; **Great Skua** [HH]. **p104: Sandwich Tern** colony & B f [DT], 1Y [DO^], N (h) [WL^], B [HH]. **p105: Black Tern** J [RM^], B f [DT], J f [HH], B [AJ^]; **Little Tern** B f [HH], B [ML]. **p106: Common Tern** B f [DT], J & B [HH]; **Arctic Tern** [HH].

p107: Roseate Tern B f [IDᴬ], J (h) [GS], B [MM]; **Arctic Tern** both [HH]. **p108: Arctic** (both), **Little & Black** Terns [HH]; **Common Tern** B [AGS], J [MD]; **Roseate Tern** [MV]; **Sandwich Tern** [SY]; **Black Tern** J [MGᴬ].

WADERS p109: Sanderling N [DT], others (4) [HH]; **Wader flock** [MGᴬ]. **p110: Flock** [DT]; **Greenshank** f [MV]; **Curlew Sandpiper** f [JPelᴬ]; **Little Ringed Plover** f [RScᴬ]; others (5) [ML]. **p111: Turnstone & Oystercatcher** [AGS], **Green Sandpiper** [Peter Gyure (Shutterstock)], **Avocet & Snipe** [DT], **Stone-curlew** [GYD], **Red-necked Phalarope** [MM], others (6) [ML]. **p112: Curlew Sandpiper** [DT]; **Little Stint** [MDanᴬ]; **Dunlin, Sanderling, Purple Sandpiper, Ringed Plover** J, **Red-necked & Grey Phalaropes & Turnstone** [HH]; **Knot** [AOᴬ]; **Ringed Plover** A **& Greenshank** [MV]; **Little Ringed Plover, Ruff & Spotted Redshank** [DOᴬ]; **Redshank** [AGS]; **Dotterel** [MRᴬ]; **Lapwing** [RdHᴬ]; **Golden Plover** [MvDᴬ]; **Grey Plover** [JvdNᴬ]. **p113: Whimbrel, Curlew, Black-tailed Godwit & Oystercatcher** [HH]; **Bar-tailed Godwit** [DOᴬ]; **Stone-curlew** [RDS], **Avocet & Green Sandpiper** [DT]; **Jack Snipe** [MRᴬ]; **Snipe** [RMᴬ]; **Woodcock** [HvDᴬ]; **Common Sandpiper** [RMᴬ]; **Wood Sandpiper** [AGS]. **p114: Oystercatcher** [AGS]; B s [AGS]; others (3) [HH]. **p115: Turnstone** B f & N/I [HH], B & B (h) [DT]; **Avocet** both [DT]. **p116: Lapwing** flock [AGS], MB f (both) & N [DT], J/I (h) [HH]. **p117: Ringed Plover** B f [MV], others (3) [HH]; **Little Ringed Plover** J f [Ron Knight (CC2.0)], B f [DOᴬ], J f & A [AGS]. **p118: Dotterel** flock [MGᴬ], FB & MB (h) [HH], A f [MRᴬ], J f [RMᴬ], J [MM]. **p119: Golden Plover** flock [HGᴬ], N/J f [AOᴬ], B [DT], N/J [HH]; **Grey Plover** (top) & B [HH], N f [RMᴬ], N/J [DT]. **p120: Jack Snipe** f [FVᴬ]; **Woodcock** f [DT]; **Snipe** f (b) & (inset) [DT], f (a) [RMᴬ], p [HH]. **p121: Woodcock** f [HvDᴬ], p [DT]; **Jack Snipe** (inset, with Snipe) & p [HH], f [MRᴬ]. **p122: Stone-curlew** f [RDS], A [GYD]; **Knot** flock [DT]; **Dunlin** flock [RMᴬ]. **p123: Sanderling, Knot, Curlew Sandpiper, Little Stint & Dunlin** all (10) [HH]. **p124: Dunlin** flock [DT], others (5) [HH]. **p125: Little Stint** J f [MDanᴬ], others (3) [HH]; **Curlew Sandpiper** B & J [HH], f [DT]. **p126: Sanderling** B Aug & N [DT], others (4) [HH]. **p127: Knot** flock [AOᴬ], N [DT], others (3) [HH]. **p128: Purple Sandpiper** all (4) [HH]. **p129: Ruff** MB (top) & A [HH], M Mar [AGS], others (4) [DT]. **p130: Common Sandpiper** (top) [DT], f (b) & f (a) [MB], p [AGS]. **p131: Wood Sandpiper** f [AGS], p [HH]; **Green Sandpiper** f (b) & f (a) [DOᴬ], p [DT]. **p132: 'Shanks' flock** [DT]; **Spotted Redshank** f [DOᴬ], B & N [DT], J [HH]; **Redshank** B f [JPelᴬ], N [DT], B p [HH]. **p133: Greenshank** J f [MV], J & B [DT]; **Redshank** B f [JPelᴬ], N [DT], B p [HH]. **p134: Black-tailed Godwit** J [HH], others (3) [DT]. **p135: Black-tailed Godwit** both [HH]; **Bar-tailed Godwit** flock & N [DT], f (a) [DOᴬ], others (4) [HH]. **p136: Curlew** (top) [AGS], others (4) [HH]. **p137: Curlew** [DT]; **Whimbrel** (top - calling) & f (b) [DT], others (3) [HH]. **p138: Grey Phalarope** J f & J/N [HH], FB [DMor]; **Red-necked Phalarope** FB f [HH], FB & MB [DT], J [AOᴬ].

LARGE WATERSIDE BIRDS p139: Herons and egrets [DK]. **p140: Grey Heron** [DT]; **Crane & Cattle Egret** [HH]; **Great White Egret** [DT]; **Little Egret** [AGS]; **Spoonbill** [DT]; **Bittern** (J) [DT]. **p141: Grey Heron** (top) & B [DT], f [HH], J & N [AGS]. **p142: Great White Egret** B & N f [HH], N [HBᴬ]; **Little Egret** B (h) [MGᴬ], N [SGᴬ], N f [RdHᴬ]; **Cattle Egret** N f [RdHᴬ], B (h) [AGS], N [DT]. **p143: Spoonbill** A f [ODᴬ], J/I f [DT], B [HH]; **Crane** both [HH].

RAILS & CRAKES p144: Moorhen A (inset) [AMᴬ], A s & J [AGS], C [DT]. **p145: Coot** flock [HH], J [AGS], others (4) [DT]. **p146: Corncrake** both [DT]; **Water Rail** f [HSᴬ], A [DT].

'GAMEBIRDS' p147: Partridge and hare (inset) [DT]; **Quail** f (b) [MRᴬ], f (a) [MV], M [HH], f (f) [DOᴬ]. **p148: Pheasant** f [DT], others (3) [AGS]. **p149: Grey Partridge** f [MV], p [DT]; **Red-legged Partridge** f [RHi], p [DT]. **p150: Red Grouse** (top) [DK], M f & F [DT], M [DMa]. **p151: Ptarmigan** M f [HH], F (h) [RTo], others (4) [HH]. **p152: Black Grouse** M (disp) [DT], F f & M [MV], M [HH], F [ML]. **p153: Capercaillie** M f & F [MV], others (3) [HH].

PIGEONS & DOVES p154: Woodpigeon p [DT], f (a) [MV], f (b) [RScᴬ]; **Collared Dove** f [RTi]; **Turtle Dove** f [RScᴬ]; **Stock Dove** f (a) [RScᴬ], f (b) [MV]; **Rock Dove** f (b) [MV], f (a) [MGᴬ]; **Flock** [AGS]. **p155: Feral pigeon** flock [Euphro (CC2.0)], dark & pale [AGS]; **Rock Dove** [HH]. **p156: Woodpigeon** all (3) [AGS]; **Stock Dove** f [MV], A [DT]. **p157: Turtle Dove** (tail illust.) [RSt], f (b) [MDanᴬ], f (a) [RScᴬ], A [DT]; **Collared Dove** (tail illust.) [RSt], f (b) & f (a) [MDanᴬ], A [RdHᴬ].

BIRDS OF PREY p158: Buzzard f (b) (left) [MGᴬ], hover [WWᴬ], f (b) others (3) [MV], f (s) [DT]. **p159: White-tailed Eagle** [HH]; others (7) [DT]. **p160: Golden Eagle** [MV]; **White-tailed Eagle** [RRᴬ]; **Buzzard** [AGS]; **Honey-buzzard** [DOᴬ]; **Red Kite** [RScᴬ]; **Marsh Harrier** F/J & F [HH]; **Carrion Crow** [AGS]. **p161: Kestrel** M [JPelᴬ], F [DT]; **Sparrowhawk** M [MB], F [MV]; **Merlin** [TMuᴬ]; **Peregrine** [MB]; **Goshawk** A [MV], J [HSᴬ]; **Hobby** [AGS]; **Osprey** [DPᴬ]; **Montagu's Harrier** M & F [HH]; **Hen Harrier** M [HGᴬ], F [DOᴬ]. **p162: Golden Eagle** A f [MV], J/I f [AGS], I f [MV], A [DK]. **p163: White-tailed Eagle** J p [HH], 2Y f [DT], A f (b) & A f (f) [MV], A p [CvRᴬ]. **p164: Buzzard** A f (a) [AGS], J f [MV], A f (s) & A p [DT]. **p165: Buzzard** f (b) [GYD], f (f) [MV]; **Honey-buzzard** F f [DT], f (f) [RMᴬ], M f (a) & M f (b) [SGᴬ], F f (b) & A p [DOᴬ]. **p166: Osprey** f [HH], others (3) [MV]. **p167: Red Kite** f (b) [DT], f (a) [ML], A p [DK], f (btm) [RScᴬ]. **p168: Marsh Harrier** f (top) & M f [DT], F f & F p [DOᴬ], M p [RPᴬ]. **p169: Hen Harrier** F f [DOᴬ], M f [SGᴬ], F p [JK], M p [Bildagentur Zoonar (Shutterstock)]; **Montagu's Harrier** f [SD], M f [DT], F p [RJSᴬ], M p [ROᴬ]. **p170: Sparrowhawk** M f & J p [MV], f f & F p [DT], J f [AOᴬ], M p [HH]. **p171: Sparrowhawk** (b) [RScᴬ], (s) [MV]; **Goshawk** FJ f & J f (inset) [HSᴬ], M p [ML], others (3) [MV]. **p172: Kestrel** M [JPelᴬ]; **Sparrowhawk** [MV]; **Merlin** J f (b) & F (p) [AOᴬ], M f (a) & M f (b) [MV], F f (a) [LSᴬ], M (p) [DK]. **p173: Kestrel** M hover [RJSᴬ], F hover [MV], M f (a) [MGᴬ], F f (a) [WSᴬ], F f (b) [RMᴬ], M f (b) [JPelᴬ], F p [DK], M p [DOᴬ]. **p174: Hobby** (top) [RScᴬ], f (b) [DOᴬ], f (a) [DT], p [DK], J (inset) [MV]. **p175: Peregrine** (top) [DT], f (b) [DOᴬ], f (a) [RMᴬ], p & A (inset) [AOᴬ].

NIGHTBIRDS p176: Nightjar [MB]; **Long-eared, Barn & Tawny Owls** [DT]. **p177: Little, Barn & Tawny Owls** [DT]; **Long-eared Owl** [HH]; **Short-eared Owl** [JPelᴬ]; **Little Owl** f [RMᴬ], A & J [GYD]. **p178: Barn Owl** all (4) [DT]. **p179: Tawny Owl** f [MRᴬ], A [MB], J [AGS]. **p180: Short-eared Owl** (top) [HH], f (b) [MB], f (a) [DOᴬ], p [AGhᴬ]. **p181: Long-eared Owl** (top) [RMᴬ], f (b) [MV], others (3) [HH]. **p182: Nightjar** all (4) [DT].

'NEAR-PASSERINES' p183: Kingfisher (top) [TMe], F [DO^], M [DT]. **p184: Cuckoo** all (5) [DT]; **Sparrowhawk** [MV]. **p185: Ring-necked Parakeet** flock [DA], f [KC], M [AGS]; **Alexandrine Parakeet** f (a) [MV]. **p186: Green Woodpecker** M f [RMB], J [RLC], F (h) [PW], M [DT]. **p187: Lesser Spotted Woodpecker** f (b) [HvDA^], f (a) [MB], F (h) & M [HH]; **Great Spotted Woodpecker** M f [Victor Tyakht (Shutterstock)], f (h) & M [DT], MJ (h) [HH].

AERIAL FEEDERS p188: Swift (top) [RSt], f (a) [DT], f (b) [AGS], nest [MG^]; **Sand Martin** f (b) [MDan^], f (a) [HS^], nest [DT]. **p189: Sand Martin** flock [WL^], f (tiny) [MG^]; **Swallow** f (tiny) [AO^], A f (b) & A f (a) [RSc^], J f [MG^], nest [DT]; **House Martin** f (tiny) [RSc^], f (b) [DT], f (a) [HH], nest [DT].

PASSERINES p190: Reed Bunting [DO^]; **Raven** [MV]; **Wren** [DT]. **p191: Yellowhammer** f & **Linnet** flock [MV]; **Skylark** flock [MG^]; others (4) [DT]. **p192: Waxwing** [HH]; others (7) [DT]. **p193: Birds** all (12) [DT].

LARKS TO WREN p194: Skylark f (b) [DT], f (a) [RSc^], (h) [AGS], p [DT]. **p195: Shorelark** f [MR^], B [DT], N/F [HH]; **Woodlark** f (s) [JOB], f (b) [RSc^], (h) & p [DT]. **p196: Tree Pipit** (display) [DT], p [RM^]; **Meadow Pipit** [HH]. **p197: Rock Pipit** (top) [AGS], p [HH]; **Water Pipit** [DT]. **p198: White Wagtail** [MG^]; **Pied Wagtail** J [AGS], F & M [DT]. **p199: Yellow Wagtail** M [VL^], J [TT]; **Grey Wagtail** J [DO^], M [RM^]. **p200: Starling** flock [DT], J, I & B [AGS], f [PM^], N [DT]. **p201: Waxwing** f [MvD^], M [HH]; **Dipper** [DT]. **p202: Dunnock** (sing) [DT], p [HH]; **Wren** (sing) & p [DT].

THRUSHES AND CHATS p203: Thrushes and chats all (6) [DT]. **p204: Blackbird** (sing) & J [DT], f [HG^], F & M [AGS]. **p205: Redwing** [LS^]; **Fieldfare** [MV]; **Blackbird** M [MG^]; F [MvD^]; **Song Thrush** [LS^]; **Mistle Thrush** [RSc^]; **Ring Ouzel** f (a) [RSc^], f (b) [MG^], FI (inset) [MB], F [SW], M [HH]. **p206: Song Thrush** f [MG^], p [AGS]; **Mistle Thrush** f [TMu^], (h) [HH]. **p207: Redwing** f [AO^], J [HH]; **Fieldfare** f [MG^], p [HH]. **p208: Robin** all (3) [DT]. **p209: Nightingale** all (3) [HH]. **p210: Redstart** M (top) [DT], F/I (inset) [WL^], M & F [AGS]. **p211: Black Redstart** (top) [MV], F/I (inset) & f [HH], F/I (btm) [HH], M & M f [DO^]. **p212: Stonechat** (top) & MN & F [AGS], M (inset) & MB (btm) [DT]. **p213: Whinchat** (top) [AGS], F/I (inset) [HG^], M [RM^], F [TMu^]. **p214: Wheatear** (top) [RM^], M f [MV], MN [HH], MB [HS^], F/I [DT].

CRESTS AND WARBLERS TO TITS p215: Crests and warblers all (7) [DT] except **Goldcrest** (hover) [MV]. **p216: Whitethroat** (top) & M [DT], J [DO^], f (h) [GYD]. **p217: Dartford Warbler** all (3) [DT]; **Lesser Whitethroat** (inset) [DT], p [MB]. **p218: Garden Warbler** [DT]; **Blackcap** M [DT], f [HH]. **p219: Goldcrest** both [AGS]; **Firecrest** (display) [HH], p [DT]. **p220: Reed Warbler** J [HH], A [DT]; **Sedge Warbler** [DT]. **p221: Grasshopper Warbler** both [DT]; **Cetti's Warbler** A [DT]. **p222: Chiffchaff** both [DT]. **p223: Wood Warbler** both [DT]; **Willow Warbler** both [HH]. **p224: Spotted Flycatcher** (top) [HH], nest [DT], p [WL^]. **p225: Pied Flycatcher** (sing) & M nest [AGS], MB [JPel^], F/J [HH]. **p226: Nuthatch** [DT]; **Treecreeper** [DT]. **p227: Bearded Tit** M f [AGS], others (3) [DT]. **p228: Long-tailed Tit** J [CJS], A [DT]; **Crested Tit** [DT]; **Tits at feeder** [DT]. **p229: Blue Tit** both [AGS]; **Great Tit** J [DT], J [AGS]. **p230: Marsh Tit** p [AGS], (h) [DT]; **Willow Tit** p & (h) [TMe]; **Blackcap** M (h) [HH]. **p231: Coal Tit** p [HH], (inset) [DT]; **Crested Tit** p [DT], (inset) [HH].

CROWS p232: Carrion Crow (h), **Jay** & rookery [DT]; **Hooded Crow** [MV]; others (6) [AGS]. **p233: Rook** A [AGS], J [HH]; **Hooded Crow** [MV]; **Carrion Crow** [DT]; **Jackdaw** [AGS]; **Raven** [ML]; **Chough** (top) & f [DT], p [ML]. **p234: Rook** f [MV], J (h) [HH], A [AM^]; **Carrion Crow** f [AGS]. **p235: Hooded Crow** both [HH]; **'hybrid'** [HvD^]; **Carrion Crow** A [DT]. **p236: Raven** (top) & f [HH], A [ML]. **p237: Jackdaw** all (3) [AGS]. **p238: Jay** f (top) [RSc^], f (btm) [MV], (inset) & main [DT]. **p239: Magpie** A main [TMe]; others (3) [DT].

FINCHES, BUNTINGS AND SPARROWS p240: Yellowhammer (h) [MV]; others (5) [DT]. **p241: Redpoll** [MB]; **Reed Bunting** MI Jan & **Linnet** flock [AGS]; **Reed Bunting** MN Nov (h) [DO^], FN Oct (h) [HH], J (h) [MB]; others (6) [DT]. **p242: Chaffinches & Bramblings** flock [AGS]; **Brambling** J [DT]; **Chaffinch** f [MV], M (inset) [DT], M p [AGS], F [MJ]. **p243: Bullfinch** both [AGS]; **Brambling** MB [HH], MN & F [HH]. **p244: Greenfinch** f (a) [MV], f b [AGS]; **Siskin** [HH]; **Goldfinch** f & flock [TMu^], feeder & A [DT], J [AGS]. **p245: Greenfinch** M [DT], F [RM^]; **Siskin** M [DT], f [HH]. **p246: Redpoll** [MR^]; **Twite** [EW^]; **Linnet** f [EW^], flock [DT], MB & F/J [AGS], MN (h) [DT]. **p247: Redpoll** F/J [DT], MB [MB]; **Twite** both [HH]. **p248: Crossbill** M, F & J [HH]; others (5) [DT]. **p249: Crossbill** [RM^]; **Scottish Crossbill** [DE]; **Parrot Crossbill** [TMe]; **Hawfinch** (top) [AGS], f [RSc^], others (3) [HH]. **p250: Corn Buntings & Yellowammers** flock [DK]; **Corn Bunting** f [MG^], (inset sing) & p [DT], (inset btm) [HH]. **p251: Snow Bunting** MB [RTo], others (4) [DT]. **p252: Yellowhammer** (top) & MB [DT], M f & F/I [MG^], FB [MV]. **p253: Cirl Bunting** (top) [RM^], F/I (h) [DO^], M & F/I [AGS]; **Yellowhammer** F (h) [HH]. **p254: Reed Bunting** (top) & FB [DT], f (s) [MG^], f (b) [HG^], MN (h) & F/I [DO^], MI (h) [AGS], MB [RM^]. **p255: House Sparrow** f [HH], MN (h) & MB [AGS]; **Tree Sparrow** A [DT].

RARE MIGRANTS AND REGULAR VAGRANTS p256: Black-browed Albatross [MG^]; **Collared Pratincole** [JPel^]; **Black-and-white Warbler** [AGS]; **American Wigeon** both [HH]; **King Eider** both [HH]. **p257: White-billed Diver** N/I [DT], B (h) [Bering Land Bridge National Preserve (CC2.0)]; **American Golden Plover** p [DMon^], f [HH]; **Black-winged Stilt** [HH]; **Long-billed Dowitcher** [HH]; **Pectoral Sandpiper** [HH]; **Temminck's Stint** [HH]; **Buff-breasted Sandpiper** [HH]; **Lesser Yellowlegs** [HH]. **p258: Ring-billed Gull** both [HH]; **Caspian Gull** [DT]; **Glossy Ibis** p [HH], f [AGS]; **Purple Heron** [HH]; **White Stork** [HH]; **Spotted Crake** [DT]; **Rough-legged Buzzard** [HH]; **Snowy Owl** [HH]. **p259: Bee-eater** [HH]; **Alpine Swift** [AGS]; **Red-rumped Swallow** [HH]; **Hoopoe** [AGS]; **Rose-coloured Starling** [HH]; **Golden Oriole** [MG^], F/I [BM^]; **Great Grey Shrike** [HH]; **Red-backed Shrike** [HH]; **Woodchat Shrike** A [RM^], J [HH]. **p260: Red-breasted Flycatcher** [HH]; **Icterine Warbler** [HH]; **Barred Warbler** [HH]; **Greenish Warbler** [HH]; **Yellow-browed Warbler** [HH]; **Pallas's Warbler** [HH]; **Dusky Warbler** [HH]; **Marsh Warbler** [HH]; **Savi's Warbler** [HG^] [AGS]. **p261: Wryneck** [RM^]; **Richard's Pipit** [RM^]; **Olive-backed Pipit** [HH]; **Bluethroat** [DT]; **Common Rosefinch** [HH]; **Little Bunting** [HH]; **Ortolan Bunting** [HH]; **Lapland Bunting** both [DT].

Index

This index includes the common English and scientific (in *italics*) names of all the birds in the book.

Bold text highlights main species accounts.

Italicized numbers indicate page(s) where comparative images or other information appear.

Regular black text is used for introductions and escapes, rare migrants and regular vagrants, or other species that are illustrated.

Short Index